The ONE YEAR

Devotional

Edited by Betsy Schmitt

Xploros

Tyndale House Publishers, Inc.
WHEATON, ILLINOIS

Visit Tyndale's exciting web site at www.tyndale.com

The One Year Jesus Bible Devotional copyright © 2002 by The Livingstone Corporation. All rights reserved.

Scripture quotations are taken from the *Holy Bible,* New Living Translation, copyright © 1996. Used by permission of Tyndale House Publishers, Inc., Wheaton, Illinois 60189. All rights reserved.

Designed by Ron Kauffman

Library of Congress Cataloging-in-Publication Data

The one year Jesus Bible devotional/Livingstone edited by Betsy Schmitt.
    p. cm.
  Includes index.
  ISBN 0-8423-7035-8 (pbk.)
  1. Jesus Christ—Biography—Devotional literature. 2. Bible. N.T. Gospels—Devotional literature. 3. Youth—Prayer-books and devotions—English. 4. Devotional calendars. I. Schmitt, Betsy.
BT306.53 .O54 2002
242'.2—dc21   2002009406

Printed in the United States of America

06 05 04 03 02
5   4   3   2

introduction

What did Jesus have to say about money, marriage, or success? What about faith, pain and suffering, or the tough issues you face in life? What does someone who lived more than 2,000 years ago have to say to you today? Plenty, if you take the time to discover the *real* Jesus—not the watered-down religious pacifist or the timid-looking person in the stained-glass window. But the Christ, the Messiah, the Savior, the *real* Jesus—in all his color, with all his power, showing up in the most unexpected places and revolutionizing the world with his life-changing message.

The *One Year Jesus Bible Devotional* will take you on an incredible year-long journey with Jesus. Through the daily readings and devotional thoughts, you will experience, in chronological order, the life, ministry, teachings, and encounters of Jesus during his time on this earth. This devotional will help you better understand Christ as your master, teacher, friend, and Savior.

The *One Year Jesus Bible Devotional* is a companion piece to *The Jesus Bible,* which is designed through the various features and notes to introduce you to Jesus, the real Jesus, in a new and fresh way. *The Jesus Bible* follows the work and purpose of Christ from the Old Testament prophecies about him to his life and ministry on earth. It records Jesus' call to radical living, first voiced nearly 2,000 years ago, that still resounds today.

Allow this devotional to deepen your relationship with the only One who offers you real answers to life's tough problems—a relationship that will last for all eternity.

Are you ready?

Reading Plan

Started Monday, September 8th

WEEK 1
- Luke 1:1-4 . . . . Eyewitness Report
- John 1:1-18 . . . . Getting the Job Done
- Matthew 1:1-17 . . . . . Faithfulness Counts
- Luke 3:23-38 . . . . A Living Legacy
- Luke 1:5-25 . . . . Beyond Reason
- Journaling . . . . Your Turn

WEEK 2
- Luke 1:26-38 . . . . Get the Message?
- Luke 1:39-56 . . . . Friend in Need
- Luke 1:57-80 . . . . The Double Announcement
- Matthew 1:18-25 . . . . . Tough Choices
- Luke 2:1-7 . . . . A Birth Fit for a Servant
- Journaling . . . . Your Turn

WEEK 3
- Luke 2:8-20 . . . . Expect the Unexpected
- Luke 2:21-40 . . . . Great Expectations
- Matthew 2:1-12 . . . . . Stargazing
- Matthew 2:13-18 . . . . Power Struggle
- Matthew 2:19-23 . . . . Under the Circumstances
- Journaling . . . . Your Turn

WEEK 4
- Luke 2:41-62 . . . . Misunderstood
- Luke 3:1-18 . . . . Walk the Talk
- Matthew 3:13-17 . . . . Tale of Two Children
- Luke 4:1-13 . . . . It's Tempting
- John 1:19-28 . . . . Point to the Light
- Journaling . . . . Your Turn

WEEK 5
- John 1:29-34 . . . . More than a Role Model
- John 1:35-51 . . . . Changing the World
- John 2:1-12 . . . . Party Time
- John 2:13-25 . . . . See-Through Hearts
- John 3:1-21 . . . . New Birth
- Journaling . . . . Your Turn

WEEK 6
- John 3:22-36 . . . . Who Gets the Glory?
- Luke 3:19-20 . . . . No Picnic
- John 4:1-26 . . . . Thirsty for Life
- John 4:27-38 . . . . The Harvest
- John 4:39-42 . . . . Real Encounter
- Journaling . . . . Your Turn

WEEK 7
- Matthew 4:12-17 . . . . Time for a Change
- John 4:46-54 . . . . Faith in Action
- Luke 4:16-30 . . . . The No-Comfort Zone
- Mark 1:16-20 . . . . Follow Me!
- Mark 1:21-28 . . . . Sabbath Fireworks
- Journaling . . . . Your Turn

WEEK 8
- Matthew 8:14-17 . . . . The Healing Touch
- Mark 1:35-39 . . . . Moving On
- Luke 5:1-11 . . . . Fishing for Results
- Mark 1:40-45 . . . . Untouchable?
- Mark 2:1-12 . . . . How Far?
- Journaling . . . . Your Turn

WEEK 9
- Matthew 9:9-13 . . . . . Jesus' Top Ten List
- Luke 5:33-39 . . . . Habit-Forming
- John 5:1-18 . . . . Against the Rules!
- John 5:19-30 . . . . It's Your Choice
- John 5:31-47 . . . . The Case for Jesus
- Journaling . . . . Your Turn

WEEK 10
- Matthew 12:1-8 . . . . . By the Rules
- Luke 6:6-11 . . . . For Mercy's Sake
- Matthew 12:15-21 . . . Super-Saints?
- Mark 3:13-19 . . . . By the Dozen
- Matthew 5:1-12 . . . . . Surprise!
- Journaling . . . . Your Turn

DAY 1 Eyewitness Report

Most honorable Theophilus:

Many people have written accounts about the events that took place among us. They used as their source material the reports circulating among us from the early disciples and other eyewitnesses of what God has done in fulfillment of his promises. Having carefully investigated all of these accounts from the beginning, I have decided to write a careful summary for you, to reassure you of the truth of all you were taught.   LUKE 1:1-4

You've probably had this happen to you: You're talking with some friends about a major event—a good one, like your local team winning a dramatic, come-from-behind victory over a heavily favored opponent, or a bad one, like a car accident or natural disaster—and everyone has an opinion. One expresses his views quietly, another states hers more vehemently, and soon it becomes a verbal free-for-all. Then someone else comes along and says, "I was there. I saw it happen." Suddenly, the entire conversation takes on a different tone because of the testimony of an eyewitness.

That's what Luke was doing when he wrote his account of the life of Jesus of Nazareth. Many people claimed to know the inside story. So Luke, a physician by training, led by the Holy Spirit, took it upon himself to investigate the claims about Jesus, giving special weight to the testimonies of eyewitnesses.

Our culture presents lots of different ideas about God, about truth, and even about Jesus himself. Doesn't it make sense to turn to eyewitnesses to form your beliefs about such important matters?

Why settle for mere opinions and speculations when someone is in front of you saying, "I was there. I saw it happen?"

In the beginning the Word already existed. He was with God, and he was God. He was in the beginning with God. He created everything there is. Nothing exists that he didn't make. Life itself was in him, and this life gives light to everyone. The light shines through the darkness, and the darkness can never extinguish it.

God sent John the Baptist to tell everyone about the light so that everyone might believe because of his testimony. John himself was not the light; he was only a witness to the light. The one who is the true light, who gives light to everyone, was going to come into the world.

But although the world was made through him, the world didn't recognize him when he came. Even in his own land and among his own people, he was not accepted. But to all who believed him and accepted him, he gave the right to become children of God. They are reborn! This is not a physical birth resulting from human passion or plan—this rebirth comes from God.

So the Word became human and lived here on earth among us. He was full of unfailing love and faithfulness. And we have seen his glory, the glory of the only Son of the Father.

John pointed him out to the people. He shouted to the crowds, "This is the one I was talking about when I said, 'Someone is coming who is far greater than I am, for he existed long before I did.'"

We have all benefited from the rich blessings he brought to us—one gracious blessing after another. For the law was given through Moses; God's unfailing love and faithfulness came through Jesus Christ. No one has ever seen God. But his only Son, who is himself God, is near to the Father's heart; he has told us about him. JOHN 1:1-18

Imagine that you are faced with an overwhelming task: the final project to end all final projects, or maybe a work assignment from your boss, Attila the Hun, Jr., who has sent countless previous victims over the edge of sanity. The problem isn't just the degree of difficulty; you don't even know where to start or how to begin.

One friend pats you on the back and shakes his head knowingly. Another gives you simplistic advice that is worth, well, about what most such advice is worth. Still another sends you a sympathy card, and a fourth yells from across the street, "Come on, you can do it! Just get started and try hard!", which would be all right, if only you had a clue what to start doing. Then another friend comes along, puts an arm around you and says, "Want me to help? I've had this course before, completed the assignment, and got an A+. Why don't you let me assist you?"

That's what happened in the incarnation of Jesus of Nazareth, God in the flesh. We humans have flailed around in futility since, well, ever since the first man and woman in the Garden. We've been trying to please God with our own efforts, an impossible task. So God entered time and space as a baby born in Bethlehem, became one of us, and not only showed us how it could be done but also did the job for us.

Here's the question: Do you think you can please God on your own, when all others have failed, or would you like Jesus' help?

| WEEK ONE | DAY 3 | # Faithfulness counts |

This is a record of the ancestors of Jesus the Messiah, a descendant of King David and of Abraham:

Abraham was the father of Isaac.
Isaac was the father of Jacob.
Jacob was the father of Judah and his brothers.
Judah was the father of Perez and Zerah (their mother was Tamar).
Perez was the father of Hezron.
Hezron was the father of Ram.
Ram was the father of Amminadab.
Amminadab was the father of Nahshon.
Nahshon was the father of Salmon.
Salmon was the father of Boaz (his mother was Rahab).
Boaz was the father of Obed (his mother was Ruth).
Obed was the father of Jesse.
Jesse was the father of King David.
David was the father of Solomon (his mother was Bathsheba, the widow of Uriah).
Solomon was the father of Rehoboam.
Rehoboam was the father of Abijah.
Abijah was the father of Asaph.
Asaph was the father of Jehoshaphat.
Jehoshaphat was the father of Jehoram.
Jehoram was the father of Uzziah.
Uzziah was the father of Jotham.
Jotham was the father of Ahaz.
Ahaz was the father of Hezekiah.
Hezekiah was the father of Manasseh.
Manasseh was the father of Amos.
Amos was the father of Josiah.
Josiah was the father of Jehoiachin and his brothers (born at the time of the exile to Babylon).
After the Babylonian exile:

Jehoiachin was the father of Shealtiel.
Shealtiel was the father of Zerubbabel.
Zerubbabel was the father of Abiud.
Abiud was the father of Eliakim.
Eliakim was the father of Azor.
Azor was the father of Zadok.
Zadok was the father of Akim.
Akim was the father of Eliud.
Eliud was the father of Eleazar.
Eleazar was the father of Matthan.
Matthan was the father of Jacob.
Jacob was the father of Joseph, the husband of Mary.
Mary was the mother of Jesus, who is called the Messiah.

All those listed above include fourteen generations from Abraham to King David, and fourteen from David's time to the Babylonian exile, and fourteen from the Babylonian exile to the Messiah.　MATTHEW 1:1-17

How many kids do you know named Amminadab, Nahshon, or Zerubbabel? When was the last time you heard a sermon about Jeconiah, Shealtiel, or Zadok? Chances are, the answers are zero and never. The people listed in verses 1-18, with a few exceptions, are not well-known biblical characters. Call them the Fellowship of the Unknown. Yet they each had a role to play in the great drama of redemption because each person mentioned here was, humanly speaking, an ancestor of Jesus on his earthly father's side. If for no other reason than that, God used them greatly to accomplish his purposes.

You may never be wealthy, powerful, or famous, but God doesn't need you to have any of those ingredients in order to use you. What he does require is that you be faithful to him. Think of some qualities of faithful people. Which of those are evident in your life? Which ones does God need to add to your mix or enhance in your life? If you're really serious about this, you could study the lives of some of these men and women and list the characteristics of faith and faithfulness you find in their lives.

Where is your faith the strongest? The weakest? Pray that God will strengthen your faith in those weak areas.

| DAY 4 ## A Living Legacy

Jesus was about thirty years old when he began his public ministry.

Jesus was known as the son of Joseph. Joseph was the son of Heli. Heli was the son of Matthat. Matthat was the son of Levi. Levi was the son of Melki. Melki was the son of Jannai. Jannai was the son of Joseph. Joseph was the son of Mattathias. Mattathias was the son of Amos. Amos was the son of Nahum. Nahum was the son of Esli. Esli was the son of Naggai. Naggai was the son of Maath. Maath was the son of Mattathias. Mattathias was the son of Semein. Semein was the son of Josech. Josech was the son of Joda. Joda was the son of Joanan. Joanan was the son of Rhesa. Rhesa was the son of Zerubbabel. Zerubbabel was the son of Shealtiel. Shealtiel was the son of Neri. Neri was the son of Melki. Melki was the son of Addi. Addi was the son of Cosam. Cosam was the son of Elmadam. Elmadam was the son of Er.   LUKE 3:23-28

If you have visited the Vietnam War Memorial in Washington, D.C., you have seen the 58,000 names etched in black stone, American men and women who gave their lives in that sad chapter in our nation's history. Whether or not you have any personal connection with any of the men and women listed there, a visit to that wall is a moving experience.

This passage lists some of the men who were forebears of Jesus' mother, Mary. Unless you are a budding Bible scholar, you probably haven't heard of most of them. They lived and died centuries ago in cultures very dissimilar to yours. But each of them made an impact, left a legacy, because they are all forebears of our Messiah, Jesus. God used each one of them to accomplish his purpose.

If you know Jesus as Lord, God used someone—or a series of someones—to bring you into a saving relationship with him. You are part of that person's legacy. Have you ever thanked that person for his or her role in your life?

Is there someone, or several someones, who would include **you** as part of their spiritual heritage?

DAY 5 Beyond Reason

It all begins with a Jewish priest, Zechariah, who lived when Herod was king of Judea. Zechariah was a member of the priestly order of Abijah. His wife, Elizabeth, was also from the priestly line of Aaron. Zechariah and Elizabeth were righteous in God's eyes, careful to obey all of the Lord's commandments and regulations. They had no children because Elizabeth was barren, and now they were both very old.

One day Zechariah was serving God in the Temple, for his order was on duty that week. As was the custom of the priests, he was chosen by lot to enter the sanctuary and burn incense in the Lord's presence. While the incense was being burned, a great crowd stood outside, praying.

Zechariah was in the sanctuary when an angel of the Lord appeared, standing to the right of the incense altar. Zechariah was overwhelmed with fear. But the angel said, "Don't be afraid, Zechariah! For God has heard your prayer, and your wife, Elizabeth, will bear you a son! And you are to name him John. You will have great joy and gladness, and many will rejoice with you at his birth, for he will be great in the eyes of the Lord. He must never touch wine or hard liquor, and he will be filled with the Holy Spirit, even before his birth. And he will persuade many Israelites to turn to the Lord their God. He will be a man with the spirit and power of Elijah, the prophet of old. He will precede the coming of the Lord, preparing the people for his arrival. He will turn the hearts of the fathers to their children, and he will change disobedient minds to accept godly wisdom."

Zechariah said to the angel, "How can I know this will happen? I'm an old man now, and my wife is also well along in years."

Then the angel said, "I am Gabriel! I stand in the very presence of God. It was he who sent me to bring you this good news! And now, since you didn't believe what I said, you won't be able to speak until the child is born. For my words will certainly come true at the proper time."

Meanwhile, the people were waiting for Zechariah to come out, wondering why he was taking so long. When he finally did come out, he couldn't speak to them. Then they realized from his gestures that he must have seen a vision in the Temple sanctuary.

He stayed at the Temple until his term of service was over, and then he returned home. Soon afterward his wife, Elizabeth, became pregnant and went into seclusion for five months. "How kind the Lord is!" she exclaimed. "He has taken away my disgrace of having no children!" LUKE 1:5-25

People react in many different ways to the news that a baby is on the way. Most soon-to-be parents are happy; some are nervous; some are outright stunned. Zechariah falls into that last category. He and his wife Elizabeth were elderly—verse 7 says they were "both very old"—and had been unable to have children. They naturally must have assumed that their childbearing opportunities had long passed. Then an angel told Zechariah that he was going to be a father after all, and Zechariah was, understandably, skeptical.

In hindsight we know the angel was right, and that Zechariah and Eliza-beth had a baby boy who grew up to be the man known as John the Baptist. But if you were in Zechariah's place and God revealed something to you that seemed to defy possibility, how would you respond?

The Christian faith does not go against reason, but it definitely goes beyond it. The Danish philosopher Søren Kierkegaard once said, "Faith is holding on to uncertainties with passionate conviction." Aspects of the faith are readily apparent to almost everyone, such as the validity of the Golden Rule (Luke 6:31) or the superiority of love over hate. But other aspects we must accept on faith, such as the virgin birth and Christ's resurrection.

Consider how you will respond when God calls you to embrace the unexpected.

Will you place your faith in your own intellect and ability to discern truth, or will you trust God and his supernatural revelation given to us in the Bible?

What did you learn about Jesus from this week's readings?

That everyone on Earth has a purpose and is in God's plan.

What reading this week had the most impact on you? Why?

Day 4, a Living Legacy, because I wonder if I am in someone's spiritual heritage.

What do you plan to do about what you have learned this week?

Trusting God with his plans for me.

Key Verse:

"No one has ever seen God. But his only Son, who is himself God, is near to the Father's heart. He has told us about him."
John 1:17-18

DAY 1   Get the Message?

In the sixth month of Elizabeth's pregnancy, God sent the angel Gabriel to Nazareth, a village in Galilee, to a virgin named Mary. She was engaged to be married to a man named Joseph, a descendant of King David. Gabriel appeared to her and said, "Greetings, favored woman! The Lord is with you!"

Confused and disturbed, Mary tried to think what the angel could mean. "Don't be frightened, Mary," the angel told her, "for God has decided to bless you! You will become pregnant and have a son, and you are to name him Jesus. He will be very great and will be called the Son of the Most High. And the Lord God will give him the throne of his ancestor David. And he will reign over Israel forever; his Kingdom will never end!"

Mary asked the angel, "But how can I have a baby? I am a virgin."

The angel replied, "The Holy Spirit will come upon you, and the power of the Most High will overshadow you. So the baby born to you will be holy, and he will be called the Son of God. What's more, your relative Elizabeth has become pregnant in her old age! People used to say she was barren, but she's already in her sixth month. For nothing is impossible with God."

Mary responded, "I am the Lord's servant, and I am willing to accept whatever he wants. May everything you have said come true." And then the angel left.   LUKE 1:26-38

Many people believe in angels. Chances are, you've even heard personal stories about angels. Yet believing in angels is quite different than getting a visit from one! First of all, forget about cute, chubby cherubs. There's a reason why most angels in the Bible began their messages with "Don't be afraid!"

Just ask Mary. When the angel Gabriel paid her a visit, her reaction was pretty normal: She was shocked, confused, and maybe even a little freaked out. Who wouldn't be when faced with a messenger of God?

But what really mattered was Mary's response to God's message. Gabriel hit Mary with the news that she was to be the mother of the Messiah, the long-awaited Savior of the world! It's here we see Mary's remarkable faith come shining through.

Mary didn't understand *how* it was going to happen, or *why* God would pick her. She wasn't even focused on the personal impact of the news—what it would mean to her reputation in town, or how Joseph was going to react. Mary chose to focus on *who* was in control of her life. To this day, Mary is called blessed because of her unshakable faith.

Where's your focus when you receive difficult news?

Like Mary, choose to focus on **who** is in control, and remember Gabriel's advice: "Don't be afraid!"

| WEEK TWO | DAY 2 | # Friend in Need |

A few days later Mary hurried to the hill country of Judea, to the town where Zechariah lived. She entered the house and greeted Elizabeth. At the sound of Mary's greeting, Elizabeth's child leaped within her, and Elizabeth was filled with the Holy Spirit.

Elizabeth gave a glad cry and exclaimed to Mary, "You are blessed by God above all other women, and your child is blessed. What an honor this is, that the mother of my Lord should visit me! When you came in and greeted me, my baby jumped for joy the instant I heard your voice! You are blessed, because you believed that the Lord would do what he said."

Mary responded,

"Oh, how I praise the Lord. How I rejoice in God my Savior! For he took notice of his lowly servant girl, and now generation after generation will call me blessed. For he, the Mighty One, is holy, and he has done great things for me. His mercy goes on from generation to generation, to all who fear him. His mighty arm does tremendous things! How he scatters the proud and haughty ones! He has taken princes from their thrones and exalted the lowly. He has satisfied the hungry with good things and sent the rich away with empty hands. And how he has helped his servant Israel! He has not forgotten his promise to be merciful. For he promised our ancestors—Abraham and his children—to be merciful to them forever."

Mary stayed with Elizabeth about three months and then went back to her own home.

LUKE 1:39-56

Mary had just received the most earth-shattering news—she, a virgin, was going to have a baby, and not just any baby, but the Messiah. So what did Mary do? Hole up in her room? No, she hurried to her cousin Elizabeth's house. This was not just a casual visit. Mary knew from Gabriel that Elizabeth was also pregnant, another miracle of God. She went to the one place where she could find encouragement and a sympathetic ear.

Elizabeth didn't know anything about Mary's pregnancy, but as soon as

Mary walked through the door, three amazing events took place: Elizabeth's baby leaped for joy within her; Elizabeth was filled with the Holy Spirit; and Elizabeth became the first to acknowledge that Mary's baby was, indeed, *her* Lord.

What encouragement that had to be for Mary! Even though Mary readily accepted the angel's news, she had to have been confused, scared, and apprehensive as to how this all would play out in her life. Yet here were affirmation, blessings, and praise for her role as God's servant.

When God gives you a difficult task to do, remember what Mary did. Look for a friend who can encourage you, support you, and affirm God's plan for you.

| WEEK TWO | DAY 3 | # The Double Announcement |

Now it was time for Elizabeth's baby to be born, and it was a boy. The word spread quickly to her neighbors and relatives that the Lord had been very kind to her, and everyone rejoiced with her.

When the baby was eight days old, all the relatives and friends came for the circumcision ceremony. They wanted to name him Zechariah, after his father. But Elizabeth said, "No! His name is John!"

"What?" they exclaimed. "There is no one in all your family by that name." So they asked the baby's father, communicating to him by making gestures. He motioned for a writing tablet, and to everyone's surprise he wrote, "His name is John!" Instantly Zechariah could speak again, and he began praising God.

Wonder fell upon the whole neighborhood, and the news of what had happened spread throughout the Judean hills. Everyone who heard about it reflected on these events and asked, "I wonder what this child will turn out to be? For the hand of the Lord is surely upon him in a special way."

Then his father, Zechariah, was filled with the Holy Spirit and gave this prophecy:

"Praise the Lord, the God of Israel, because he has visited his people and redeemed them. He has sent us a mighty Savior from the royal line of his servant David, just as he promised through his holy prophets long ago. Now we will be saved from our enemies and from all who hate us. He has been merciful to our ancestors by remembering his sacred covenant with them, the covenant he gave to our ancestor Abraham. We have been rescued from our enemies, so we can serve God without fear, in holiness and righteousness forever.

"And you, my little son, will be called the prophet of the Most High, because you will prepare the way for the Lord. You will tell his people how to find salvation through forgiveness of their sins. Because of God's tender mercy, the light from heaven is about to break upon us, to give light to those who sit in darkness and in the shadow of death, and to guide us to the path of peace."[*]

John grew up and became strong in spirit. Then he lived out in the wilderness until he began his public ministry to Israel.   LUKE 1:57-80

Typically, new parents send out birth announcements *after* the baby is born. For the arrival of John the Baptist, the order was reversed. The birth announcement came before his parents even knew of the pregnancy!

From the very beginning, events surrounding this child's birth were unique—an angelic announcement concerning his birth; the parents old enough to be grandparents; the father struck dumb for doubting the angel's announcement. Even his name was not what people expected. This would not be an ordinary child.

So what was all the fuss about? Zechariah's first words after his speech was restored revealed another startling fact: God had a special job in store for John. He would be God's spokesman, announcing the birth of yet another baby—Jesus the Messiah! John was called to prepare the people's hearts for the coming of the Lord.

No wonder Zechariah couldn't stop praising God. Not only would the long-awaited Messiah come in his lifetime, but *his* son would play a key role in the Messiah's life and ministry. Incredible!

The incredible news for us today is that we, too, are called by God to prepare others for Jesus. Whenever you invite a friend to church, take time to help someone, share with a stranger, you are preparing the way for Jesus to come into someone else's heart.

Incredible.

Who among your friends needs to hear about Jesus? Pray that you will have an opportunity to prepare the way for Jesus in your friend's heart.

| DAY 4 # tough choices

Now this is how Jesus the Messiah was born. His mother, Mary, was engaged to be married to Joseph. But while she was still a virgin, she became pregnant by the Holy Spirit. Joseph, her fiancé, being a just man, decided to break the engagement quietly, so as not to disgrace her publicly.

As he considered this, he fell asleep, and an angel of the Lord appeared to him in a dream. "Joseph, son of David," the angel said, "do not be afraid to go ahead with your marriage to Mary. For the child within her has been conceived by the Holy Spirit. And she will have a son, and you are to name him Jesus, for he will save his people from their sins." All of this happened to fulfill the Lord's message through his prophet:

"Look! The virgin will conceive a child! She will give birth to a son, and he will be called Immanuel (meaning, God is with us)."

When Joseph woke up, he did what the angel of the Lord commanded. He brought Mary home to be his wife, but she remained a virgin until her son was born. And Joseph named him Jesus.   MATTHEW 1:18-25

No guy wants to hear that his girlfriend is pregnant. But that's exactly the news Joseph heard from Mary. And she was the girl he was about to marry! Not only that, Joseph knew the baby wasn't his. Can't you just hear the rumors starting to spread through the small, dusty town of Nazareth?

Joseph probably considered what he believed were his only options: 1) Divorce her quietly, sparing himself and Mary from scandal; or 2) stone her to death, as was his right under Jewish custom. Being "a just man" and sensitive to Mary's situation, Joseph chose option number one. But then an angel appeared to him and gave him a third option: Marry her.

Joseph hadn't even considered this option, probably because it would have been humiliating for him to go through with the marriage at this point. But God, through an angelic dream, helped Joseph to see that this *was* the best decision.

When you have a tough choice to make or face an "impossible" situation, ask God for his guidance and wisdom. As in Joseph's situation, there may be a third option to a situation that you have not even considered.

Look for the God-option in your impossible situation.

A Birth Fit for a servant

At that time the Roman emperor, Augustus, decreed that a census should be taken throughout the Roman Empire. (This was the first census taken when Quirinius was governor of Syria.) All returned to their own towns to register for this census. And because Joseph was a descendant of King David, he had to go to Bethlehem in Judea, David's ancient home. He traveled there from the village of Nazareth in Galilee. He took with him Mary, his fiancé,e, who was obviously pregnant by this time.

And while they were there, the time came for her baby to be born. She gave birth to her first child, a son. She wrapped him snugly in strips of cloth and laid him in a manger, because there was no room for them in the village inn. LUKE 2:1-7

Life is filled with expectations. There are expectations about the future, about where to go to college, about a future mate, about the type of career to pursue. Sometimes our hopes and dreams are met; sometimes we have to live with disappointment when our hopes are not realized.

The Jewish people had certain expectations about the Messiah. They were looking for a mighty king, the Messiah-King who would be born in a royal palace with all the accompanying fanfare. They were looking for a warrior who would come and drive out the hated Romans and establish the city of Jerusalem to its former glory. What they weren't expecting was a baby, born in a dirty, dingy feed trough to a couple of insignificant, unknown people.

Yet this was the scene where God chose to enter our world as a tiny, helpless baby in the most crude and stark conditions. These were the people God chose to use: a young girl whose faith was big enough to believe God's promise and a young man who struggled to do the right thing.

As you read about Jesus' life and ministry, remember the manger. Nothing about this God-man met the expectations of the people he came to save: not those he chose to befriend, not his teachings, nor his choice to die on a cross.

What are your expectations about Jesus? Which of these should be changed in light of the manger?

What did you learn about Jesus from this week's readings?

What reading this week had the most impact on you? Why?

What do you plan to do about what you have learned this week?

Key Verse:

WEEK THREE

| DAY 1 ## Expect the unexpected

That night some shepherds were in the fields outside the village, guarding their flocks of sheep. Suddenly, an angel of the Lord appeared among them, and the radiance of the Lord's glory surrounded them. They were terribly frightened, but the angel reassured them. "Don't be afraid," he said. "I bring you good news of great joy for everyone! The Savior— yes, the Messiah, the Lord—has been born tonight in Bethlehem, the city of David! And this is how you will recognize him: You will find a baby lying in a manger, wrapped snugly in strips of cloth!"

Suddenly, the angel was joined by a vast host of others—the armies of heaven—praising God:

"Glory to God in the highest heaven, and peace on earth to all whom God favors."

When the angels had returned to heaven, the shepherds said to each other, "Come on, let's go to Bethlehem! Let's see this wonderful thing that has happened, which the Lord has told us about."

They ran to the village and found Mary and Joseph. And there was the baby, lying in the manger. Then the shepherds told everyone what had happened and what the angel had said to them about this child. All who heard the shepherds' story were astonished, but Mary quietly treasured these things in her heart and thought about them often. The shepherds went back to their fields and flocks, glorifying and praising God for what the angels had told them, and because they had seen the child, just as the angel had said.   LUKE 2:8-20

It's probably a safe bet that you've never had an angel appear to you. Don't feel left out; very few people ever have. So it would be natural to be a bit overwhelmed, not to mention terrified, if an angel—or a bunch of angels— suddenly showed up in your neighborhood. How would *you* react?

When angels appeared to the shepherds on the hillside outside Bethlehem that first Christmas Eve, the shepherds were petrified. When they heard the angels' message of the Messiah born in a manger (a feed trough of all things!) in the town of David (Bethlehem of all places!), no doubt they were perplexed as well. Who would have dreamed the Savior, Christ the Lord, would come in such a fashion?

God delights in doing the unexpected, the unlikely, the unbelievable. Don't be surprised if he tells *you* to do something unconventional. When he does, learn a lesson from those humble shepherds. Instead of ignoring God's message or running from it, move *toward* him and his plans for you.

Allow God to lead you. You may be amazed or even frightened, but you will not be bored.

| DAY 2 Great Expectations

Eight days later, when the baby was circumcised, he was named Jesus, the name given him by the angel even before he was conceived.

Then it was time for the purification offering, as required by the law of Moses after the birth of a child; so his parents took him to Jerusalem to present him to the Lord. The law of the Lord says, "If a woman's first child is a boy, he must be dedicated to the Lord." So they offered a sacrifice according to what was required in the law of the Lord—"either a pair of turtledoves or two young pigeons."

Now there was a man named Simeon who lived in Jerusalem. He was a righteous man and very devout. He was filled with the Holy Spirit, and he eagerly expected the Messiah to come and rescue Israel. The Holy Spirit had revealed to him that he would not die until he had seen the Lord's Messiah. That day the Spirit led him to the Temple. So when Mary and Joseph came to present the baby Jesus to the Lord as the law required, Simeon was there. He took the child in his arms and praised God, saying,

> "Lord, now I can die in peace! As you promised me, I have seen the Savior you have given to all people. He is a light to reveal God to the nations, and he is the glory of your people Israel!"

Joseph and Mary were amazed at what was being said about Jesus. Then Simeon blessed them, and he said to Mary, "This child will be rejected by many in Israel, and it will be their undoing. But he will be the greatest joy to many others. Thus, the deepest thoughts of many hearts will be revealed. And a sword will pierce your very soul."

Anna, a prophet, was also there in the Temple. She was the daughter of Phanuel, of the tribe of Asher, and was very old. She was a widow, for her husband had died when they had been married only seven years. She was now eighty-four years old. She never left the Temple but stayed there day and night, worshiping God with fasting and prayer. She came along just as Simeon was talking with Mary and Joseph, and she began praising God. She talked about Jesus to everyone who had been waiting for the promised King to come and deliver Jerusalem.

When Jesus' parents had fulfilled all the requirements of the law of the Lord, they returned home to Nazareth in Galilee. There the child grew up healthy and strong. He was filled with wisdom beyond his years, and God placed his special favor upon him.   LUKE 2:21-40

Parents are filled with pride and excitement when a baby is born, especially a first child. Your parents felt that way when you were born, too, even if the excitement has worn off a bit. Joseph and Mary had even more reason than other parents to feel a sense of anticipation about their first-born considering the events surrounding their son's birth, but most likely, they didn't expect the type of reception that their baby received when they visited the temple. Old Simeon, a prophet, and Anna, a prophetess, individually pronounced God's special blessing upon the baby Jesus. Joseph and Mary must have marveled—and worried—about what it all meant.

God has a purpose for you as well. There are no accidental children, no spare people, and certainly no unnecessary Christians. Angels did not herald your arrival on planet Earth, and your first church attendance was not marked with pronouncements from prophets and prophetesses. But if you have received Christ as your Lord, you *are* chosen by God and called according to his purpose.

As you read the Bible and talk with God in prayer, ask him to show you what your purpose is.

WEEK THREE | DAY 3 ## stargazing

Jesus was born in the town of Bethlehem in Judea, during the reign of King Herod. About that time some wise men from eastern lands arrived in Jerusalem, asking, "Where is the newborn king of the Jews? We have seen his star as it arose, and we have come to worship him."

Herod was deeply disturbed by their question, as was all of Jerusalem. He called a meeting of the leading priests and teachers of religious law. "Where did the prophets say the Messiah would be born?" he asked them.

"In Bethlehem," they said, "for this is what the prophet wrote:

'O Bethlehem of Judah, you are not just a lowly village in Judah, for a ruler will come from you who will be the shepherd for my people Israel.'"

Then Herod sent a private message to the wise men, asking them to come see him. At this meeting he learned the exact time when they first saw the star. Then he told them, "Go to Bethlehem and search carefully for the child. And when you find him, come back and tell me so that I can go and worship him, too!"

After this interview the wise men went their way. Once again the star appeared to them, guiding them to Bethlehem. It went ahead of them and stopped over the place where the child was. When they saw the star, they were filled with joy! They entered the house where the child and his mother, Mary, were, and they fell down before him and worshiped him.

Then they opened their treasure chests and gave him gifts of gold, frankincense, and myrrh. But when it was time to leave, they went home another way, because God had warned them in a dream not to return to Herod.   MATTHEW 2:1-12

People today look for wisdom various places and many different forms. They consult experts, research books, search the Internet, write to newspaper columnists, and so forth. Back in Bible times there were some wise men called magi who consulted the night sky. They were such experts on the stars that when they saw a new star appear in the sky, they recognized it as the star of the promised Messiah.

These wise men traveled for many days following that star. It led them to Jerusalem where they asked, "where is the one who has been born king of the Jews?" When they found him, they gave him gifts, bowed down and worshiped him.

This shows that wisdom can be found in many different places and in many different ways.

Be open to how God may want to speak to you—whether it's through a friend, his Word, circumstances, or even nature.

| WEEK THREE | DAY 4 | power struggle |

After the wise men were gone, an angel of the Lord appeared to Joseph in a dream. "Get up and flee to Egypt with the child and his mother," the angel said. "Stay there until I tell you to return, because Herod is going to try to kill the child." That night Joseph left for Egypt with the child and Mary, his mother, and they stayed there until Herod's death. This fulfilled what the Lord had spoken through the prophet: "I called my Son out of Egypt."

Herod was furious when he learned that the wise men had outwitted him. He sent soldiers to kill all the boys in and around Bethlehem who were two years old and under, because the wise men had told him the star first appeared to them about two years earlier. Herod's brutal action fulfilled the prophecy of Jeremiah:

"A cry of anguish is heard in Ramah—weeping and mourning unrestrained. Rachel weeps for her children, refusing to be comforted—for they are dead."

MATTHEW 2:13-18

What a monstrous act of unspeakable evil: killing all boys in and around Bethlehem who were two years old and under. Why would Herod do such a terrible thing?

Herod correctly understood that no one can serve two kings. You can pledge allegiance to one, or none at all, but you cannot submit to two. News of another king born in his kingdom presented a threat to Herod's power, even if that other king was still a baby.

Men and women who attain some level of power in this world often become very jealous of their positions. They don't like anyone or anything that challenges their authority. This is one reason the gospel of Jesus Christ has always been contrary to the dominant culture: it says that all authority in this life is limited and temporary, and that ultimate, eternal authority rests in the nail-scarred hands of King Jesus. Even today that message makes many powerful (and some not-so-powerful) people uncomfortable, and Christians may very well have to choose which king they will follow: the temporary leaders of this world, or the eternal King of kings.

You make many choices in life—who your friends are, what you do with your free time, what your activities are. What do these say about who is king in your life?

|DAY 5   under the circumstances

When Herod died, an angel of the Lord appeared in a dream to Joseph in Egypt and told him, "Get up and take the child and his mother back to the land of Israel, because those who were trying to kill the child are dead." So Joseph returned immediately to Israel with Jesus and his mother. But when he learned that the new ruler was Herod's son Archelaus, he was afraid. Then, in another dream, he was warned to go to Galilee. So they went and lived in a town called Nazareth. This fulfilled what was spoken by the prophets concerning the Messiah: "He will be called a Nazarene."   MATTHEW 2:19-23

God reveals his will to us in different ways. He speaks to us through the Bible, through prayer, through other people, and also through circumstances. On this occasion, he used circumstances to give Mary's husband, Joseph, important guidance.

Joseph believed that Archelaus, Herod's son and successor, posed a threat to his family's lives and safety. Indeed, Archelaus was an extremely violent man who started his reign by slaughtering three thousand influential people.

So instead of moving to some place in Judea, where Archelaus reigned, Joseph took Mary and Jesus back to Nazareth in Galilee. In a dream God confirmed Joseph's decision to avoid Judea. This is something God does not ordinarily do. Remember, God will never guide us in a way that contradicts what he tells us in the Bible. For example, if, through prayer, you discern that God is leading you to become a millionaire by selling illegal drugs or auctioning off your little brother to the highest bidder, you have misunderstood. God ordains our circumstances under his sovereign control to lead us in making decisions that honor him and build up others.

What has God been trying to tell you through your circumstances, your contacts with others, and your Bible readings?

What did you learn about Jesus from this week's readings?

What reading this week had the most impact on you? Why?

What do you plan to do about what you have learned this week?

Key Verse:

| DAY 1 ## Misunderstood

Every year Jesus' parents went to Jerusalem for the Passover festival. When Jesus was twelve years old, they attended the festival as usual. After the celebration was over, they started home to Nazareth, but Jesus stayed behind in Jerusalem. His parents didn't miss him at first, because they assumed he was with friends among the other travelers. But when he didn't show up that evening, they started to look for him among their relatives and friends. When they couldn't find him, they went back to Jerusalem to search for him there. Three days later they finally discovered him. He was in the Temple, sitting among the religious teachers, discussing deep questions with them. And all who heard him were amazed at his understanding and his answers.

His parents didn't know what to think. "Son!" his mother said to him. "Why have you done this to us? Your father and I have been frantic, searching for you everywhere."

"But why did you need to search?" he asked. "You should have known that I would be in my Father's house." But they didn't understand what he meant.

Then he returned to Nazareth with them and was obedient to them; and his mother stored all these things in her heart. So Jesus grew both in height and in wisdom, and he was loved by God and by all who knew him. LUKE 2:11-52

No doubt at least one time in your life you have felt misunderstood, even by those who ought to know you best. Imagine—Jesus had the same experience.

Joseph and Mary—who should have known that their son was no ordinary boy—lost track of him once on the way home from Jerusalem. Certainly Jesus is not the only teenager to have ever gotten separated from his parents, but most don't end up in a question-and-answer session with religious leaders. That, however, is where the young Messiah was when his parents finally found him. They scolded him for worrying them so badly.

Even though Jesus told his anxious parents that they "should have known that I would be in my Father's house," he obediently returned with his earthly parents and lived under their authority for another eighteen years.

If Jesus willingly obeyed **his** earthly parents—even when misunderstood—how much more should we honor our mothers and fathers?

walk the talk

It was now the fifteenth year of the reign of Tiberius, the Roman emperor. Pilate was governor over Judea; Herod Antipas was ruler over Galilee; his brother Philip was ruler over Iturea and Traconitis; Lysanias was ruler over Abilene. Annas and Caiaphas were the high priests. At this time a message from God came to John son of Zechariah, who was living out in the wilderness. Then John went from place to place on both sides of the Jordan River, preaching that people should be baptized to show that they had turned from their sins and turned to God to be forgiven. Isaiah had spoken of John when he said,

"He is a voice shouting in the wilderness: 'Prepare a pathway for the Lord's coming! Make a straight road for him! Fill in the valleys, and level the mountains and hills! Straighten the curves, and smooth out the rough places! And then all people will see the salvation sent from God.'"

Here is a sample of John's preaching to the crowds that came for baptism: "You brood of snakes! Who warned you to flee God's coming judgment? Prove by the way you live that you have really turned from your sins and turned to God. Don't just say, 'We're safe—we're the descendants of Abraham.' That proves nothing. God can change these stones here into children of Abraham. Even now the ax of God's judgment is poised, ready to sever your roots. Yes, every tree that does not produce good fruit will be chopped down and thrown into the fire."

The crowd asked, "What should we do?"

John replied, "If you have two coats, give one to the poor. If you have food, share it with those who are hungry."

Even corrupt tax collectors came to be baptized and asked, "Teacher, what should we do?"

"Show your honesty," he replied. "Make sure you collect no more taxes than the Roman government requires you to."

"What should we do?" asked some soldiers.

John replied, "Don't extort money, and don't accuse people of things you know they didn't do. And be content with your pay."

Everyone was expecting the Messiah to come soon, and they were eager to know whether John might be the Messiah. John answered their questions by saying, "I baptize with water; but someone is coming soon who is greater than I am—so much greater that I am not even worthy to be his slave. He will baptize you with the Holy Spirit and with fire. He is ready to separate the chaff from the grain with his winnowing fork. Then he will clean up the threshing area, storing the grain in his barn but burning the chaff with never-ending fire." John used many such warnings as he announced the Good News to the people.   LUKE 3:1-18

You probably have heard the expression, "You can talk the talk, but can you walk the walk"? People say this because it's easy to *say* you're going to do something, or that you're really great at some sport or skill, but it's harder to back it up such boasts. Talk is cheap.

John the Baptist challenged those who came into the wilderness to hear him to "prove by the way you live that you have really turned from your sins and turned to God." In other words, back up your claims of being religious with action. If you say you are a Christian, what in your life proves what you claim?

For example, don't just say you love God; show up consistently at your church's worship services and tell him yourself. Worship with sincerity, "in spirit and in truth" (John 4:24). Don't just say you love your neighbor; show it with acts of kindness, compassion and even sacrifice. Don't just say you're a Christian; seek to be Christlike in your actions, words, attitudes and relationships.

You can talk the talk, but can you walk the walk? You can, by God's grace.

DAY 3 TaLe of Two chiLdren

WEEK FOUR

Then Jesus went from Galilee to the Jordan River to be baptized by John. But John didn't want to baptize him. "I am the one who needs to be baptized by you," he said, "so why are you coming to me?"

But Jesus said, "It must be done, because we must do everything that is right." So then John baptized him.

After his baptism, as Jesus came up out of the water, the heavens were opened and he saw the Spirit of God descending like a dove and settling on him. And a voice from heaven said, "This is my beloved Son, and I am fully pleased with him." MATTHEW 3:13-17

Imagine that a man has two sons. He loves them both unconditionally. The first son is a model child: loving, obedient, respectful, glad to be with his father. The second child is not. Sullen, withdrawn, disobedient and disrespectful, he tolerates his father, but does not enjoy his company nor seek him out willingly. Which one does the father love?

He loves them both. Parental love is not contingent upon the behavior of the child. But with which one is the father most pleased? No contest. He's far more pleased, for obvious reasons, with his first son.

Jesus was the only Son of his heavenly Father. Their love for each other was perfect. In all areas of his life, he exhibited complete obedience to his Father. Jesus certainly didn't need to be baptized—a ritual symbolizing repentance for sins. But he did it out of loving obedience and a desire to honor his Father. So God said, "This is my beloved Son, and I am fully pleased with him."

If you are a believer, then you, too, are God's child (John 1:12).

Which kind of child are you in your relationship with your heavenly Father?

It's Tempting

Then Jesus, full of the Holy Spirit, left the Jordan River. He was led by the Spirit to go out into the wilderness, where the Devil tempted him for forty days. He ate nothing all that time and was very hungry.

Then the Devil said to him, "If you are the Son of God, change this stone into a loaf of bread."

But Jesus told him, "No! The Scriptures say, 'People need more than bread for their life.'"

Then the Devil took him up and revealed to him all the kingdoms of the world in a moment of time. The Devil told him, "I will give you the glory of these kingdoms and authority over them—because they are mine to give to anyone I please. I will give it all to you if you will bow down and worship me."

Jesus replied, "The Scriptures say,

'You must worship the Lord your God; serve only him.'"

Then the Devil took him to Jerusalem, to the highest point of the Temple, and said, "If you are the Son of God, jump off! For the Scriptures say,

'He orders his angels to protect and guard you. And they will hold you with their hands to keep you from striking your foot on a stone.'"

Jesus responded, "The Scriptures also say, 'Do not test the Lord your God.'"

When the Devil had finished tempting Jesus, he left him until the next opportunity came.

LUKE 4:1-13

If you knew an earthquake was coming, you would prepare for it. You would find a safe place, a doorway perhaps, away from windows and potential falling objects. If you had enough time, you would leave the danger area altogether. The problem is, earthquakes don't give any warning.

Temptation often operates the same way. It hits unannounced when we are unprepared. When it comes, we would do well to remember that Jesus was tempted in the wilderness. There, Satan tried to tempt Jesus in several different ways. In each case Jesus saw through Satan's scheme to subvert God's plan and answered his adversary with Scripture. That's a good plan for us as well.

More importantly, this passage also shows that our Savior understands what it's like to face temptations. This was not the only time Jesus was tempted; he was tempted many times. Hebrews 4:15 tells us, "This High Priest of ours understands our weaknesses, for he faced all of the same temptations we do, yet he did not sin."

When we are tempted, as we often will be, knowing how Jesus handled such circumstances can help a lot. Knowing that he went through it, too, provides great comfort.

DAY 5 point to the Light

WEEK FOUR

This was the testimony of John when the Jewish leaders sent priests and Temple assistants from Jerusalem to ask John whether he claimed to be the Messiah. He flatly denied it. "I am not the Messiah," he said.

"Well then, who are you?" they asked. "Are you Elijah?"

"No," he replied.

"Are you the Prophet?"

"No."

"Then who are you? Tell us, so we can give an answer to those who sent us. What do you have to say about yourself?"

John replied in the words of Isaiah:

"I am a voice shouting in the wilderness, 'Prepare a straight pathway for the Lord's coming!'"

Then those who were sent by the Pharisees asked him, "If you aren't the Messiah or Elijah or the Prophet, what right do you have to baptize?"

John told them, "I baptize with water, but right here in the crowd is someone you do not know, who will soon begin his ministry. I am not even worthy to be his slave." This incident took place at Bethany, a village east of the Jordan River, where John was baptizing.

JOHN 1:19-28

Remember what it's like to have someone point a flashlight directly into your eyes in an otherwise darkened room? Of course. It looks very bright at the time, so bright you can't see anything else for a few moments. But if someone points that light at you in broad daylight, you barely even notice.

The greater light of the sun totally overwhelms the puny light of the flash-light.

John the Baptist was a very important person in God's plan: he introduced the Savior to Israel. In fact, Jesus once said no one ever born was greater than John (Luke 7:28). Even so, John knew that his main job was to prepare the way for Jesus and to worship him. So he said he was a small, momentary light whose job was to point to the one true Light.

Our role is to worship Christ and enjoy getting to know him better day by day. Along the way, we get to introduce others to the one who has changed our lives.

John pointed to Jesus. That's really all we have to do, too.

What did you learn about Jesus from this week's readings?

What reading this week had the most impact on you? Why?

What do you plan to do about what you have learned this week?

Key Verse:

WEEK FIVE

| DAY 1 | ## more than a role model

The next day John saw Jesus coming toward him and said, "Look! There is the Lamb of God who takes away the sin of the world! He is the one I was talking about when I said, 'Soon a man is coming who is far greater than I am, for he existed long before I did.' I didn't know he was the one, but I have been baptizing with water in order to point him out to Israel."

Then John said, "I saw the Holy Spirit descending like a dove from heaven and resting upon him. I didn't know he was the one, but when God sent me to baptize with water, he told me, 'When you see the Holy Spirit descending and resting upon someone, he is the one you are looking for. He is the one who baptizes with the Holy Spirit.' I saw this happen to Jesus, so I testify that he is the Son of God."   JOHN 1:29-34

A lot of people, including many non-Christians, see Jesus as a positive role model. He certainly *is* that; in fact, he is without question the greatest role model who ever lived. But he's more than that. Much more.

John called Jesus "the Lamb of God, who takes away the sin of the world." This means that Jesus' role goes beyond just being a good example. He is the *atoning sacrifice*—the payment for our sins. He suffered and died on a cross to bring sinful men, women and young people back to a holy God. He made payment in his own blood for a debt that we owed but could never pay.

This is what sets Christianity apart from all other religions. Every faith has a set of beliefs and teachings that it holds to be true. Christianity alone says that its founder not only taught great truths, but also died and resurrected to empower his followers to live by those truths. He is the sacrificial Lamb who paid the ultimate price for our redemption.

When someone asks you if you have any heroes, tell them you have one, and his name is Jesus. Not just because of how he lived, but how—and **why**—he died.

changing the world

The following day, John was again standing with two of his disciples. As Jesus walked by, John looked at him and then declared, "Look! There is the Lamb of God!" Then John's two disciples turned and followed Jesus.

Jesus looked around and saw them following. "What do you want?" he asked them.

They replied, "Rabbi" (which means Teacher), "where are you staying?"

"Come and see," he said. It was about four o'clock in the afternoon when they went with him to the place, and they stayed there the rest of the day.

Andrew, Simon Peter's brother, was one of these men who had heard what John said and then followed Jesus. The first thing Andrew did was to find his brother, Simon, and tell him, "We have found the Messiah" (which means the Christ).

Then Andrew brought Simon to meet Jesus. Looking intently at Simon, Jesus said, "You are Simon, the son of John—but you will be called Cephas" (which means Peter).

The next day Jesus decided to go to Galilee. He found Philip and said to him, "Come, be my disciple." Philip was from Bethsaida, Andrew and Peter's hometown.

Philip went off to look for Nathanael and told him, "We have found the very person Moses and the prophets wrote about! His name is Jesus, the son of Joseph from Nazareth."

"Nazareth!" exclaimed Nathanael. "Can anything good come from there?"

"Just come and see for yourself," Philip said.

As they approached, Jesus said, "Here comes an honest man—a true son of Israel."

"How do you know about me?" Nathanael asked.

And Jesus replied, "I could see you under the fig tree before Philip found you."

Nathanael replied, "Teacher, you are the Son of God—the King of Israel!"

Jesus asked him, "Do you believe all this just because I told you I had seen you under the fig tree? You will see greater things than this." Then he said, "The truth is, you will all see heaven open and the angels of God going up and down upon the Son of Man."

JOHN 1:35-51

How does a person change the world?

Karl Marx started with a handful of university students and ignited a movement that eventually held over a billion people under the merciless tyranny of Communism. Jesus started with a small band of nobodies in an insignificant corner of the Roman Empire, and he also launched a revolution. But his was different from the Communist revolution. It *liberates* rather than *enslaves*. Marx's ideas now lie on the scrap heap of history with other failed ideologies. Jesus' revolution continues on, changing lives and entire cultures, larger today and growing faster than ever before.

Sociologist Margaret Mead once said, "Never doubt that a small group of thoughtful, committed citizens can change the world; indeed, it's the only thing that ever has."

You may not be famous, talented, wealthy or powerful. But if you want to change the world, join with the hundreds of millions of others down through the ages who have committed their hearts, souls, and minds to Jesus.

How do you change your school, your neighborhood, your home? One life at a time!

DAY 3 Party Time

WEEK FIVE

The next day Jesus' mother was a guest at a wedding celebration in the village of Cana in Galilee. Jesus and his disciples were also invited to the celebration. The wine supply ran out during the festivities, so Jesus' mother spoke to him about the problem. "They have no more wine," she told him.

"How does that concern you and me?" Jesus asked. "My time has not yet come."

But his mother told the servants, "Do whatever he tells you."

Six stone waterpots were standing there; they were used for Jewish ceremonial purposes and held twenty to thirty gallons each. Jesus told the servants, "Fill the jars with water." When the jars had been filled to the brim, he said, "Dip some out and take it to the master of ceremonies." So they followed his instructions.

When the master of ceremonies tasted the water that was now wine, not knowing where it had come from (though, of course, the servants knew), he called the bridegroom over. "Usually a host serves the best wine first," he said. "Then, when everyone is full and doesn't care, he brings out the less expensive wines. But you have kept the best until now!"

This miraculous sign at Cana in Galilee was Jesus' first display of his glory. And his disciples believed in him.

After the wedding he went to Capernaum for a few days with his mother, his brothers, and his disciples.   JOHN 2:1-12

Sometimes individual Christians or even whole churches give the impression that to follow Jesus is to say good-bye to anything remotely resembling fun. Their Ten Commandments all begin with "Thou shalt not," and just to make sure you don't enjoy life, they add a few dozen more prohibitions.

No one is suggesting the Christian life is a non-stop party. It involves sacrifice, discipline, and yes, sometimes suffering. But look where we find Jesus in John 2:1-1—a wedding celebration. And not only was Jesus in attendance, he also helped keep the party going in a very real and practical way—he turned water into wine. This drives some *Thou shalt not*-types crazy, but it's true.

The truth is that Jesus was the life of the party. He had a reputation for enjoying life to its fullest and enjoying the people around him. He feasted along with fasting. He partied along with praying. He welcomed company as well as solitude.

Follow Jesus. You may be surprised where he takes you.

DAY 4 see-Through Hearts

It was time for the annual Passover celebration, and Jesus went to Jerusalem. In the Temple area he saw merchants selling cattle, sheep, and doves for sacrifices; and he saw money changers behind their counters. Jesus made a whip from some ropes and chased them all out of the Temple. He drove out the sheep and oxen, scattered the money changers' coins over the floor, and turned over their tables. Then, going over to the people who sold doves, he told them, "Get these things out of here. Don't turn my Father's house into a market-place!"

Then his disciples remembered this prophecy from the Scriptures: "Passion for God's house burns within me."

"What right do you have to do these things?" the Jewish leaders demanded. "If you have this authority from God, show us a miraculous sign to prove it."

"All right," Jesus replied. "Destroy this temple, and in three days I will raise it up."

"What!" they exclaimed. "It took forty-six years to build this Temple, and you can do it in three days?" But by "this temple," Jesus meant his body. After he was raised from the dead, the disciples remembered that he had said this. And they believed both Jesus and the Scriptures.

Because of the miraculous signs he did in Jerusalem at the Passover celebration, many people were convinced that he was indeed the Messiah. But Jesus didn't trust them, because he knew what people were really like. No one needed to tell him about human nature.

JOHN 2:13-25

Appearances can be deceiving. Many people seem nice enough on the outside but have a mean streak just below the surface. Others have a gruff exterior that hides a soft heart.

In this passage, Jesus demonstrates an uncanny ability to see through to the hearts of people and situations that others completely misunderstand. His Father's house (the temple) was built to be a place of worship; greedy men turned it into a crass marketplace. Jesus called them on their sin and presumptuousness.

When Jesus referred to his own body as "this temple," they thought he was talking about bricks and mortar. Crowds gathered to watch him perform miracles, apparently signing up to be his followers; he knew most of them were really only there to see a magic act. Jesus saw through each of them. Today he still sees through them—and us.

When you pray, remember: God already knows what is in your heart.

Be honest with God about what scares you and encourages you; what makes you glad or apprehensive; who you love as well as who you find it difficult to love.

DAY 5 New Birth

After dark one evening, a Jewish religious leader named Nicodemus, a Pharisee, came to speak with Jesus. "Teacher," he said, "we all know that God has sent you to teach us. Your miraculous signs are proof enough that God is with you."

Jesus replied, "I assure you, unless you are born again, you can never see the Kingdom of God."

"What do you mean?" exclaimed Nicodemus. "How can an old man go back into his mother's womb and be born again?"

Jesus replied, "The truth is, no one can enter the Kingdom of God without being born of water and the Spirit. Humans can reproduce only human life, but the Holy Spirit gives new life from heaven. So don't be surprised at my statement that you must be born again. Just as you can hear the wind but can't tell where it comes from or where it is going, so you can't explain how people are born of the Spirit."

"What do you mean?" Nicodemus asked.

Jesus replied, "You are a respected Jewish teacher, and yet you don't understand these things? I assure you, I am telling you what we know and have seen, and yet you won't believe us. But if you don't even believe me when I tell you about things that happen here on earth, how can you possibly believe if I tell you what is going on in heaven? For only I, the Son of Man, have come to earth and will return to heaven again. And as Moses lifted up the bronze snake on a pole in the wilderness, so I, the Son of Man, must be lifted up on a pole, so that everyone who believes in me will have eternal life.

"For God so loved the world that he gave his only Son, so that everyone who believes in him will not perish but have eternal life. God did not send his Son into the world to condemn it, but to save it.

"There is no judgment awaiting those who trust him. But those who do not trust him have already been judged for not believing in the only Son of God. Their judgment is based on this fact: The light from heaven came into the world, but they loved the darkness more than the light, for their actions were evil. They hate the light because they want to sin in the darkness. They stay away from the light for fear their sins will be exposed and they will be punished. But those who do what is right come to the light gladly, so everyone can see that they are doing what God wants." JOHN 3:1-21

This passage, one of the best known in the entire Bible, contains one of its most important statements: "You must be born again." It also includes its most beloved promise: "For God so loved the world that he gave his only Son, so that everyone who believes in him will not perish but have eternal life."

To be a Christian—to have eternal life—is not a matter of doing good deeds, avoiding certain sins, or getting involved in church activities. All those are worthwhile. But you can do good deeds till you drop from exhaustion, avoid sins with great dedication, even serve on every committee in your church and *still* miss the mark.

To be a Christian means that you *believe* in Jesus as your Lord and Savior and *accept* by faith the payment he made on the cross for your sins. This kind of faith is not mere religious lip service but gut-level trust in Jesus to save your soul. That's what it takes to be born again.

Everyone must decide to either trust in Jesus for salvation or in someone or something else. Your parents cannot make the decision for you, nor can your church, youth pastor, best friend, or anyone else. It's *your* decision.

If you haven't already made this all-important decision, why not reread John 3:1-21 and do so right now?

What did you learn about Jesus from this week's readings?

What reading this week had the most impact on you? Why?

What do you plan to do about what you have learned this week?

Key Verse:

WEEK SIX

| DAY 1 | who Gets the Glory?

Afterward Jesus and his disciples left Jerusalem, but they stayed in Judea for a while and baptized there.

At this time John the Baptist was baptizing at Aenon, near Salim, because there was plenty of water there and people kept coming to him for baptism. This was before John was put into prison. At that time a certain Jew began an argument with John's disciples over ceremonial cleansing. John's disciples came to him and said, Teacher, the man you met on the other side of the Jordan River, the one you said was the Messiah, is also baptizing people. And everybody is going over there instead of coming here to us". JOHN 3:22-26

"Hey, John—remember that guy Jesus you baptized? Well, he's upstream there baptizing even more people than you are!" Imagine one of John's loyal disciples coming to him, breathless, a worried look on his face, having scouted out "the competition."

"What are we going to do, John?"

Unfortunately, much of the church's history has been characterized by jealousy and unhealthy competitiveness. These things are still with us. But consider how John the Baptist responded to the news of Jesus' growing ministry—He rejoiced that Jesus had come and that God's kingdom was advancing. He ended any argument or divisiveness among his followers by letting them know that Jesus was first in his life.

When you feel those pangs of jealousy when someone else is chosen for the solo in the church choir, or the pull to compete when another youth group member is honored for his work on the mission trip, remember John the Baptist.

Put Jesus at the center of everything you do and rejoice when Christ is honored by others' actions.

| DAY 2 **NO picnic**

John also publicly criticized Herod Antipas, ruler of Galilee, for marrying Herodias, his brother's wife, and for many other wrongs he had done. So Herod put John in prison, adding this sin to his many others.   LUKE 3:19-20

If you are nice and follow Jesus faithfully, everyone will like you and life will go well for you. Right?

Not necessarily. Life is not always a picnic for God's people, even his best and most faithful ones. John the Baptist was doing what God had called him to do as a prophet: to speak the truth no matter what. For his faithfulness John was thrown into Herod's prison and eventually was beheaded.

God does not promise his people an easy time of it. In fact, the record of the Bible and church history shows quite the opposite. The ones who follow God most devotedly often suffer the most. Why does God allow this? We simply don't know.

Isaiah 55:8-9 says, "'My thoughts are completely different from yours,' says the LORD. 'And my ways are far beyond anything you could imagine. For just as the heavens are higher than the earth, so are my ways higher than your ways and my thoughts higher than your thoughts.'"

Living for Jesus does not guarantee us an easy life. It does, however, assure that our life will be meaningful.

| DAY 3 **Thirsty for Life**

Jesus learned that the Pharisees had heard, "Jesus is baptizing and making more disciples than John" (though Jesus himself didn't baptize them—his disciples did). So he left Judea to return to Galilee.

He had to go through Samaria on the way. Eventually he came to the Samaritan village of Sychar, near the parcel of ground that Jacob gave to his son Joseph. Jacob's well was there; and Jesus, tired from the long walk, sat wearily beside the well about noontime. Soon a Samaritan woman came to draw water, and Jesus said to her, "Please give me a drink." He was alone at the time because his disciples had gone into the village to buy some food.

The woman was surprised, for Jews refuse to have anything to do with Samaritans. She said to Jesus, "You are a Jew, and I am a Samaritan woman. Why are you asking me for a drink?"

Jesus replied, "If you only knew the gift God has for you and who I am, you would ask me, and I would give you living water."

"But sir, you don't have a rope or a bucket," she said, "and this is a very deep well. Where would you get this living water? And besides, are you greater than our ancestor Jacob who gave us this well? How can you offer better water than he and his sons and his cattle enjoyed?"

Jesus replied, "People soon become thirsty again after drinking this water. But the water I give them takes away thirst altogether. It becomes a perpetual spring within them, giving them eternal life."

"Please, sir," the woman said, "give me some of that water! Then I'll never be thirsty again, and I won't have to come here to haul water."

"Go and get your husband," Jesus told her.

"I don't have a husband," the woman replied.

Jesus said, "You're right! You don't have a husband—for you have had five husbands, and you aren't even married to the man you're living with now."

"Sir," the woman said, "you must be a prophet. So tell me, why is it that you Jews insist that Jerusalem is the only place of worship, while we Samaritans claim it is here at Mount Gerizim, where our ancestors worshiped?"

Jesus replied, "Believe me, the time is coming when it will no longer matter whether you worship the Father here or in Jerusalem. You Samaritans know so little about the one you worship, while we Jews know all about him, for salvation comes through the Jews. But the time is coming and is already here when true worshipers will worship the Father in spirit and in truth. The Father is looking for anyone who will worship him that way. For God is Spirit, so those who worship him must worship in spirit and in truth."

The woman said, "I know the Messiah will come—the one who is called Christ. When he comes, he will explain everything to us."

Then Jesus told her, "I am the Messiah!"   JOHN 4:1-26

Friendships, parties, football games, concerts, dating, movies—everyone wants to enjoy life, to experience it to the fullest. Some people make wise choices about where to go to satisfy that desire, looking to parents, teachers, coaches, youth pastors, sports, music, and studies. Others choose negative and destructive influences like drugs, gangs, or dark and perverse musical acts. Whichever way we choose, we all have something in common: We're all thirsty for life.

The Samaritan woman whom Jesus encountered at the well outside Sychar was looking for the best life she could find for herself. Her search had led her to marry five men and she now lived with another man to whom she was not married. Jesus saw not only her sins, but also her deepest need: to know him as her Messiah.

When you look for the best way to satisfy your thirsty and hungry soul, remember the Samaritan woman.

Begin and end your search with Jesus, the living Word, and with the Bible, the written Word.

The Harvest

Just then his disciples arrived. They were astonished to find him talking to a woman, but none of them asked him why he was doing it or what they had been discussing. The woman left her water jar beside the well and went back to the village and told everyone, "Come and meet a man who told me everything I ever did! Can this be the Messiah?" So the people came streaming from the village to see him.

Meanwhile, the disciples were urging Jesus to eat. "No," he said, "I have food you don't know about."

"Who brought it to him?" the disciples asked each other.

Then Jesus explained: "My nourishment comes from doing the will of God, who sent me, and from finishing his work. Do you think the work of harvesting will not begin until the summer ends four months from now? Look around you! Vast fields are ripening all around us and are ready now for the harvest. The harvesters are paid good wages, and the fruit they harvest is people brought to eternal life. What joy awaits both the planter and the harvester alike! You know the saying, 'One person plants and someone else harvests.' And it's true. I sent you to harvest where you didn't plant; others had already done the work, and you will gather the harvest." JOHN 4:27-38

Take a moment during school and look around the classroom. What do you see? Most likely you see a group of teens much like yourself, some looking bored, others talking animatedly about their plans for the weekend. Some of these kids you know, some you don't know as well.

Now take another look. See them with Jesus' eyes. What do you see now? Do you see the harvest? Do you see some kids who are hurting, some who don't have a clue what they want to do with their life, some who are angry or hostile toward adults, some who are confused? Do you see a group of kids who *need* Jesus, just like the people did back in the disciples' time?

Jesus told his earliest followers that the harvest is all around and is *ready* for harvesters to do their work. He tells us the same thing today. If we take our relationship with Jesus seriously we will see that we are called to work in this harvest. He wants us to tell the people around us about the eternal life that is found through faith in Christ.

Jesus said that the harvest is ready. Are you?

| DAY 5   ReaL Encounter

Many Samaritans from the village believed in Jesus because the woman had said, "He told me everything I ever did!" When they came out to see him, they begged him to stay at their village. So he stayed for two days, long enough for many of them to hear his message and believe. Then they said to the woman, "Now we believe because we have heard him ourselves, not just because of what you told us. He is indeed the Savior of the world."

JOHN 4:39-42

Think about it. The Samaritan woman probably had a reputation in her town—and based on what we learn about her in Scripture (4:16-18), not a particularly good one. Yet when she returned to her village and told others about her encounter with Jesus, they listened to her *and* believed in Christ.

Think about it! Something must have radically changed in this woman for others to accept her word so readily. Because of her bad reputation, they could have easily dismissed her, saying, "Oh, sure, you've got yet another man in your life!" But *something about her* had changed, and it caused others in her village to investigate the man whom she had met. When they actually met Jesus and heard him speak, they were eager to believe that "He is indeed the Savior of the world."

Jesus has that effect upon people. He is able to change lives just like he changed the Samaritan woman's life. When this happens, the news is just too good to keep to yourself.

How has your encounter with Jesus changed your life? What would your friends say about this?

What did you learn about Jesus from this week's readings?

What reading this week had the most impact on you? Why?

What do you plan to do about what you have learned this week?

Key Verse:

| DAY 1 ## time for a change

When Jesus heard that John had been arrested, he left Judea and returned to Galilee. But instead of going to Nazareth, he went to Capernaum, beside the Sea of Galilee, in the region of Zebulun and Naphtali. This fulfilled Isaiah's prophecy:

"In the land of Zebulun and of Naphtali, beside the sea, beyond the Jordan River— in Galilee where so many Gentiles live—the people who sat in darkness have seen a great light. And for those who lived in the land where death casts its shadow, a light has shined."

From then on, Jesus began to preach, "Turn from your sins and turn to God, because the Kingdom of Heaven is near." MATTHEW 4:12-17

Jesus' first sermon was very simple. Its central theme was this: Turn from your sins because the kingdom of heaven is near.

Jesus was talking about repentance. He wanted people to change their attitudes about sin and turn away from it. This means that instead of loving our sins, actively flaunting God's commands, or even being apathetic about them, Jesus wants us to do an about-face. We are to turn *away* from sin and *toward* God. This is not always easy, and it requires us to look to him for help and the power to obey him when the pressure is on.

Repentance is not a one-time-only event. It is an ongoing lifestyle of desiring to please God, asking his help to do so and looking to him for forgiveness when we fail. Jesus' basic message is as applicable today as when he first proclaimed it 2000 years ago: Turn from your sin because the kingdom of heaven is near.

Is there sin in your life—your thoughts, words, attitudes, behaviors, or relationships—for which you should repent?

Faith in Action

In the course of his journey through Galilee, he arrived at the town of Cana, where he had turned the water into wine. There was a government official in the city of Capernaum whose son was very sick. When he heard that Jesus had come from Judea and was traveling in Galilee, he went over to Cana. He found Jesus and begged him to come to Capernaum with him to heal his son, who was about to die.

Jesus asked, "Must I do miraculous signs and wonders before you people will believe in me?"

The official pleaded, "Lord, please come now before my little boy dies."

Then Jesus told him, "Go back home. Your son will live!" And the man believed Jesus' word and started home.

While he was on his way, some of his servants met him with the news that his son was alive and well. He asked them when the boy had begun to feel better, and they replied, "Yesterday afternoon at one o'clock his fever suddenly disappeared!" Then the father realized it was the same time that Jesus had told him, "Your son will live." And the officer and his entire household believed in Jesus. This was Jesus' second miraculous sign in Galilee after coming from Judea.   JOHN 4:46-54

Check out what this government official did. First, he traveled 20 miles to see Jesus and ask for his help. The man was most likely one of the king's officers, but he called Jesus *Lord,* putting himself under Jesus' authority. He asked the Lord to help heal his sick child, and he believed Jesus' promise that the child would live. The man asked, believed, and then *obeyed* Jesus and returned home. This man not only believed what Jesus said, but he acted on it, demonstrating his faith.

Faith is more than just believing what Jesus says. It isn't enough to say we believe that Jesus can take care of all our problems. Clearly the Bible teaches that, and it's true. But faith also requires obedience. We need to *act* as if Jesus can do what he says.

Next time you pray for Jesus to help you with a specific problem or need, put your faith into action.

Live as though you believe Jesus will do what he says. That's faith in action.

DAY 3 | the NO-comfort zone

When he came to the village of Nazareth, his boyhood home, he went as usual to the synagogue on the Sabbath and stood up to read the Scriptures. The scroll containing the messages of Isaiah the prophet was handed to him, and he unrolled the scroll to the place where it says:

"The Spirit of the Lord is upon me, for he has appointed me to preach Good News to the poor. He has sent me to proclaim that captives will be released, that the blind will see, that the downtrodden will be freed from their oppressors, and that the time of the Lord's favor has come."

He rolled up the scroll, handed it back to the attendant, and sat down. Everyone in the synagogue stared at him intently. Then he said, "This Scripture has come true today before your very eyes!"

All who were there spoke well of him and were amazed by the gracious words that fell from his lips. "How can this be?" they asked. "Isn't this Joseph's son?"

Then he said, "Probably you will quote me that proverb, 'Physician, heal yourself'—meaning, 'Why don't you do miracles here in your hometown like those you did in Capernaum?' But the truth is, no prophet is accepted in his own hometown.

"Certainly there were many widows in Israel who needed help in Elijah's time, when there was no rain for three and a half years and hunger stalked the land. Yet Elijah was not sent to any of them. He was sent instead to a widow of Zarephath—a foreigner in the land of Sidon. Or think of the prophet Elisha, who healed Naaman, a Syrian, rather than the many lepers in Israel who needed help."

When they heard this, the people in the synagogue were furious. Jumping up, they mobbed him and took him to the edge of the hill on which the city was built. They intended to push him over the cliff, but he slipped away through the crowd and left them.

LUKE 4:16-30

If you attend your church's worship services regularly, you probably occasionally feel like you've heard it all before. Imagine how Jesus must have felt! He attended the synagogue in Nazareth week after week and listened to men read words he himself had inspired.

But one day something very different took place. Jesus himself taught from the prophet Isaiah's words, which point to him—to Jesus Christ. At first this was well received, until people realized the implications of his message. Jesus was talking about *them*, and comparing them to the unbelieving citizens of ancient Israel. Not only that, Jesus implied that the gospel be offered even to the despised Gentiles! As the level of discomfort grew, people's attitudes toward Jesus changed drastically.

If you take the gospel seriously, aspects of it will move you out of your comfort zone, perhaps **way** out. When that happens, go where he leads, and trust Jesus to steady you.

| DAY 4 # FOLLOW ME!

One day as Jesus was walking along the shores of the Sea of Galilee, he saw Simon and his brother, Andrew, fishing with a net, for they were commercial fishermen. Jesus called out to them, "Come, be my disciples, and I will show you how to fish for people!" And they left their nets at once and went with him.

A little farther up the shore Jesus saw Zebedee's sons, James and John, in a boat mending their nets. He called them, too, and immediately they left their father, Zebedee, in the boat with the hired men and went with him.   MARK 1:16-20

As you read these verses, you may get the impression that one day some men were fishing in the Sea of Galilee when a stranger named Jesus came by, said, "Follow me," and they dropped everything and went. Not exactly.

They had met him previously, had heard him speak, and undoubtedly had been thinking about him and his message. They may have been talking it over with one another. When he came and called them, they were ready.

Are you giving serious consideration to following Jesus? Wonderful! It is the most important decision you will ever make—one that has *eternal* consequences. Follow the example of these fishermen and think it through very carefully. It will change your entire life. It will affect what you do for a career, and how you do it. It will impact your decisions about marriage. It will greatly influence how you spend your time and your money, what kinds of recreation you enjoy, and how you conduct your relationships.

Following Jesus as Lord will radically shape every area of your life, just as surely as it caused those fishermen to leave their boats and their nets and embark on the adventure of a lifetime.

DAY 5 sabbath fireworks

Jesus and his companions went to the town of Capernaum, and every Sabbath day he went into the synagogue and taught the people. They were amazed at his teaching, for he taught as one who had real authority—quite unlike the teachers of religious law.

A man possessed by an evil spirit was in the synagogue, and he began shouting, "Why are you bothering us, Jesus of Nazareth? Have you come to destroy us? I know who you are—the Holy One sent from God!"

Jesus cut him short. "Be silent! Come out of the man." At that, the evil spirit screamed and threw the man into a convulsion, but then he left him.

Amazement gripped the audience, and they began to discuss what had happened. "What sort of new teaching is this?" they asked excitedly. "It has such authority! Even evil spirits obey his orders!" The news of what he had done spread quickly through that entire area of Galilee. MARK 1:21-28

When was the last time you saw something truly amazing happen in a worship service?

The people of Capernaum were not expecting anything out of the ordinary that Sabbath, either. The bulletin did not say:

- Call to worship
- Welcome
- Message from the Scriptures
- Exorcism
- Benediction

The people were expecting another typical synagogue service; instead, they saw a supernatural confrontation between the Son of God and a demon-possessed man. Picture it: an evil spirit face-to-face with God himself. No wonder he cried out! He was way out of his league, and he knew it. And notice that the demon had a good grasp of who Jesus is, calling him "the Holy One sent from God!"

Worship services are not intended to be spectacular manifestations of supernatural conflict. They are designed for worship, to glorify God, build up his people, and advance his kingdom. But when the kingdom of God invades the kingdoms of this world with power and authority, fireworks follow.

Don't be surprised if your world is rocked as you worship its Creator.

What did you learn about Jesus from this week's readings?

What reading this week had the most impact on you? Why?

What do you plan to do about what you have learned this week?

Key Verse:

WEEKEIGHT

| DAY 1 ## The Healing Touch

When Jesus arrived at Peter's house, Peter's mother-in-law was in bed with a high fever. But when Jesus touched her hand, the fever left her. Then she got up and prepared a meal for him.

That evening many demon-possessed people were brought to Jesus. All the spirits fled when he commanded them to leave; and he healed all the sick. This fulfilled the word of the Lord through Isaiah, who said, "He took our sicknesses and removed our diseases." MATTHEW 8:14-17

The gods of other religions are distant, remote, and not intimately involved with creation. Only Christianity gives us a God who is so concerned with his creatures that he actually became one of us.

Jesus was God. Yet he lived a truly human life. He breathed our air, ate our food, and walked our roads. He touched and healed the sick, the blind, the lame, and the demon-possessed. God cares enough about us to become one of us, to get his hands dirty with the grime and the problems of his people.

Historically, Christians have followed Jesus' example in extending mercy and compassion to the sick and suffering, the outcast and oppressed, the orphan and widow. In times of crisis, disease, natural disaster, and war, Christians rush in to help while others rush to escape. We do this not to earn Christ's love but as a response to his love.

Jesus' healing miracles were just a taste of what the whole world will one day experience in God's kingdom.

Look for ways you can extend Jesus' healing, love, and compassion to others. In this way bring a touch of heaven to a needy earth.

DAY 2 ## moving on

The next morning Jesus awoke long before daybreak and went out alone into the wilderness to pray. Later Simon and the others went out to find him. They said, "Everyone is asking for you."

But he replied, "We must go on to other towns as well, and I will preach to them, too, because that is why I came." So he traveled throughout the region of Galilee, preaching in the synagogues and expelling demons from many people.   MARK 1:35-39

If you were a preacher, and you were experiencing tremendous success and popular adulation in a town, wouldn't you stay and enjoy it? Most people would, but Jesus didn't.

After seeing marvelous results with his work in Capernaum, Jesus got up early the next morning, spent time talking with his Father, and decided to move on. Why? He had certainly experienced enough hostility and rejection in other places. Why not stay and bask in the acceptance for a while?

Simply put, Jesus had a job to do. He was focused on his mission to reach as many people as possible in the surrounding towns, to proclaim the good news of God's love and salvation to them all. Beyond that, he wanted to get that message to the whole world. Obviously, he succeeded—you're reading that story now.

Jesus didn't allow success, fame, or complacency to deter him from completing his mission.

When God gives you a task, follow Jesus' example. Start moving and don't let anything sidetrack you.

DAY 3 Fishing for Results

One day as Jesus was preaching on the shore of the Sea of Galilee, great crowds pressed in on him to listen to the word of God. He noticed two empty boats at the water's edge, for the fishermen had left them and were washing their nets. Stepping into one of the boats, Jesus asked Simon, its owner, to push it out into the water. So he sat in the boat and taught the crowds from there.

When he had finished speaking, he said to Simon, "Now go out where it is deeper and let down your nets, and you will catch many fish."

"Master," Simon replied, "we worked hard all last night and didn't catch a thing. But if you say so, we'll try again." And this time their nets were so full they began to tear! A shout for help brought their partners in the other boat, and soon both boats were filled with fish and on the verge of sinking.

When Simon Peter realized what had happened, he fell to his knees before Jesus and said, "Oh, Lord, please leave me—I'm too much of a sinner to be around you." For he was awe-struck by the size of their catch, as were the others with him. His partners, James and John, the sons of Zebedee, were also amazed.

Jesus replied to Simon, "Don't be afraid! From now on you'll be fishing for people!" And as soon as they landed, they left everything and followed Jesus.   LUKE 5:1-11

Jesus probably made his living as a carpenter. Yet here he was telling veteran fishermen how to get a better catch. Peter was understandably hesitant to do as Jesus said. After all, he had spent his entire life up to that time on the water. Still, he decided to do what Jesus asked of him. He and the others were rewarded with a huge catch of fish.

Some people today dismiss Jesus because he lived so long ago. He taught people from a different time and culture. What relevancy could his teachings possibly have for today? When he lived among us, Jesus reached out to people from different backgrounds and education. And he continues to break through all barriers and concepts. His message and teachings are as fresh and relevant today as they were that day by the Sea of Galilee.

There is something about Jesus that compels us to respond, even if he directs us to do things that don't make much sense at the time. That's when faith and trust come in. Remember Peter, and put out into the deep water.

Trusting in Jesus means being willing to take that first step.

| DAY 4   # untouchabLe?

A man with leprosy came and knelt in front of Jesus, begging to be healed. "If you want to, you can make me well again," he said.

Moved with pity, Jesus touched him. "I want to," he said. "Be healed!" Instantly the leprosy disappeared—the man was healed. Then Jesus sent him on his way and told him sternly, "Go right over to the priest and let him examine you. Don't talk to anyone along the way. Take along the offering required in the law of Moses for those who have been healed of leprosy, so everyone will have proof of your healing."

But as the man went on his way, he spread the news, telling everyone what had happened to him. As a result, such crowds soon surrounded Jesus that he couldn't enter a town anywhere publicly. He had to stay out in the secluded places, and people from everywhere came to him there.   MARK 1:40-45

God reaches out to the most unlikely people. If you had asked someone in first-century Palestine who the Messiah would visit, they might have listed many different kinds of people. But lepers undoubtedly would have been very last on the list.

Lepers were the absolute outcasts of Jewish society. The word *leprosy* covered a number of different kinds of skin diseases, but all lepers were considered unclean and were shunned. No one interacted with a leper. Most importantly, no one ever willingly *touched* one.

But Jesus did. He touched the untouchable and loved the unlovable. He still does this.

Who do you know who seems an unlikely candidate for God's love? Someone at school, at work, on the team, or in your family? Pray for that person, and ask God to use you to bring Christ into his or her life.

The last person on your list may be the next one on God's list.

|DAY 5   HOW Far?

Several days later Jesus returned to Capernaum, and the news of his arrival spread quickly through the town. Soon the house where he was staying was so packed with visitors that there wasn't room for one more person, not even outside the door. And he preached the word to them. Four men arrived carrying a paralyzed man on a mat. They couldn't get to Jesus through the crowd, so they dug through the clay roof above his head. Then they lowered the sick man on his mat, right down in front of Jesus. Seeing their faith, Jesus said to the paralyzed man, "My son, your sins are forgiven."

But some of the teachers of religious law who were sitting there said to themselves, "What? This is blasphemy! Who but God can forgive sins!"

Jesus knew what they were discussing among themselves, so he said to them, "Why do you think this is blasphemy? Is it easier to say to the paralyzed man, 'Your sins are forgiven' or 'Get up, pick up your mat, and walk'? I will prove that I, the Son of Man, have the authority on earth to forgive sins." Then Jesus turned to the paralyzed man and said, "Stand up, take your mat, and go on home, because you are healed!"

The man jumped up, took the mat, and pushed his way through the stunned onlookers. Then they all praised God. "We've never seen anything like this before!" they exclaimed.

MARK 2:1-12

How far would you go to bring a friend to Jesus?

This passage tells the amazing story of Jesus' healing of a paralyzed man. But it's also the story of the man's friends and all they did to get him to Jesus for healing. The poor man obviously needed healing and so couldn't get himself to Jesus. So his friends did for him what he could not do for himself. They even removed part of a roof to get the paralyzed man to the Lord.

What a great picture of salvation! Apart from Christ, we are all spiritual cripples, unable to help ourselves. Then, someone comes along, has compassion on us in our helpless state, and brings us to Jesus through word and example. Just as in this story, Jesus forgives our sins *and* heals us. Thank God for his amazing compassion, and for people who care enough to tell others about it.

How far would you go to bring a friend to Jesus?

What did you learn about Jesus from this week's readings?

What reading this week had the most impact on you? Why?

What do you plan to do about what you have learned this week?

Key Verse:

DAY 1 | Jesus' Top Ten List

As Jesus was going down the road, he saw Matthew sitting at his tax-collection booth. "Come, be my disciple," Jesus said to him. So Matthew got up and followed him.

That night Matthew invited Jesus and his disciples to be his dinner guests, along with his fellow tax collectors and many other notorious sinners. The Pharisees were indignant. "Why does your teacher eat with such scum?" they asked his disciples.

When he heard this, Jesus replied, "Healthy people don't need a doctor—sick people do." Then he added, "Now go and learn the meaning of this Scripture: 'I want you to be merciful, I don't want your sacrifices.' For I have come to call sinners, not those who think they are already good enough." MATTHEW 9:9-13

If Jesus were to come to your school, who do you think he would hang out with? The most popular kids, the student government officers, the best athletes, the cheerleaders? Well, maybe.

Jesus might very well spend time with any or all of those people if they wanted him to. But it is more likely that he would gravitate toward people nobody else wants to be around. That is what Jesus did in ancient Israel. He spent time with tax collectors, prostitutes, lepers, the outcast, and the socially unacceptable—not exactly a *Who's Who* of ancient Palestine.

God is not impressed with anyone's résumé or yearbook biography. God loves us in spite of what we are, not because of it. He seems to take particular delight in the lowly because they are so much more aware of their need for him.

Wherever you fit—if you consider yourself an outcast or one of the in-crowd—Jesus came to be with people exactly like you.

Habit-Forming

The religious leaders complained that Jesus' disciples were feasting instead of fasting. "John the Baptist's disciples always fast and pray," they declared, "and so do the disciples of the Pharisees. Why are yours always feasting?"

Jesus asked, "Do wedding guests fast while celebrating with the groom? Someday he will be taken away from them, and then they will fast."

Then Jesus gave them this illustration: "No one tears a piece of cloth from a new garment and uses it to patch an old garment. For then the new garment would be torn, and the patch wouldn't even match the old garment. And no one puts new wine into old wineskins. The new wine would burst the old skins, spilling the wine and ruining the skins. New wine must be put into new wineskins. But no one who drinks the old wine seems to want the fresh and the new. 'The old is better,' they say." LUKE 5:33-39

Old habits die hard. People easily become accustomed to doing things in one particular manner and find it hard to change their ways even when something better comes along. Think about it. How comfortable are your grandparents with a computer?

The Pharisees and the teachers of the law were accustomed to thinking of their faith in terms of self-denial and observance of religious laws. Then along came Jesus with his talk of weddings, banquets, joy in heaven, and freedom in this life. The old mental machinery of the Pharisees couldn't switch gears to keep up with him

As you experience the joy and freedom of following Jesus, some people may say you're not serious, sober, or solemn enough. Don't worry about such talk. They said the same thing about Jesus.

Embrace the freedom and joy of following Christ!

|DAY 3 # aqainst the RuLes!

Afterward Jesus returned to Jerusalem for one of the Jewish holy days. Inside the city, near the Sheep Gate, was the pool of Bethesda, with five covered porches. Crowds of sick people—blind, lame, or paralyzed—lay on the porches. One of the men lying there had been sick for thirty-eight years. When Jesus saw him and knew how long he had been ill, he asked him, "Would you like to get well?"

"I can't, sir," the sick man said, "for I have no one to help me into the pool when the water is stirred up. While I am trying to get there, someone else always gets in ahead of me."

Jesus told him, "Stand up, pick up your sleeping mat, and walk!"

Instantly, the man was healed! He rolled up the mat and began walking! But this miracle happened on the Sabbath day. So the Jewish leaders objected. They said to the man who was cured, "You can't work on the Sabbath! It's illegal to carry that sleeping mat!"

He replied, "The man who healed me said to me, 'Pick up your sleeping mat and walk'."

"Who said such a thing as that?" they demanded.

The man didn't know, for Jesus had disappeared into the crowd. But afterward Jesus found him in the Temple and told him, "Now you are well; so stop sinning, or something even worse may happen to you." Then the man went to find the Jewish leaders and told them it was Jesus who had healed him.

So the Jewish leaders began harassing Jesus for breaking the Sabbath rules. But Jesus replied, "My Father never stops working, so why should I?" So the Jewish leaders tried all the more to kill him. In addition to disobeying the Sabbath rules, he had spoken of God as his Father, thereby making himself equal with God.   JOHN 5:1-18

When Jesus comes into a person's life, things change. Guilt and confusion give way to peace and clarity. Sometimes invalids even get up and leave their sickbeds behind, as happened in this passage.

The healing of a crippled man should have been good news, but not everyone in Jerusalem saw it that way. Some religious leaders were offended that this man would carry his mat on the Sabbath. This was against the Jewish law. Amazing! A man who had been an invalid for 38 years was healed. He could walk again. But these people were more concerned about religious rules. No wonder Jesus felt frustrated with them.

We follow a Messiah who is more concerned about people than procedure. He often works in ways that seem unorthodox and even scandalous, using the most unlikely methods.

Don't let rules, traditions, or a "that's the way things are" attitude keep you from seeing God at work in your life.

it's your choice

Jesus replied, "I assure you, the Son can do nothing by himself. He does only what he sees the Father doing. Whatever the Father does, the Son also does. For the Father loves the Son and tells him everything he is doing, and the Son will do far greater things than healing this man. You will be astonished at what he does. He will even raise from the dead anyone he wants to, just as the Father does. And the Father leaves all judgment to his Son, so that everyone will honor the Son, just as they honor the Father. But if you refuse to honor the Son, then you are certainly not honoring the Father who sent him.

"I assure you, those who listen to my message and believe in God who sent me have eternal life. They will never be condemned for their sins, but they have already passed from death into life.

"And I assure you that the time is coming, in fact it is here, when the dead will hear my voice—the voice of the Son of God. And those who listen will live. The Father has life in himself, and he has granted his Son to have life in himself. And he has given him authority to judge all mankind because he is the Son of Man. Don't be so surprised! Indeed, the time is coming when all the dead in their graves will hear the voice of God's Son, and they will rise again. Those who have done good will rise to eternal life, and those who have continued in evil will rise to judgment. But I do nothing without consulting the Father. I judge as I am told. And my judgment is absolutely just, because it is according to the will of God who sent me; it is not merely my own.   JOHN 5:19-30

We live in a time when many different worldviews compete for our attention and allegiance. Some people claim that all these viewpoints are equally valid and even that it is wrong to believe one way is superior to the others. But Jesus says he is the only one that gives life.

Jesus doesn't leave this incredible claim unsupported. He backed up what he said with an impressive list of credentials: Everything he said comes from God, his Father; He has been handed all authority from God himself; He will rise from the dead; He does nothing without God's say-so. We know Christ's claims are true because we have seen the results.

The true test of any set of beliefs is how well those beliefs work in the real world. Christianity is by far the most positive, life-affirming force the world has ever seen. All over the world hospitals, orphanages, and schools have been built in Jesus' name. Poor people receive assistance, the hungry are fed, women's and children's rights are advanced all because Jesus said we should do this. Magnificent works of art have been created and music composed for his glory.

Contrast this with other religions and viewpoints that produce death, destruction, and discord wherever they go. Moses urged the people of Israel to "choose life" (Deuteronomy 30:19)—an admonition that is as important today as ever.

Jesus said those who listen to his message have eternal life and have already passed from death into life. Listen to him, and **choose life.**

|DAY 5 # The case for jesus

"If I were to testify on my own behalf, my testimony would not be valid. But someone else is also testifying about me, and I can assure you that everything he says about me is true. In fact, you sent messengers to listen to John the Baptist, and he preached the truth. But the best testimony about me is not from a man, though I have reminded you about John's testimony so you might be saved. John shone brightly for a while, and you benefited and rejoiced. But I have a greater witness than John—my teachings and my miracles. They have been assigned to me by the Father, and they testify that the Father has sent me. And the Father himself has also testified about me. You have never heard his voice or seen him face to face, and you do not have his message in your hearts, because you do not believe me—the one he sent to you.

"You search the Scriptures because you believe they give you eternal life. But the Scriptures point to me! Yet you refuse to come to me so that I can give you this eternal life.

"Your approval or disapproval means nothing to me, because I know you don't have God's love within you. For I have come to you representing my Father, and you refuse to welcome me, even though you readily accept others who represent only themselves. No wonder you can't believe! For you gladly honor each other, but you don't care about the honor that comes from God alone.

"Yet it is not I who will accuse you of this before the Father. Moses will accuse you! Yes, Moses, on whom you set your hopes. But if you had believed Moses, you would have believed me because he wrote about me. And since you don't believe what he wrote, how will you believe what I say?" JOHN 5:31-47

If you have ever been involved with a courtroom trial, or even watched one on TV, you understand how crucial the witnesses' testimony is. One credible eyewitness can sway an entire case.

In this passage Jesus makes his case for being the Messiah, the one and only Son of God. Jewish law required two to three witnesses to prove a claim. Jesus calls five: John the Baptist; Jesus' own teachings and miracles; the Father; the Scriptures; and Moses.

Case closed.

Well, not quite. Even though the testimony is clear and the evidence for Jesus is overwhelming, each of us must render our own verdict: Will we follow the evidence and embrace Christ as Lord, or ignore it and choose to worship some lesser god?

Head knowledge is not enough. Jesus wants a commitment of your heart and will. What's your verdict?

What did you learn about Jesus from this week's readings?

What reading this week had the most impact on you? Why?

What do you plan to do about what you have learned this week?

Key Verse:

DAY 1	## By the Rules

At about that time Jesus was walking through some grainfields on the Sabbath. His disciples were hungry, so they began breaking off heads of wheat and eating the grain. Some Pharisees saw them do it and protested, "Your disciples shouldn't be doing that! It's against the law to work by harvesting grain on the Sabbath."

But Jesus said to them, "Haven't you ever read in the Scriptures what King David did when he and his companions were hungry? He went into the house of God, and they ate the special bread reserved for the priests alone. That was breaking the law, too. And haven't you ever read in the law of Moses that the priests on duty in the Temple may work on the Sabbath? I tell you, there is one here who is even greater than the Temple! But you would not have condemned those who aren't guilty if you knew the meaning of this Scripture: 'I want you to be merciful; I don't want your sacrifices.' For I, the Son of Man, am master even of the Sabbath."   MATTHEW 12:1-8

When someone becomes a drug addict or grossly overweight, the problem is not the drugs or the food. Instead, that person has taken something intended for good—such as drugs made for medical treatment—and used them in a manner that is harmful.

That's what the Pharisees did with the Sabbath. The Sabbath was given for the good of humankind. It was designed to make sure employers didn't make people work too much. One day in seven was set aside to rest, play, and remember the God who gives us all good things. It was intended to be a *blessing*; the Pharisees had made it a *burden*.

In his response to the Pharisees, Jesus pointed to the *intent* behind the law of the Sabbath, rather than the *letter* of the law. While the Pharisees were more interested in keeping the rules, Jesus reminded them of what was most important—making sure the attitude of the heart toward God was right.

When you're tempted to live strictly by the rules and expect others to do the same, remember what Jesus said: "I want you to be merciful; I don't want your sacrifices."

For Mercy's sake

On another Sabbath day, a man with a deformed right hand was in the synagogue while Jesus was teaching. The teachers of religious law and the Pharisees watched closely to see whether Jesus would heal the man on the Sabbath, because they were eager to find some legal charge to bring against him. But Jesus knew their thoughts. He said to the man with the deformed hand, "Come and stand here where everyone can see." So the man came forward. Then Jesus said to his critics, "I have a question for you. Is it legal to do good deeds on the Sabbath, or is it a day for doing harm? Is this a day to save life or to destroy it?" He looked around at them one by one and then said to the man, "Reach out your hand." The man reached out his hand, and it became normal again! At this, the enemies of Jesus were wild with rage and began to discuss what to do with him.   LUKE 6:6-11

You probably have met someone of the type—the boy in class who puts everyone down, or the girl at the lunch table who has to knock each person who walks by. Some people just live to criticize others. They look to find fault in everyone and everything. Such a critical spirit is cancer to the soul—the soul of the *critic*.

Jesus' opponents were afflicted with it. This passage says they were watching Jesus closely just to see if he would do something for which they could accuse him. Instead of rejoicing that the man's hand was restored to normal, they blew their fuses over what they perceived to be a breach of protocol. Imagine—they missed a miracle because it wasn't done according to their rules and regulations!

Whenever there was a clash between religious formality and real human need, Jesus always chose to meet the need.

When you face such choices, remember our compassionate—and often unconventional—Savior, and lean in the direction of mercy.

DAY 3 super-saints?

But Jesus knew what they were planning. He left that area, and many people followed him. He healed all the sick among them, but he warned them not to say who he was. This fulfilled the prophecy of Isaiah concerning him:

"Look at my Servant, whom I have chosen. He is my Beloved, and I am very pleased with him. I will put my Spirit upon him, and he will proclaim justice to the nations.

"He will not fight or shout; he will not raise his voice in public. He will not crush those who are weak, or quench the smallest hope, until he brings full justice with his final victory. And his name will be the hope of all the world." MATTHEW 12:15-21

We read about them in books and articles and hear about them in church— the super-saints who accomplish great things for God against overwhelming odds. Thank God for such people!

Keep in mind, though, that the reason we hear about them is because their stories are exceptional. Most of us will never be featured in books and movies. We often struggle through our days, trying to be faithful to live like Jesus, but failing again and again. Don't let those failures hang too heavily on your soul. Jesus cares just as much for you as that missionary or evangelist you read about. In fact, this passage seems to have the struggling believer in mind: "He will not crush those who are weak, or quench the smallest hope, until he brings full justice with his final victory."

From Christ's perspective, we are all weak and frail, *including* that great man or woman of the faith you admire so much. He or she is worthy of admiration, but also just as dependent on God's grace as you.

Lean on Jesus for your strength, your hope, and your victory.

By the Dozen

Afterward Jesus went up on a mountain and called the ones he wanted to go with him. And they came to him. Then he selected twelve of them to be his regular companions, calling them apostles. He sent them out to preach, and he gave them authority to cast out demons. These are the names of the twelve he chose:

Simon (he renamed him Peter), James and John (the sons of Zebedee, but Jesus nick-named them "Sons of Thunder"), Andrew, Philip, Bartholomew, Matthew, Thomas, James (son of Alphaeus), Thaddaeus, Simon (the Zealot), Judas Iscariot (who later betrayed him).

MARK 3:13-19

If you wanted to change the world, what kind of people would you ask to help launch your revolution? People who have money, power, fame, and prestige, perhaps some famous athletes, movie stars, and other influential men and women?

Jesus called twelve men to be his team, to carry his message of love, hope, and salvation to the world. None of them were superstars by the world's standards. In fact, the first man listed, Simon Peter, would one day deny even knowing Jesus. The last name, Judas, belonged to the man who betrayed Christ into the hands of his executioners. It's almost beyond belief that Jesus, God himself, would use men like this, and that he *still* uses such men, women, and young people.

The English evangelist John Wesley once wrote: "Give me a hundred men who fear nothing but sin, and desire nothing but God, and I will shake the world. I care not a straw whether they be clergymen or laymen; and such alone will overthrow the kingdom of Satan and build up the kingdom of God on earth."

No matter who you are or what you've done, Jesus can use you, if you're willing.

DAY 5 surprise!

One day as the crowds were gathering, Jesus went up the mountainside with his disciples and sat down to teach them.

This is what he taught them:

"God blesses those who realize their need for him, for the Kingdom of Heaven is given to them.

God blesses those who mourn, for they will be comforted.

God blesses those who are gentle and lowly, for the whole earth will belong to them.

God blesses those who are hungry and thirsty for justice, for they will receive it in full.

God blesses those who are merciful, for they will be shown mercy.

God blesses those whose hearts are pure, for they will see God.

God blesses those who work for peace, for they will be called the children of God.

God blesses those who are persecuted because they live for God, for the Kingdom of Heaven is theirs.

"God blesses you when you are mocked and persecuted and lied about because you are my followers. Be happy about it! Be very glad! For a great reward awaits you in heaven. And remember, the ancient prophets were persecuted, too."   MATTHEW 5:1-12

Has Jesus surprised you lately? Has he answered a real long-shot prayer, showed you something new in the Bible, or done something radical in your life that really got your attention? If not, you may not be paying close enough attention to what he is saying to you and doing with you.

Jesus came into this world to turn the world's reasoning upside-down. Take a look at Matthew 5:1-12, the beginning of what is commonly known as the Sermon on the Mount, and see what Jesus revealed about his Father's heart. God blesses those who realize how needy they are. Those who mourn. Those who are gentle and lowly. Aren't these facts unexpected and refreshing?

F. R. Maltby captured the essence of these verses this way: "Jesus promised his disciples three things—that they would be completely fearless, absurdly happy, and in constant trouble."

If you're serious about being a Christian, you will undoubtedly find yourself doing some very unconventional things in unconventional ways with unconventional people.

Don't be surprised with what Jesus has planned for you.

What did you learn about Jesus from this week's readings?

What reading this week had the most impact on you? Why?

What do you plan to do about what you have learned this week?

Key Verse:

WEEK ELEVEN

| DAY 1 | ## Be Like Jesus

"You are the salt of the earth. But what good is salt if it has lost its flavor? Can you make it useful again? It will be thrown out and trampled underfoot as worthless. You are the light of the world—like a city on a mountain, glowing in the night for all to see. Don't hide your light under a basket! Instead, put it on a stand and let it shine for all. In the same way, let your good deeds shine out for all to see, so that everyone will praise your heavenly Father."

MATTHEW 5:13-16

As Christians, Jesus calls us to be salt and light in the world. Salt adds flavor; so we're called to flavor the world, shake things up, and challenge the status quo, just like he did. In the ancient world, salt was also used as a preservative; so we're called to keep the world from decaying and falling further into moral and spiritual decline.

Jesus also calls us to be light. Light illuminates. So we're to speak truth and expose falsehood. Light also purifies, like radiation used in cancer therapy. So we are to be agents of holiness in a sin-sick culture. And light is a source of heat. So we are to be warm and welcoming of others.

Notice that both salt and light have positive and negative attributes, opposing what is evil and wrong and highlighting what is good and right. Can you imagine what our culture would be like without the influence of Christ? It would become dark and cold, bland and colorless, cruel and unjust.

Follow Jesus and you will stay salty and your light will shine.

DAY 2 Making the Grade

"Don't misunderstand why I have come. I did not come to abolish the law of Moses or the writings of the prophets. No, I came to fulfill them. I assure you, until heaven and earth disappear, even the smallest detail of God's law will remain until its purpose is achieved. So if you break the smallest commandment and teach others to do the same, you will be the least in the Kingdom of Heaven. But anyone who obeys God's laws and teaches them will be great in the Kingdom of Heaven.

"But I warn you—unless you obey God better than the teachers of religious law and the Pharisees do, you can't enter the Kingdom of Heaven at all!   MATTHEW 5:17-20

Reading this passage makes you feel like a first-year guitar student competing against Eric Clapton, or a junior varsity wannabe going one-on-one against Kobe Bryant. The bar is set impossibly high! Who could possibly say he or she "obey[s] God better than the teachers of religious law and the Pharisees [did]"? Why would Jesus say we have to do the impossible?

Because it *is* impossible for us. That's the point: Attaining eternal life is beyond us. We need help. So Jesus came to do for us what we are unable to do for ourselves. If we could be good enough on our own, however difficult it is, God would let us do it. He wouldn't have sacrificed his Son to accomplish what we could do ourselves.

Salvation through faith in Jesus is the gift of God, period. If you have it, be thankful. If you're not sure about it, talk to someone who can help, like a parent, a youth pastor, or a minister.

Accept God's gift today. It won't cost you anything, but it will last you an eternity.

	DAY 3	# The Other Dimension

"You have heard that the law of Moses says, 'Do not murder. If you commit murder, you are subject to judgment.' But I say, if you are angry with someone, you are subject to judgment! If you call someone an idiot, you are in danger of being brought before the high council. And if you curse someone, you are in danger of the fires of hell.

"So if you are standing before the altar in the Temple, offering a sacrifice to God, and you suddenly remember that someone has something against you, leave your sacrifice there beside the altar. Go and be reconciled to that person. Then come and offer your sacrifice to God. Come to terms quickly with your enemy before it is too late and you are dragged into court, handed over to an officer, and thrown in jail. I assure you that you won't be free again until you have paid the last penny." MATTHEW 5:21-26

It's easy to love God. After all, he is perfectly holy, just, loving, and forgiving. He loves us so much he sent his only Son to die in our place. What is there about him not to love?

On the other hand, loving one another is a bit more challenging. Humans, even the best of us, are not always holy, just, loving, nor forgiving. We sometimes lie to one another, we disappoint each other, and often we are just downright unlovable. Love that guy who just cut you off on the highway? Forget about it!

Yet Jesus calls his followers to have harmonious relations with one another as well as with God. In fact, Jesus said that our relationships with each other are so important that if there is a problem with someone else, we need to try to make it right *before* we go to worship!

Our lives take place on two dimensions: the vertical dimension, which is our relationship with God; and the horizontal dimension, our relationships with one another. We are to have right relationships both ways.

God in Christ took the initiative to move toward you in the vertical dimension. Is there someone you need to move toward in the horizontal dimension?

DAY 4 ## do what?

"You have heard that the law of Moses says, 'Do not commit adultery.' But I say, anyone who even looks at a woman with lust in his eye has already committed adultery with her in his heart. So if your eye—even if it is your good eye—causes you to lust, gouge it out and throw it away. It is better for you to lose one part of your body than for your whole body to be thrown into hell. And if your hand—even if it is your stronger hand—causes you to sin, cut it off and throw it away. It is better for you to lose one part of your body than for your whole body to be thrown into hell."   MATTHEW 5:27-30

When reading the Bible, every once in a while you come upon a passage that brings you to a complete standstill. This is one of those passages. What *is* Jesus talking about here—gouging out our eyes, cutting off our hands?

Jesus is talking figuratively. He's not really saying any of us should gouge out an eye or cut off a hand. He is talking about dealing with the sin in our lives. You know, that bad habit that is hard to get rid of, or that secret sinful desire that we enjoy thinking about.

Jesus wants us to know that it is *far better* to experience the pain involved with getting rid of sinful habits or desires than to allow them to result in judgment and punishment later. It is very difficult to take the necessary steps to remove that sinfulness from our lives. But it's a lot less painful than the alternative.

Take a look at your own life. Is anything there that causes you to sin? If so, begin the process of dealing with it.

| DAY 5 # TWO are one

"You have heard that the law of Moses says, 'A man can divorce his wife by merely giving her a letter of divorce.' But I say that a man who divorces his wife, unless she has been unfaithful, causes her to commit adultery. And anyone who marries a divorced woman commits adultery." MATTHEW 5:31-32

Marriage was a messy proposition in the time of Christ, just as it is today. Husbands and wives fought and split up. Religious leaders argued over what kinds of divorces were legitimate.

Jesus' words on the subject were a bombshell then, and they are still disturbing today. (See also Matthew 19:5-9.) God designed marriage to be permanent. God *allows* divorce for reasons of adultery, but he never commands it or desires it.

Marriage is the most important and intimate of all human bonds, and if it were only that, it would be precious indeed. But marriage is a *covenant*—literally, a blood oath—between parties, and in this case, the parties are a man, a woman, and God himself. The Bible does make certain limited provisions for ending a marriage (see 1 Corinthians 7:10-16), but God's plan now is as it was in the Garden of Eden: one man, one woman, for life.

The bottom line is, God hates divorce (Malachi 2:16). It robs him of glory and wounds everyone involved. Even if you come from a broken home, resolve now with God's help to marry wisely and marry for keeps.

Marriage is God's idea, not ours. Pray that if you marry, your marriage will honor God.

What did you learn about Jesus from this week's readings?

What reading this week had the most impact on you? Why?

What do you plan to do about what you have learned this week?

Key Verse:

WEEKTWELVE

| DAY 1 ## yes or no

"Again, you have heard that the law of Moses says, 'Do not break your vows; you must carry out the vows you have made to the Lord.' But I say, don't make any vows! If you say, 'By heaven!' it is a sacred vow because heaven is God's throne. And if you say, 'By the earth!' it is a sacred vow because the earth is his footstool. And don't swear, 'By Jerusalem!' for Jerusalem is the city of the great King. Don't even swear, 'By my head!' for you can't turn one hair white or black. Just say a simple, 'Yes, I will,' or 'No, I won't.' Your word is enough. To strengthen your promise with a vow shows that something is wrong."   MATTHEW 5:33-37

We live in an age of nonstop communication through TV, radio, movies, the Internet, newspapers, books, and magazines. Teachers give lectures, candidates make speeches, and preachers deliver sermons. In order to be heard above it all, talk gets louder, raunchier, and more aggressive. Today, people even use God's name as mere punctuation or as an epithet.

Enough.

Jesus says we should keep our speech simple. When was the last time you heard a politician, an athlete, actor, or other celebrity answer a question with a simple yes or no? This happens so rarely it is noticeable by its stark contrast.

Yet, as Jesus points out, there is power and clarity in such succinctness. If you make it your practice to answer others, especially adults, briefly and respectfully, you will stand out. More importantly, you will honor God and obey Jesus' clear teaching.

If you have trouble exercising verbal restraint, ask God to help you. He'll answer with a clear, unequivocal yes.

"You have heard that the law of Moses says, 'If an eye is injured, injure the eye of the person who did it. If a tooth gets knocked out, knock out the tooth of the person who did it.' But I say, don't resist an evil person! If you are slapped on the right cheek, turn the other, too. If you are ordered to court and your shirt is taken from you, give your coat, too. If a soldier demands that you carry his gear for a mile, carry it two miles. Give to those who ask, and don't turn away from those who want to borrow."   MATTHEW 5:38-42

Be honest. At times you just don't feel like doing what the Bible says. Every Christian has those times when he or she doesn't want to pay the price of following Jesus. The Christian life makes demands on us that go way beyond what we would ask of ourselves.

It's hard to turn the other cheek. It's hard to go the second mile. It's hard to give without asking anything in return. But if we wait till we *feel* like doing those things, we'll never do them. It takes an act of *will*, or a daily series of such acts, to submit ourselves to the lordship of Christ, to give him the right to order our minds, guide our emotions, shape our decisions, influence our relationships, and so forth.

Vance Havner says, "Jesus demands greater allegiance than any dictator who ever lived. The difference is, Jesus is entitled to it."

What choices do you need to make in order to live for Christ?

| DAY 3 ## The Jesus Challenge

"You have heard that the law of Moses says, 'Love your neighbor' and hate your enemy. But I say, love your enemies! Pray for those who persecute you! In that way, you will be acting as true children of your Father in heaven. For he gives his sunlight to both the evil and the good, and he sends rain on the just and on the unjust, too. If you love only those who love you, what good is that? Even corrupt tax collectors do that much. If you are kind only to your friends, how are you different from anyone else? Even pagans do that. But you are to be perfect, even as your Father in heaven is perfect." MATTHEW 5:43-48

If you were to invent your own religion, would you teach your followers to love their enemies? To pray for those who persecuted them? Probably not. Nobody does these things.

Nobody except people serious about being like Jesus. He calls his disciples to a lifestyle that is radically different from the rest of the world's. It's hard to love an enemy. It's difficult to pray for someone who is unkind or hateful toward you. We cannot do this in our own strength. It takes the supernatural work of the Holy Spirit to give us the desire and ability to do it. We must ask Jesus for the grace to treat others, even our enemies, as he treated us when we were his enemies.

Paul wrote in Romans 5:10: "For since we were restored to friendship with God by the death of his Son while we were still his enemies, we will certainly be delivered from eternal punishment by his life."

The late British author G. K. Chesterton wrote, "It is not that Christianity has been tried and found wanting; rather, Christianity has been found difficult and left untried."

To whom can you show Jesus' love today? Take the challenge; give it a try!

| DAY 4 Guaranteed!

"Take care! Don't do your good deeds publicly, to be admired, because then you will lose the reward from your Father in heaven. When you give a gift to someone in need, don't shout about it as the hypocrites do—blowing trumpets in the synagogues and streets to call attention to their acts of charity! I assure you, they have received all the reward they will ever get. But when you give to someone, don't tell your left hand what your right hand is doing. Give your gifts in secret, and your Father, who knows all secrets, will reward you."

MATTHEW 6:1-4

Someone conducted an interesting though troubling study with teenagers in a distressed inner city neighborhood. He asked them: "If you had a choice, would you rather be given ten dollars right now or one hundred dollars a month from now?" Almost all of them said they'd choose the ten dollars on the spot. Why? Because they weren't sure they'd be alive to collect the money later.

In this passage, Jesus says that when we perform acts of charity, we can make a choice between two kinds of prizes. We can choose the immediate reward of the applause of people or the eternal reward of the approval of our heavenly Father. The better choice is obvious. Man's approval is fickle and temporary; God's approval is unchanging and eternal.

Those who follow Christ often perform acts of service, compassion, and charity when no one else but God notices or cares.

God promises an everlasting blessing upon us for our faithfulness. Choose this reward.

DAY 5 # The Model Prayer

"And now about prayer. When you pray, don't be like the hypocrites who love to pray publicly on street corners and in the synagogues where everyone can see them. I assure you, that is all the reward they will ever get. But when you pray, go away by yourself, shut the door behind you, and pray to your Father secretly. Then your Father, who knows all secrets, will reward you.

"When you pray, don't babble on and on as people of other religions do. They think their prayers are answered only by repeating their words again and again. Don't be like them, because your Father knows exactly what you need even before you ask him! Pray like this:

Our Father in heaven, may your name be honored.
May your Kingdom come soon.
May your will be done here on earth, just as it is in heaven.
Give us our food for today, and forgive us our sins, just as we have forgiven those who have sinned against us.
And don't let us yield to temptation, but deliver us from the evil one.

"If you forgive those who sin against you, your heavenly Father will forgive you. But if you refuse to forgive others, your Father will not forgive your sins."   MATTHEW 6:5-15

This prayer is commonly called the Lord's Prayer. In it Jesus models the way we are to pray. He does not say we are to use these exact words as a dull, meaningless repetition. He says, "When you pray, pray like this"—assuming that we will be people of prayer. Here are some thoughts and insights into what Jesus meant when he gave us this prayer model.

"Our Father in heaven" is a term of intimacy that is followed by the prayer, "May your name be honored." *Honored* comes from the same root word that means holy, revered, respected, and treated with dignity.

"May your Kingdom come soon. May your will be done here on earth, just as it is in heaven." This expression of longing for the rule of God indicates that we're ready to submit to him as King and Lord.

"Give us our food for today." For the people of Jesus' day this was not just a figure of speech.

"Forgive us our sins, just as we have forgiven those who have sinned against us." How well have you forgiven others?

"Don't let us yield to temptation, but deliver us from the evil one." In other words, "Protect us, for we are frail."

Keep these thoughts in mind next time you recite the the Lord's Prayer. Why not say it as part of your devotions today?

What did you learn about Jesus from this week's readings?

What reading this week had the most impact on you? Why?

What do you plan to do about what you have learned this week?

Key Verse:

WEEK THIRTEEN

| DAY 1 ## Quiet Time

"And when you fast, don't make it obvious, as the hypocrites do, who try to look pale and disheveled so people will admire them for their fasting. I assure you, that is the only reward they will ever get. But when you fast, comb your hair and wash your face. Then no one will suspect you are fasting, except your Father, who knows what you do in secret. And your Father, who knows all secrets, will reward you."   MATTHEW 6:16-18

Let's say you have successfully read through the entire Bible in one year. You have to tell someone about your accomplishment—or do you? Take a look at how Jesus reacts to those who make their religious habits a matter of public knowledge.

On the surface it appears that Jesus is addressing the topic of fasting—the dos and don'ts of going without food in order to spend time in prayer. But if you dig a little deeper, you'll discover that Jesus is actually talking about hypocrisy among the religious leaders; that is, fasting in order to make a good impression on others.

What is Jesus' point? God is concerned with our heart and our motives. Jesus praised those who quietly go about the business of prayer, giving, making sacrifices, helping others, or spending time in the Word. Are we out to impress our friends and youth pastor with our super holiness, or are we trying to develop a deeper relationship with Christ?

It's not about quality time or quantity time, but about quiet time between you and Jesus.

HeavenLy investments

"Don't store up treasures here on earth, where they can be eaten by moths and get rusty, and where thieves break in and steal. Store your treasures in heaven, where they will never become moth-eaten or rusty and where they will be safe from thieves. Wherever your treasure is, there your heart and thoughts will also be.

"Your eye is a lamp for your body. A pure eye lets sunshine into your soul. But an evil eye shuts out the light and plunges you into darkness. If the light you think you have is really darkness, how deep that darkness will be!

"No one can serve two masters. For you will hate one and love the other, or be devoted to one and despise the other. You cannot serve both God and money."   MATTHEW 6:19-24

What is truly important to you? Not to your parents, friends, youth pastor, or the majority of kids in your school, but to *you*? Before you start your list, answer the following questions:

How do you spend your down time? After school is out, after your job is done and homework finished, what do you do when you can do whatever you want?

How do you spend your money? After you've taken care of whatever obligations you have, how do you use any cash you have left over?

When you answer those questions, you have a good start on answering the question of what is really important in your life. Is there room in your day and in your budget for God and what's important to him? Do you spend any of your time or money pursuing him and advancing his kingdom?

Jesus said, "Wherever your treasure is, there your heart and thoughts will also be." Time and money are two of the most precious elements in our lives.

Where do you invest your treasures—in Jesus, or in this world?

| DAY 3 # Kingdom Living

"So I tell you, don't worry about everyday life—whether you have enough food, drink, and clothes. Doesn't life consist of more than food and clothing? Look at the birds. They don't need to plant or harvest or put food in barns because your heavenly Father feeds them. And you are far more valuable to him than they are. Can all your worries add a single moment to your life? Of course not.

"And why worry about your clothes? Look at the lilies and how they grow. They don't work or make their clothing, yet Solomon in all his glory was not dressed as beautifully as they are. And if God cares so wonderfully for flowers that are here today and gone tomorrow, won't he more surely care for you? You have so little faith!

"So don't worry about having enough food or drink or clothing. Why be like the pagans who are so deeply concerned about these things? Your heavenly Father already knows all your needs, and he will give you all you need from day to day if you live for him and make the Kingdom of God your primary concern.

"So don't worry about tomorrow, for tomorrow will bring its own worries. Today's trouble is enough for today."   MATTHEW 6:25-34

Missionary Jim Elliot, killed by Auca Indians in Ecuador in 1956, is remembered for being a courageous and faithful servant of Jesus Christ. He is also remembered for something he wrote in his diary not long before he died: "He is no fool who gives up what he cannot keep in order to gain what he cannot lose."

Young people are inundated with so many messages from modern culture. Many of these focus on self: self-esteem, self-respect, self-fulfillment. Nothing is inherently wrong with any of these things. But Jesus' message is more about self-sacrifice and self-denial than self-seeking. Christ wants to pry the world's suction cups off our hearts—materialism, hedonism, cynicism, and self-ism in all its forms—so that we can focus on what is truly, eternally important.

Is your day filled with nonstop activities designed to please yourself? Or are you committed to make the kingdom of God your primary concern?

Stop judging others, and you will not be judged. For others will treat you as you treat them. Whatever measure you use in judging others, it will be used to measure how you are judged. And why worry about a speck in your friend's eye when you have a log in your own? How can you think of saying, "Let me help you get rid of that speck in your eye," when you can't see past the log in your own eye? Hypocrite! First get rid of the log from your own eye; then perhaps you will see well enough to deal with the speck in your friend's eye.

Don't give what is holy to unholy people. Don't give pearls to swine! They will trample the pearls, then turn and attack you.   MATTHEW 7:1-6

If you committed a serious sin—something scandalous that everyone knew about—would you (a) show up for church that Sunday, or (b) run in the opposite direction? Far too many Christians would, if they were honest, have to choose (b). Why? How has the church gained the reputation for being a repository of judgment?

Simply put, too many of us have forgotten Jesus' words in Matthew 7:1: "Stop judging others, and you will not be judged." Instead, we seem to love to point the accusing finger at the one who stumbles and falls, and the bigger the stumble, the more fingers point. But Jesus, the best person planet Earth has ever seen, warned us not to judge. He clearly and unequivocally condemned the sin of hypocrisy, leveling his harshest criticisms at people who professed to love God but put others down for their frailties.

When someone you know falls into sin, don't be too quick to join the chorus of the critical. That person may need someone to help find the way back to peace with God.

If you ever stumble into sin, look for someone who takes Jesus' words in Matthew 7:1-6 seriously.

DAY 5 Hang in There!

Keep on asking, and you will be given what you ask for. Keep on looking, and you will find. Keep on knocking, and the door will be opened. For everyone who asks, receives. Everyone who seeks, finds. And the door is opened to everyone who knocks. You parents—if your children ask for a loaf of bread, do you give them a stone instead? Or if they ask for a fish, do you give them a snake? Of course not! If you sinful people know how to give good gifts to your children, how much more will your heavenly Father give good gifts to those who ask him.

Do for others what you would like them to do for you. This is a summary of all that is taught in the law and the prophets.   MATTHEW 7:7-12

If you have been a Christian very long you have probably had the experience of praying faithfully for a friend or family member with no apparent results. When that person seems uninterested, unchanged, and as far from God as ever, you may have grown discouraged and just about given up hope. Don't!

Whether you are praying for someone's salvation or any other legitimate need, don't grow weary and quit just because God does not work according to your timetable. Jesus tells us to keep on asking, keep on looking, and keep on knocking. In other words, *hang in there!* Jesus wants us to know that God is a good Father and he cares more about your friend or loved one than even you do.

God is not reluctant to work in the lives of the people we care about. He does, however, require willingness on their part, and that may be the battleground in which we need to be praying. He also may want to teach us perseverance and tenacity in prayer.

Your prayers may not seem change your friends or loved ones, but they will almost certainly change **you.**

What did you learn about Jesus from this week's readings?

What reading this week had the most impact on you? Why?

What do you plan to do about what you have learned this week?

Key Verse:

DAY 1 The Easy way out

"You can enter God's Kingdom only through the narrow gate. The highway to hell is broad, and its gate is wide for the many who choose the easy way. But the gateway to life is small, and the road is narrow, and only a few ever find it." MATTHEW 7:13-14

Most people have taken the easy way out at one time or another in their lives, maybe by cheating on an exam or looking the other way when a friend was in need. In your spiritual life you also can choose an easy way. But first, check out what Jesus had to say about this.

He described the road to the kingdom of God as having a very narrow entrance. And this road is narrow like one set in a forest among thick under-brush and trees. Only those willing to make an effort will find it. But this isn't meant to discourage you, God promises not to disappoint those who truly *seek* the kingdom (Matthew 7:7).

But you must purposefully set out to find this path and then remain on it in order to enter the kingdom of God. You won't stumble upon it by accident and then walk right into the kingdom. Contrast this with the path to hell. It is a wide path that is easy to find—all you have to do is follow the crowd. However, this has a consequence: the easy path ends with destruction.

Are you a *seeker*—someone who's hungry to find the truth? Or are you a *tag-along*—someone who's just following the crowd?

Start seeking God's way for yourself. Only the right path will lead you to the right place.

"Beware of false prophets who come disguised as harmless sheep, but are really wolves that will tear you apart. You can detect them by the way they act, just as you can identify a tree by its fruit. You don't pick grapes from thornbushes, or figs from thistles. A healthy tree produces good fruit, and an unhealthy tree produces bad fruit. A good tree can't produce bad fruit, and a bad tree can't produce good fruit. So every tree that does not produce good fruit is chopped down and thrown into the fire. Yes, the way to identify a tree or a person is by the kind of fruit that is produced."   MATTHEW 7:15-20

So what does a *real* Christian look like anyway? A likely answer is this: It is someone who professes faith in Christ, attends church, reads and studies the Bible, and whose actions tend to reflect Christ's teaching. On the other hand, a person who habitually cheats on tests, lies, or hurts others is probably not a Christian.

In Old Testament times God's message was given through prophets. When a prophet spoke, people paid attention. But there was one problem: a lot of counterfeit prophets were roaming around the land. They acted like real prophets and even used the same religious-sounding words. But instead of serving God they used their positions for money and power.

In the New Testament, Jesus warned his followers about such false prophets, who *profess* to follow him but are really promoting their own agenda. So what's the trick in telling a true prophet from a false one? Look at their fruit—the results of their labor expressed in their way of living.

What does your life say about you? Do you say you believe in Christ, while your actions express what you *really* believe?

Ask your pastor or a trusted friend to tell you if they see a difference between what you say and what you do.

| DAY 3   # what's Holding you up?

"Not all people who sound religious are really godly. They may refer to me as 'Lord,' but they still won't enter the Kingdom of Heaven. The decisive issue is whether they obey my Father in heaven. On judgment day many will tell me, 'Lord, Lord, we prophesied in your name and cast out demons in your name and performed many miracles in your name.' But I will reply, 'I never knew you. Go away; the things you did were unauthorized.'

"Anyone who listens to my teaching and obeys me is wise, like a person who builds a house on solid rock. Though the rain comes in torrents and the floodwaters rise and the winds beat against that house, it won't collapse, because it is built on rock. But anyone who hears my teaching and ignores it is foolish, like a person who builds a house on sand. When the rains and floods come and the winds beat against that house, it will fall with a mighty crash."

After Jesus finished speaking, the crowds were amazed at his teaching, for he taught as one who had real authority—quite unlike the teachers of religious law.   MATTHEW 7.21-29

What's the most important part of a house? The roof or the windows? Maybe it's the door or the walls. Actually, it's the foundation. Hidden beneath the house, the foundation holds everything up. That's why it's important to place a building's foundation on solid ground—just ask anyone who has seen a house fall into a ocean or slide off a hillside during a storm.

Jesus said that people, like houses, need to have strong foundations. Many realize this fact too late, after things begin to fall apart. When trouble hits them, there's nothing to hold on to because they neglected to place their foundation on solid rock.

Jesus himself is the firm foundation for your life. The Bible contains the instructions on how to build upon that foundation. Knowing Christ's words but not following them gives you no support when difficult times come. But when you build your life upon Christ you're able to withstand all kinds of hardship.

Are you building your life on the solid rock of Jesus Christ and the truth of the Bible, or on the unstable sand of worldly ways?

| DAY 4 # The Proper Authority

When Jesus had finished saying all this, he went back to Capernaum. Now the highly valued slave of a Roman officer was sick and near death. When the officer heard about Jesus, he sent some respected Jewish leaders to ask him to come and heal his slave. So they earnestly begged Jesus to come with them and help the man. "If anyone deserves your help, it is he," they said, "for he loves the Jews and even built a synagogue for us."

So Jesus went with them. But just before they arrived at the house, the officer sent some friends to say, "Lord, don't trouble yourself by coming to my home, for I am not worthy of such an honor. I am not even worthy to come and meet you. Just say the word from where you are, and my servant will be healed. I know because I am under the authority of my superior officers, and I have authority over my soldiers. I only need to say, 'Go,' and they go, or 'Come,' and they come. And if I say to my slaves, 'Do this or that,' they do it."

When Jesus heard this, he was amazed. Turning to the crowd, he said, "I tell you, I haven't seen faith like this in all the land of Israel!" And when the officer's friends returned to his house, they found the slave completely healed.   LUKE 7:1-10

Everyone has authority figures in their life: a boss, parents, teachers, a coach, or a pastor. It is a rare individual who answers to no one. In this passage we meet a Roman officer who was no stranger to authority. He answered to those above him in the military chain of command. He also was the commander of over one hundred soldiers in the Palestinian outpost of Capernaum.

This career soldier was selected for his position not only for his courage, but also for his intellect and ability to make decisions. He was accustomed to giving orders and having them obeyed, was comfortable being in a position of power, and recognized authority in others.

When this man's favorite servant fell deathly ill, the powerful soldier was powerless. He knew he needed help from an authority greater than himself. He needed Jesus, the only one who could possibly heal his servant. But he didn't personally approach Jesus, nor did he ask Jesus to come to him. Rather he spoke these words of faith, "Just say the word from where you are, and my servant will be healed."

The truth is that everyone is under Chirst's authority. When we acknowledge this in our daily lives we display our faith.

Whose authority do you seek when you are in a tough situation? Where do you go when you feel powerless?

DAY 5 **Better than Hollywood's zombies**

Soon afterward Jesus went with his disciples to the village of Nain, with a great crowd follow-ing him. A funeral procession was coming out as he approached the village gate. The boy who had died was the only son of a widow, and many mourners from the village were with her. When the Lord saw her, his heart overflowed with compassion. "Don't cry!" he said. Then he walked over to the coffin and touched it, and the bearers stopped. "Young man," he said, "get up." Then the dead boy sat up and began to talk to those around him! And Jesus gave him back to his mother.

Great fear swept the crowd, and they praised God, saying, "A mighty prophet has risen among us," and "We have seen the hand of God at work today." The report of what Jesus had done that day spread all over Judea and even out across its borders.   LUKE 7:11-17

In horror films, it's never good when dead people start coming back to life. Even though it's just Hollywood, this can be very scary. The resurrection scene described in this passage starts out with sadness and fear but ends with people gaining a better understanding of Jesus.

A widow's only son had died. This meant trouble because her only source of love and support had passed away. All she could hope for was a life of poverty and loneliness. As the tears dropped, her heart broke. Jesus' heart broke, too. So he stepped in and brought the widow's son back to life. Jesus wasn't putting on a show for the crowd. The Bible isn't like Hollywood. He did this out of compassion for the widow. He understood her pain and knew exactly how to comfort her.

Are you afraid that your hurts are too big for Jesus to fix? The Bible tells this story to encourage you to take those hurts to the Lord.

Don't hesitate to share your pain and frustration with Jesus. He cares for you more than anyone else. Jesus can comfort you.

What did you learn about Jesus from this week's readings?

What reading this week had the most impact on you? Why?

What do you plan to do about what you have learned this week?

Key Verse:

| DAY 1 ## Two kinds of Hearts

The disciples of John the Baptist told John about everything Jesus was doing. So John called for two of his disciples, and he sent them to the Lord to ask him, "Are you the Messiah we've been expecting, or should we keep looking for someone else?"

John's two disciples found Jesus and said to him, "John the Baptist sent us to ask, 'Are you the Messiah we've been expecting, or should we keep looking for someone else?'"

At that very time, he cured many people of their various diseases, and he cast out evil spirits and restored sight to the blind. Then he told John's disciples, "Go back to John and tell him what you have seen and heard—the blind see, the lame walk, the lepers are cured, the deaf hear, the dead are raised to life, and the Good News is being preached to the poor. And tell him, 'God blesses those who are not offended by me.'. . .

"How shall I describe this generation?" Jesus asked. "With what will I compare them? They are like a group of children playing a game in the public square. They complain to their friends, 'We played wedding songs, and you weren't happy, so we played funeral songs, but you weren't sad.' For John the Baptist didn't drink wine and he often fasted, and you say, 'He's demon possessed.' And I, the Son of Man, feast and drink, and you say, 'He's a glutton and a drunkard, and a friend of the worst sort of sinners!' But wisdom is shown to be right by the lives of those who follow it."   LUKE 7:18-23, 31-35

People who really desire to know the truth adjust their thinking as they discover new insights. Others stubbornly hold on to their views even when those views are proved to be wrong. This is seen in today's Scripture reading.

When John the Baptist heard Jesus was in town, he didn't mess around. He bluntly asked him: "Are you the Messiah?" John didn't want a theological debate; he wanted an answer. So Jesus gave scriptural evidence that John would recognize. The result? John put his trust in Jesus.

The Pharisees, on the other hand, operated with closed hearts. Even though they knew the Scriptures, they chose not to acknowledge Jesus as the Messiah. To them, Jesus was a drunkard and John was demon-possessed! Their viewpoint was skewed because they weren't actually seeking the truth.

Do you read the Bible only to justify your own point of view? Or are you searching with an open heart, ready to be transformed by the truth?

God promises that if you seek the truth, you **will** find it.

DAY 2 you Think you're so smart

Then Jesus began to denounce the cities where he had done most of his miracles, because they hadn't turned from their sins and turned to God. "What horrors await you, Korazin and Bethsaida! For if the miracles I did in you had been done in wicked Tyre and Sidon, their people would have sat in deep repentance long ago, clothed in sackcloth and throwing ashes on their heads to show their remorse. I assure you, Tyre and Sidon will be better off on the judgment day than you! And you people of Capernaum, will you be exalted to heaven? No, you will be brought down to the place of the dead. For if the miracles I did for you had been done in Sodom, it would still be here today. I assure you, Sodom will be better off on the judgment day than you."

Then Jesus prayed this prayer: "O Father, Lord of heaven and earth, thank you for hiding the truth from those who think themselves so wise and clever, and for revealing it to the childlike. Yes, Father, it pleased you to do it this way!

"My Father has given me authority over everything. No one really knows the Son except the Father, and no one really knows the Father except the Son and those to whom the Son chooses to reveal him."

Then Jesus said, "Come to me, all of you who are weary and carry heavy burdens, and I will give you rest. Take my yoke upon you. Let me teach you, because I am humble and gentle, and you will find rest for your souls. For my yoke fits perfectly, and the burden I give you is light."   MATTHEW 11:20-30

Who's the smartest person you know? How do you know that he or she is so intelligent? Before you answer, consider today's Scripture reading.

Some people in Jesus' day thought they were pretty clever. But God gave them *tons* of signs through Jesus' miracles, and they still did not believe in him. Instead, they rationalized the miracles away with their "superior" intellect. They thought they had God figured out. But God can't be kept in a box, least of all the box of the human mind! The knowledge of God comes only through a relationship with Jesus Christ.

God can't be understood though natural human wisdom. That's why he welcomes with open arms the childlike, humble people of this world. When such people come to the Father, they receive a revelation of the truth.

If you have questions about God, that's okay! Just remember that God hides the truth from those who think they are wise and clever and reveals it to the childlike.

What preconceived ideas do you have about God? Tell the Lord that you are willing to change them.

one way to say Thanks

One of the Pharisees asked Jesus to come to his home for a meal, so Jesus accepted the invitation and sat down to eat. A certain immoral woman heard he was there and brought a beautiful jar filled with expensive perfume. Then she knelt behind him at his feet, weeping. Her tears fell on his feet, and she wiped them off with her hair. Then she kept kissing his feet and putting perfume on them.

When the Pharisee who was the host saw what was happening and who the woman was, he said to himself, "This proves that Jesus is no prophet. If God had really sent him, he would know what kind of woman is touching him. She's a sinner!"

Then Jesus spoke up and answered his thoughts. "Simon," he said to the Pharisee, "I have something to say to you."

"All right, Teacher," Simon replied, "go ahead."

Then Jesus told him this story: "A man loaned money to two people—five hundred pieces of silver to one and fifty pieces to the other. But neither of them could repay him, so he kindly forgave them both, canceling their debts. Who do you suppose loved him more after that?"

Simon answered, "I suppose the one for whom he canceled the larger debt."

"That's right," Jesus said. Then he turned to the woman and said to Simon, "Look at this woman kneeling here. When I entered your home, you didn't offer me water to wash the dust from my feet, but she has washed them with her tears and wiped them with her hair. You didn't give me a kiss of greeting, but she has kissed my feet again and again from the time I first came in. You neglected the courtesy of olive oil to anoint my head, but she has anointed my feet with rare perfume. I tell you, her sins—and they are many—have been forgiven, so she has shown me much love. But a person who is forgiven little shows only little love." Then Jesus said to the woman, "Your sins are forgiven."

The men at the table said among themselves, "Who does this man think he is, going around forgiving sins?"

And Jesus said to the woman, "Your faith has saved you; go in peace." LUKE 7:36-50

Imagine a prostitute showing up uninvited at an important banquet. This actually happened in the house of a respected Pharisee who was hosting a dinner for Jesus Christ. This must have raised a few eyebrows! Yet that low woman came with a high purpose—to express her love and thankfulness to her Savior.

In contrast to this prostitute, the Pharisee had neglected to perform common welcoming rituals for the Lord. Maybe he thought that his superior position meant he didn't need to treat Jesus as an equal. Yet the prostitute knew she was a sinner and was deeply thankful to the Lord. This revealed her faith, and Jesus forgave her sins.

Are you grateful to Jesus for his forgiveness? How can you say "thank you" to him today?

| DAY 4 | # Road Tripping with Jesus

Not long afterward Jesus began a tour of the nearby cities and villages to announce the Good News concerning the Kingdom of God. He took his twelve disciples with him, along with some women he had healed and from whom he had cast out evil spirits. Among them were Mary Magdalene, from whom he had cast out seven demons; Joanna, the wife of Chuza, Herod's business manager; Susanna; and many others who were contributing from their own resources to support Jesus and his disciples. LUKE 8:1-3

Road trips are great. There is something exhilarating about traveling on the open road with a bunch of close friends. Relationships formed along the way make such trips memorable. Look at the people Jesus chose to bring with him when he took to the road.

Naturally, there were the twelve disciples. But not many people know that some of Lord's fellow travelers were women. While that's not a big deal today, in the culture of Jesus' day women were a lower class than men. So Jesus spent time with women to show his respect for them as equals.

These were women of all kinds. One was the wife of a powerful political leader. Another had been possessed by demons. Some were wealthy women who helped fund the whole trip. Each woman had a special role to play in Jesus' band.

If you had the chance to travel with Jesus, what role do you think you would play? Organizer? Encourager? Servant? God has made you the way you are for a purpose.

Don't be afraid to use your unique gifts to serve God!

| DAY 5 # choosing sides

Then a demon-possessed man, who was both blind and unable to talk, was brought to Jesus. He healed the man so that he could both speak and see. The crowd was amazed. "Could it be that Jesus is the Son of David, the Messiah?" they wondered out loud.

But when the Pharisees heard about the miracle, they said, "No wonder he can cast out demons. He gets his power from Satan, the prince of demons."

Jesus knew their thoughts and replied, "Any kingdom at war with itself is doomed. A city or home divided against itself is doomed. And if Satan is casting out Satan, he is fighting against himself. His own kingdom will not survive. And if I am empowered by the prince of demons, what about your own followers? They cast out demons, too, so they will judge you for what you have said. But if I am casting out demons by the Spirit of God, then the Kingdom of God has arrived among you. Let me illustrate this. You can't enter a strong man's house and rob him without first tying him up. Only then can his house be robbed! Anyone who isn't helping me opposes me, and anyone who isn't working with me is actually working against me.

"Every sin or blasphemy can be forgiven—except blasphemy against the Holy Spirit, which can never be forgiven. Anyone who blasphemes against me, the Son of Man, can be forgiven, but blasphemy against the Holy Spirit will never be forgiven, either in this world or in the world to come." MATTHEW 12:22-32

When it comes to Jesus Christ, you can't ride the fence. You have to make a decision—either you're for him or against him. This Scripture describes one of those situations.

The Pharisees credited Jesus' power to Satan. In doing so they cursed the the Holy Spirit, the real source of Jesus' power. This gave Jesus a good reason to point out that, in the spiritual realm, it's all or nothing.

He asked them, "Why would Satan try to cast out Satan?" This just doesn't make sense. You're either working to advance Satan's power or to further Christ's kingdom. It's easy for us to lose sight of this spiritual truth and try to stay in a gray area between the two kingdoms. However, Christ's message makes it impossible to remain neutral.

If you're not for Jesus, a door is open for Satan to use you. Whose side are you on?

What did you learn about Jesus from this week's readings?

What reading this week had the most impact on you? Why?

What do you plan to do about what you have learned this week?

Key Verse:

WEEK SIXTEEN

DAY 1 Just Give me a sign!

One day some teachers of religious law and Pharisees came to Jesus and said, "Teacher, we want you to show us a miraculous sign to prove that you are from God."

But Jesus replied, "Only an evil, faithless generation would ask for a miraculous sign; but the only sign I will give them is the sign of the prophet Jonah. For as Jonah was in the belly of the great fish for three days and three nights, so I, the Son of Man, will be in the heart of the earth for three days and three nights. The people of Nineveh will rise up against this generation on judgment day and condemn it, because they repented at the preaching of Jonah. And now someone greater than Jonah is here—and you refuse to repent. The queen of Sheba will also rise up against this generation on judgment day and condemn it, because she came from a distant land to hear the wisdom of Solomon. And now someone greater than Solomon is here—and you refuse to listen to him.

"When an evil spirit leaves a person, it goes into the desert, seeking rest but finding none. Then it says, 'I will return to the person I came from.' So it returns and finds its former home empty, swept, and clean. Then the spirit finds seven other spirits more evil than itself, and they all enter the person and live there. And so that person is worse off than before. That will be the experience of this evil generation." MATTHEW 12:38-45

"Why can't you give me a sign? Just one little sign? Then I'll believe!" Be honest, have you ever said this to the Lord? The Pharisees did. And Jesus' answer was surprising.

Jesus told them that the sign *had already been given*. It was not in the many miracles he was doing at the time but was seen in the Old Testament book of Jonah! Jonah's three-day stay in the belly of the great fish fore-shadowed the three days that Jesus would lie in the tomb after his cruci-fixion. This means that the sign the Pharasees wanted would be seen in Christ's resurrection from the dead.

There were two reasons why the Pharisees would get no other sign. First, they didn't want to *listen*; second, they didn't want to *repent*. It's no different today. Our requests for signs from God come from our non-listening, unrepen-tant hearts. The fact is, even if a sign did come, we wouldn't recognize or believe it. In our communication with God, the disconnect is always on our end, not on his. So resist the urge to plead for a sign.

Don't question God. Instead ask yourself these questions:
"Do I have unrepented sin in my life?"
"Am I **really** listening to God?"

|DAY 2 # A Part of the Family

Jesus' mother and brothers arrived at the house where he was teaching. They stood outside and sent word for him to come out and talk with them. There was a crowd around Jesus, and someone said, "Your mother and your brothers and sisters are outside, asking for you."

Jesus replied, "Who is my mother? Who are my brothers?" Then he looked at those around him and said, "These are my mother and brothers. Anyone who does God's will is my brother and sister and mother." MARK 3:31-35

One day, Jesus was teaching to a packed house. When his mother and brothers showed up they couldn't get in to see him. So they sent word to let Jesus know that they were there and he responded in a way that seems harsh. Actually, Jesus was using his family to make a point about *another* family—the family of God.

Jesus taught that when we do God's will, we align ourselves with God. Since he, the Son of God, always does the will of God, following him enables us to have a relationship with the Father. And this relationship isn't vague. We become children in God's own family, a brother or sister of Christ.

Are you part of the spiritual family of God? Have you found a church group or fellowship that connects you with your spiritual brothers and sisters?

The relationships you build in God's family will last for eternity.

DAY 3	# The master storyteller

Once again Jesus began teaching by the lakeshore. There was such a large crowd along the shore that he got into a boat and sat down and spoke from there. He began to teach the people by telling many stories such as this one:

"Listen! A farmer went out to plant some seed. As he scattered it across his field, some seed fell on a footpath, and the birds came and ate it. Other seed fell on shallow soil with underlying rock. The plant sprang up quickly, but it soon wilted beneath the hot sun and died because the roots had no nourishment in the shallow soil. Other seed fell among thorns that shot up and choked out the tender blades so that it produced no grain. Still other seed fell on fertile soil and produced a crop that was thirty, sixty, and even a hundred times as much as had been planted." Then he said, "Anyone who is willing to hear should listen and understand!" MARK 4:1-9

People love to hear a good storyteller weave a tale. Stories have the ability to help even the youngest of young children grasp difficult ideas. Jesus told stories all the time, and today's Scripture tells a story that hit home for the farmers in his audience. As Jesus filled their minds with pictures of seeds, soil, sun, and harvest—images that were part of their daily lives—he connected with his audience on a personal level. This is one of the marks of a good storyteller.

In the parable of the soils, Jesus' images helped the people connect *abstract* ideas like godliness and open-heartedness with the *concrete* ideas of dirt and rocks. Those with open hearts and minds learned deep truths from Jesus' parables. These people didn't just come to *listen* to a nice story, they desired to *understand* and be transformed by Jesus' teaching.

Do you want to gain a deeper understanding of God? What everyday objects or pictures could you use to help you get a better grasp of spiritual truths?

With the right story, ordinary objects in your life can become constant reminders of God's truths.

After They Heard the Message

Later, when Jesus was alone with the twelve disciples and with the others who were gathered around, they asked him, "What do your stories mean?"

He replied, "You are permitted to understand the secret about the Kingdom of God. But I am using these stories to conceal everything about it from outsiders, so that the Scriptures might be fulfilled:

'They see what I do, but they don't perceive its meaning. They hear my words, but they don't understand. So they will not turn from their sins and be forgiven.'

"But if you can't understand this story, how will you understand all the others I am going to tell? The farmer I talked about is the one who brings God's message to others. The seed that fell on the hard path represents those who hear the message, but then Satan comes at once and takes it away from them. The rocky soil represents those who hear the message and receive it with joy. But like young plants in such soil, their roots don't go very deep. At first they get along fine, but they wilt as soon as they have problems or are persecuted because they believe the word. The thorny ground represents those who hear and accept the Good News, but all too quickly the message is crowded out by the cares of this life, the lure of wealth, and the desire for nice things, so no crop is produced. But the good soil represents those who hear and accept God's message and produce a huge harvest—thirty, sixty, or even a hundred times as much as had been planted." MARK 4:10-20

No one likes the feeling of being lost, but with a little help from a map or a passerby you can get back on the right track. After hearing Jesus' parable of the soils, the twelve disciples felt a little lost. Fortunately, Jesus took time to tell them the true meaning of his story.

Jesus explained that the four soils refer to four different ways people's hearts receive the message of God. Each person *hears* the message. What matters is what they do with the message *after* they hear it. Only one person's heart willingly accepted the seed of God's Word and so it grew. In the end, only that person produced a harvest for God.

Have you allowed God's Word to be planted in your heart? If so, it will produce a harvest of good fruit. In other words, your faith is confirmed and affirmed by your way of life.

If your friends and family were to describe you, what spiritual fruit would they mention?

| DAY 5   # time to Grow

Jesus also said, "Here is another illustration of what the Kingdom of God is like: A farmer planted seeds in a field, and then he went on with his other activities. As the days went by, the seeds sprouted and grew without the farmer's help, because the earth produces crops on its own. First a leaf blade pushes through, then the heads of wheat are formed, and finally the grain ripens. And as soon as the grain is ready, the farmer comes and harvests it with a sickle."   MARK 4:26-29

Have you ever seen the cycle of growth from the emerging shoots of spring, to the explosion of summer green, to the brilliant resolution of harvest gold? Jesus used these phases of plant growth to describe the development of faith. Just as a plant grows slowly over the months, faith is also a growth process. *It takes time.*

When you're struggling through trials and doubts, you can find comfort in the knowledge that God is the one who makes your faith mature. Sometimes this means pruning. Other times it means sunshine or rain. Your job is simply to have a heart that is open to God.

In what ways is God helping you grow to spiritual maturity? Ask God to enable you to grow through all the seasons of your life.

What did you learn about Jesus from this week's readings?

What reading this week had the most impact on you? Why?

What do you plan to do about what you have learned this week?

Key Verse:

DAY 1 waiting for a weeding

Here is another story Jesus told: "The Kingdom of Heaven is like a farmer who planted good seed in his field. But that night as everyone slept, his enemy came and planted weeds among the wheat. When the crop began to grow and produce grain, the weeds also grew. The farmer's servants came and told him, 'Sir, the field where you planted that good seed is full of weeds!'

"'An enemy has done it!' the farmer exclaimed.

"'Shall we pull out the weeds?' they asked.

"He replied, 'No, you'll hurt the wheat if you do. Let both grow together until the harvest. Then I will tell the harvesters to sort out the weeds and burn them and to put the wheat in the barn.'" MATTHEW 13:24-30

Farmers do all they can to eliminate weeds from their crops because weeds crowd out the good stuff. Once a field has too many weeds, however, wise farmers know that they'd better leave the weeds so they can salvage some of the crop. This is also true in a spiritual sense.

In Jesus' parable an enemy had planted weeds a farmer's field of grain. Instead of pulling out the weeds, the farmer allowed them to grow along with the wheat. Likewise, believers, the wheat, must live each day among unbelievers, the weeds.

As Christians it's tempting to surround ourselves only with other believers. If we do this we run the risk of losing contact with the world around us. But God calls us to shine as his lights *in the world*. That means showing God's love and friendship to all people, especially those who don't already have a relationship with Christ.

Do you prefer to spend all your time surrounded by other Christians? How could you show God's love to the unbelievers in your life?

| DAY 2   small Beginnings

Here is another illustration Jesus used: "The Kingdom of Heaven is like a mustard seed planted in a field. It is the smallest of all seeds, but it becomes the largest of garden plants and grows into a tree where birds can come and find shelter in its branches."

MATTHEW 13:31-32

Compare a single seed with a giant tree. It's amazing that such magnificent life could come from an item so tiny. God's kingdom had a small start like this, and it's not done growing.

Jesus' audience was expecting a kingdom with a great king, yet Jesus compared the kingdom of Heaven to a mustard seed, the *smallest of all seeds*. Jesus wasn't worried about small beginnings. He saw potential in tiny seeds of faith.

Jesus sees potential in you, too. From the time you began to follow Christ, you became part of the ever-growing kingdom of God. As believers unite, this kingdom impacts the world more and more. But it all starts with the faith of *individual* people.

Do you feel your faith is too small to be effective? When was the last time you offered a helping hand? A listening ear? Can you take some time this week to show your neighbor God's love?

Often the smallest seeds grow into the tallest trees.

| DAY 3 ## just a little bit of yeast

Jesus also used this illustration: "The Kingdom of Heaven is like yeast used by a woman making bread. Even though she used a large amount of flour, the yeast permeated every part of the dough."

Jesus always used stories and illustrations like these when speaking to the crowds. In fact, he never spoke to them without using such parables. This fulfilled the prophecy that said, "I will speak to you in parables. I will explain mysteries hidden since the creation of the world." MATTHEW 13:33-35

In all of his *breaking* of bread, Jesus must have learned a thing or two about the *baking* of bread. Undoubtedly he understood the importance of yeast. A loaf of bread only needs a small amount but forget the yeast and the bread can't rise.

Although yeast is often used as a negative symbol in the Bible, in this passage the yeast represents the spreading of God's kingdom. Every time a new person trusts in Christ, the Kingdom of God grows. And once we come in contact with this yeast, we are never the same.

The wonderful thing about yeast is that it only takes a little to cause the dough to grow many times its size. In other words, you aren't responsible for sharing God's love with the entire world. Share a just little faith with your family or classmates and then watch it grow.

A little bit of God's love goes a long way in the growth of the kingdom.

Then, leaving the crowds outside, Jesus went into the house. His disciples said, "Please explain the story of the weeds in the field."

"All right," he said. "I, the Son of Man, am the farmer who plants the good seed. The field is the world, and the good seed represents the people of the Kingdom. The weeds are the people who belong to the evil one. The enemy who planted the weeds among the wheat is the Devil. The harvest is the end of the world, and the harvesters are the angels.

"Just as the weeds are separated out and burned, so it will be at the end of the world. I, the Son of Man, will send my angels, and they will remove from my Kingdom everything that causes sin and all who do evil, and they will throw them into the furnace and burn them. There will be weeping and gnashing of teeth. Then the godly will shine like the sun in their Father's Kingdom. Anyone who is willing to hear should listen and understand!"

MATTHEW 13:36-43

To farmers, the autumn harvest represents a job well done. Their patience and hard work pays off and a large crop rewards them. Similarly the end of the world is God's harvest.

When Jesus explained the parable of the weeds, he compared the harvest with the final judgment of God. During God's judgment the just are separated from the unjust. Those who belong to Satan will first be separated from the godly. Then they will be separated from God.

Jesus' description of the punishment for sin is blunt and horrible. It goes directly against our indifferent attitudes. We sometimes think that if we just don't *think* about God's judgment we can live like we want and avoid punishment. But in the end, sin cannot exist in the presence of the perfect God. Nor can anyone who refuses to give up sin.

If you died today, would you be part of God's good crop? Do you have sin in your life that you haven't yet confessed yet to God? If you confess, God is faithful to forgive all your sins.

Don't wait until harvest time!

DAY 5 An Exciting Discovery

The Kingdom of Heaven is like a treasure that a man discovered hidden in a field. In his excitement, he hid it again and sold everything he owned to get enough money to buy the field—and to get the treasure, too! MATTHEW 13:44

Did you ever have the pleasure of rummaging through old boxes in your grandparent's attic? This is fun. You can discover all sorts of hidden treasures. Today's Scripture shows what one man did when he discovered a treasure in a field.

The man may have decided to take a shortcut through a neighbor's field. His path led him past a small object jutting out of the ground. When he investigated and saw it was buried treasure, he started to get excited. He had to have it! So he bought the whole field just to get the treasure.

The true treasure that's waiting to be discovered is the kingdom of God. The good news is that God has written a map in each person's heart to help that person find it. If we're willing to look deeply and join in the search, an amazing friendship with God awaits us. God *wants* us to be excited about finding him.

Are you eagerly seeking a relationship with God? What people around you are truly excited about finding God?

Don't let anyone convince you that following Christ means having a boring life. Being part of God's kingdom is exciting!

What did you learn about Jesus from this week's readings?

What reading this week had the most impact on you? Why?

What do you plan to do about what you have learned this week?

Key Verse:

WEEKEIGHTEEN

| DAY 1 ## worth More than Anything

Again, the Kingdom of Heaven is like a pearl merchant on the lookout for choice pearls. When he discovered a pearl of great value, he sold everything he owned and bought it!
MATTHEW 13:45-46

Here Jesus describes a merchant who had spent his whole life buying and selling pearls. His eye was trained to spot the good ones. So when he came upon *the* pearl, he knew he had the find of a lifetime and sold all he owned just to possess it. To him the pearl was priceless.

The Kingdom of Heaven is like that pearl—more valuable than *anything* else we might have. Like the merchant, we should take whatever steps are necessary to obtain it—whether it's giving up an activity that distracts us from Jesus, breaking off a harmful relationship, or quitting a bad habit.

Sadly, there are those who put careers, power, money, or possessions before Jesus. They are losing out on the most valuable thing they could possibly have—a place in the eternal kingdom of God.

What's distracting you from Jesus? Are you willing to give that up for the sake of the kingdom?

Christ's free offer of salvation is the most valuable gift you will ever receive.

Again, the Kingdom of Heaven is like a fishing net that is thrown into the water and gathers fish of every kind. When the net is full, they drag it up onto the shore, sit down, sort the good fish into crates, and throw the bad ones away. That is the way it will be at the end of the world. The angels will come and separate the wicked people from the godly, throwing the wicked into the fire. There will be weeping and gnashing of teeth. Do you understand?"

"Yes," they said, "we do."

Then he added, "Every teacher of religious law who has become a disciple in the Kingdom of Heaven is like a person who brings out of the storehouse the new teachings as well as the old."   MATTHEW 13:47-52

If you've attended church for a while, you probably know the people who frequently participate in the church's activities. It's natural to assume that these same folks are likely to be standing with you one day before God's heavenly throne.

Jesus gives a picture of that final judgment that is different than what you might expect. The kingdom is described as a fishing net that gathers up *all* people, not just believers. We do not know who is who in that net. Only God can tell the good from the bad fish. We may be shocked to discover the result of that judgment. Some people whom we expect to be in God's kingdom may not be there. Others whom we don't expect will be there with us.

Your job is twofold: First make sure that your own relationship with the Lord is secure and healthy. Then, be faithful to share the gospel with others.

In the same Boat

One day Jesus said to his disciples, "Let's cross over to the other side of the lake." So they got into a boat and started out. On the way across, Jesus lay down for a nap, and while he was sleeping the wind began to rise. A fierce storm developed that threatened to swamp them, and they were in real danger.

The disciples woke him up, shouting, "Master, Master, we're going to drown!"

So Jesus rebuked the wind and the raging waves. The storm stopped and all was calm! Then he asked them, "Where is your faith?"

And they were filled with awe and amazement. They said to one another, "Who is this man, that even the winds and waves obey him?"   LUKE 8:22-25

The storms of life can be terrifying—like losing a friend in a car crash or discovering that a loved one has cancer.

In this passage we see the disciples in a terrifying storm at sea. They are literally fighting for their lives. In a panic they awaken Jesus, not to ask him for help, not to beg him to save them, but to tell him the end has come. They thought they were going to die. The disciples had forgotten who was in the boat with them. Jesus, God himself, was the only one who could possibly save them.

At times, we react the same way. When faced with overwhelming problems, we tend to panic, to believe that there is no way out, and that we are going down with the ship. That's when we need to remember that Jesus is with us and turn to him in faith.

In the middle of life's storms, remember that Jesus is with you. He will see you through.

touching the outcasts

So they arrived at the other side of the lake, in the land of the Gerasenes. Just as Jesus was climbing from the boat, a man possessed by an evil spirit ran out from a cemetery to meet him. This man lived among the tombs and could not be restrained, even with a chain. Whenever he was put into chains and shackles—as he often was—he snapped the chains from his wrists and smashed the shackles. No one was strong enough to control him. All day long and throughout the night, he would wander among the tombs and in the hills, screaming and hitting himself with stones.

When Jesus was still some distance away, the man saw him. He ran to meet Jesus and fell down before him. He gave a terrible scream, shrieking, "Why are you bothering me, Jesus, Son of the Most High God? For God's sake, don't torture me!" For Jesus had already said to the spirit, "Come out of the man, you evil spirit."

Then Jesus asked, "What is your name?"

And the spirit replied, "Legion, because there are many of us here inside this man." Then the spirits begged him again and again not to send them to some distant place. There happened to be a large herd of pigs feeding on the hillside nearby. "Send us into those pigs," the evil spirits begged. Jesus gave them permission. So the evil spirits came out of the man and entered the pigs, and the entire herd of two thousand pigs plunged down the steep hillside into the lake, where they drowned.

The herdsmen fled to the nearby city and the surrounding countryside, spreading the news as they ran. Everyone rushed out to see for themselves. A crowd soon gathered around Jesus, but they were frightened when they saw the man who had been demon possessed, for he was sitting there fully clothed and perfectly sane. Those who had seen what happened to the man and to the pigs told everyone about it, and the crowd began pleading with Jesus to go away and leave them alone.

When Jesus got back into the boat, the man who had been demon possessed begged to go, too. But Jesus said, "No, go home to your friends, and tell them what wonderful things the Lord has done for you and how merciful he has been." So the man started off to visit the Ten Towns of that region and began to tell everyone about the great things Jesus had done for him; and everyone was amazed at what he told them. MARK 5:1-20

Travel across this country, and in every city you can see people living on the street. For them, finding a place to sleep, eat, and clean up is a constant struggle. Very few people are willing to help them. Some even cross the street if they spy a street person approaching.

But Jesus purposefully engaged such off-limits people. He wasn't afraid to get involved with the people whom others ignored. In fact, this portion of Scripture shows Jesus in a Gentile land healing a Gentile man who had been rejected by his *own* society! No self-respecting Jewish person would be caught dead in a Gentile country, let alone talking with a demon-possessed native.

Jesus knows that *all people* need his love. What prevents you from sharing the good news with others?

Pray that God will transform you into a messenger of Christ's love.

| WEEK EIGHTEEN | DAY 5 | # A crowd of Disbelief |

When Jesus went back across to the other side of the lake, a large crowd gathered around him on the shore. A leader of the local synagogue, whose name was Jairus, came and fell down before him, pleading with him to heal his little daughter. "She is about to die," he said in desperation. "Please come and place your hands on her; heal her so she can live."

Jesus went with him, and the crowd thronged behind. And there was a woman in the crowd who had had a hemorrhage for twelve years. She had suffered a great deal from many doctors through the years and had spent everything she had to pay them, but she had gotten no better. In fact, she was worse. She had heard about Jesus, so she came up behind him through the crowd and touched the fringe of his robe. For she thought to herself, "If I can just touch his clothing, I will be healed." Immediately the bleeding stopped, and she could feel that she had been healed!

Jesus realized at once that healing power had gone out from him, so he turned around in the crowd and asked, "Who touched my clothes?"

His disciples said to him, "All this crowd is pressing around you. How can you ask, 'Who touched me?'"

But he kept on looking around to see who had done it. Then the frightened woman, trembling at the realization of what had happened to her, came and fell at his feet and told him what she had done. And he said to her, "Daughter, your faith has made you well. Go in peace. You have been healed."

While he was still speaking to her, messengers arrived from Jairus's home with the message, "Your daughter is dead. There's no use troubling the Teacher now."

But Jesus ignored their comments and said to Jairus, "Don't be afraid. Just trust me." Then Jesus stopped the crowd and wouldn't let anyone go with him except Peter and James and John. When they came to the home of the synagogue leader, Jesus saw the commotion and the weeping and wailing. He went inside and spoke to the people. "Why all this weeping and commotion?" he asked. "The child isn't dead; she is only asleep."

The crowd laughed at him, but he told them all to go outside. Then he took the girl's father and mother and his three disciples into the room where the girl was lying. Holding her hand, he said to her, "Get up, little girl!" And the girl, who was twelve years old, immediately stood up and walked around! Her parents were absolutely overwhelmed. Jesus commanded them not to tell anyone what had happened, and he told them to give her something to eat.   MARK 5:21-43

Jesus seems to have had a crowd following him wherever he went. In this passage a crowd followed Jesus to see if he could do a miracle. A woman in the crowd secretly touched him and was healed. Shortly after this he faced another crowd who doubted his power and laughed at him.

Jairus pressed through that doubting crowd and asked Jesus to bring his daughter back to life. Both the woman and Jairus show *individual faith*. Their faith caused them to stand out in the crowd. Jesus still works through your faith even in the midst of a crowd of disbelief.

Reactions to your faith will range from confused disbelief to snickering insults. How will such reactions affect you?

Ignore others' disbelief and trust in Jesus.

What did you learn about Jesus from this week's readings?

What reading this week had the most impact on you? Why?

What do you plan to do about what you have learned this week?

Key Verse:

WEEKNINETEEN

| DAY 1 **Getting to the Doctor**

After Jesus left the girl's home, two blind men followed along behind him, shouting, "Son of David, have mercy on us!"

They went right into the house where he was staying, and Jesus asked them, "Do you believe I can make you see?"

"Yes, Lord," they told him, "we do."

Then he touched their eyes and said, "Because of your faith, it will happen." And suddenly they could see! Jesus sternly warned them, "Don't tell anyone about this." But instead, they spread his fame all over the region.

When they left, some people brought to him a man who couldn't speak because he was possessed by a demon. So Jesus cast out the demon, and instantly the man could talk. The crowds marveled. "Nothing like this has ever happened in Israel!" they exclaimed.

But the Pharisees said, "He can cast out demons because he is empowered by the prince of demons." MATTHEW 9:27-34

If you're sick, you go to the doctor's office. If you're *really* sick, you need someone to take you to the doctor's office. This portion of Scripture shows how three people visited Doctor Jesus.

The two blind men didn't find it hard to believe that Jesus could heal their blindness. After all, he had just raised a girl from the dead. They were determined to see the doctor. Nothing was going to stop them. So they boldly marched right up to Jesus and asked for healing. On their heels came a demon-possessed man who was so weak that he had to be carried to Jesus. The Lord healed each of these people because they came in faith.

Have you been hurting lately? Jesus wants you to boldly come to him. Does someone you know need some help in getting to Jesus? Be a friend and bring them to the Doctor.

Go to Christ in faith.

Jesus left that part of the country and returned with his disciples to Nazareth, his hometown. The next Sabbath he began teaching in the synagogue, and many who heard him were astonished. They asked, "Where did he get all his wisdom and the power to perform such miracles? He's just the carpenter, the son of Mary and brother of James, Joseph, Judas, and Simon. And his sisters live right here among us." They were deeply offended and refused to believe in him.

Then Jesus told them, "A prophet is honored everywhere except in his own hometown and among his relatives and his own family." And because of their unbelief, he couldn't do any mighty miracles among them except to place his hands on a few sick people and heal them. And he was amazed at their unbelief.

Then Jesus went out from village to village, teaching.   MARK 6:1-6

Remember the kid who was klutzy in grade school but became the star gymnast in high school? Or the girl who was gawky in sixth grade but was voted homecoming queen? People often grow up differently than we would have predicted.

The people of Nazareth thought they knew their hometown boy, Jesus. When they looked at him they saw the son of a carpenter. They knew him as child playing with all the other children in the neighborhood. So it came as a shock to hear this same Jesus claim to be the Messiah. In fact, Jesus' claims actually offended the people who should have been his biggest fans.

The people of Nazareth had preconceived ideas about Jesus. They couldn't see who Jesus really was. Even today people have preconceived ideas about Jesus. For example, they say he was merely a great teacher and a morally upright man. These ideas prevent them from seeing Jesus as he really is—as God, as man, as Savior, and as King.

See Jesus for who he really is.

DAY 3 workers Needed!

Jesus traveled through all the cities and villages of that area, teaching in the synagogues and announcing the Good News about the Kingdom. And wherever he went, he healed people of every sort of disease and illness. He felt great pity for the crowds that came, because their problems were so great and they didn't know where to go for help. They were like sheep without a shepherd. He said to his disciples, "The harvest is so great, but the workers are so few. So pray to the Lord who is in charge of the harvest; ask him to send out more workers for his fields." MATTHEW 9:35-38

When you look around at the kids in your homeroom at school, what do you see? A bunch of familiar faces? Or do you see your classmates as Jesus does—as people in need of the Savior?

Everywhere Jesus went he saw a spiritual harvest—people in need of the good news about God's kingdom. The need was so great that Jesus told his followers to pray that the Father would send *more* workers to reach the lost.

Just as in Jesus' time, the harvest today is great and the workers are few. Jesus didn't come to earth to sit around. He came to work and he expects his followers to do the same.

Are you a worker for the kingdom of God? You can start by praying for one or two people. Then look for opportunities to share the gospel with them. This is how to participate in God's great harvest.

Pray that the Lord of the harvest will put you to work.

| DAY 4 # Doing the work

Jesus called his twelve disciples to him and gave them authority to cast out evil spirits and to heal every kind of disease and illness. Here are the names of the twelve apostles:

first Simon (also called Peter), then Andrew (Peter's brother), James (son of Zebedee), John (James's brother), Philip, Bartholomew, Thomas, Matthew (the tax collector), James (son of Alphaeus), Thaddaeus, Simon (the Zealot), Judas Iscariot (who later betrayed him).

Jesus sent the twelve disciples out with these instructions: "Don't go to the Gentiles or the Samaritans, but only to the people of Israel—God's lost sheep. Go and announce to them that the Kingdom of Heaven is near. Heal the sick, raise the dead, cure those with leprosy, and cast out demons. Give as freely as you have received!

"Don't take any money with you. Don't carry a traveler's bag with an extra coat and sandals or even a walking stick. Don't hesitate to accept hospitality, because those who work deserve to be fed. Whenever you enter a city or village, search for a worthy man and stay in his home until you leave for the next town. When you are invited into someone's home, give it your blessing. If it turns out to be a worthy home, let your blessing stand; if it is not, take back the blessing. If a village doesn't welcome you or listen to you, shake off the dust of that place from your feet as you leave. I assure you, the wicked cities of Sodom and Gomorrah will be better off on the judgment day than that place will be.

"Look, I am sending you out as sheep among wolves. Be as wary as snakes and harmless as doves."   MATTHEW 10:1-16

Ask any sheep rancher to tell you about the chances a lone sheep has against a pack of wolves. It's a fact of a nature that the wolves will kill the sheep. So why does Jesus tell his disciples that he is sending them out as sheep among wolves? To discourage them? To make them give up and go home? No, Jesus is preparing his followers for the reality of this world. He wants to alert us to the opposition that we will certainly encounter as we live for him.

In the second part of Jesus' instructions he instructs us to "be as wary as snakes and harmless as doves." This means that we need to be wise about the way we carry the gospel to others. We should be careful and stay out of harm's way, like a snake. We are not to act like wolves and attack others with the truth, rather be like doves, harmless yet attractive, presenting the gospel in a gentle way.

Be open to others' needs and wise about how you present the gospel to them.

| DAY 5 # ReaLity DiscipLeship

But beware! For you will be handed over to the courts and beaten in the synagogues. And you must stand trial before governors and kings because you are my followers. This will be your opportunity to tell them about me—yes, to witness to the world. When you are arrested, don't worry about what to say in your defense, because you will be given the right words at the right time. For it won't be you doing the talking—it will be the Spirit of your Father speaking through you.

Brother will betray brother to death, fathers will betray their own children, and children will rise against their parents and cause them to be killed. And everyone will hate you because of your allegiance to me. But those who endure to the end will be saved. When you are persecuted in one town, flee to the next. I assure you that I, the Son of Man, will return before you have reached all the towns of Israel. . . .

Don't be afraid of those who want to kill you. They can only kill your body; they cannot touch your soul. Fear only God, who can destroy both soul and body in hell. Not even a sparrow, worth only half a penny, can fall to the ground without your Father knowing it. And the very hairs on your head are all numbered. So don't be afraid; you are more valuable to him than a whole flock of sparrows.

If anyone acknowledges me publicly here on earth, I will openly acknowledge that person before my Father in heaven. But if anyone denies me here on earth, I will deny that person before my Father in heaven.   MATTHEW 10:17-23, 28-33

The melodramatic music swells as the soap-opera doctor enters the hospital room. Everyone waits as he approaches the bed. The soap-opera patient grabs his hand, "Give it to me straight, doc," he rasps, "I can take it." Can you take straight talk about following Jesus?

In this passage Jesus tells it like it is, describing the stark reality awaiting his followers: The world will hate you; you will be persecuted; you will stand trial; you may even die for your faith. He wants his followers to understand the full cost of being his disciple. He doesn't sugarcoat it. But he does tell of the incredible rewards awaiting those who remain faithful in his work: You will be saved; God will care for you and protect your eternal soul; you will be given the right words at the right time; Christ will acknowledge you before the Father.

Are you going to play it safe or will you risk it all for God's kingdom?

Jesus' eternal rewards are worth far more than anything this world can offer.

What did you learn about Jesus from this week's readings?

What reading this week had the most impact on you? Why?

What do you plan to do about what you have learned this week?

Key Verse:

DAY 1 making the choice

Herod Antipas, the king, soon heard about Jesus, because people everywhere were talking about him. Some were saying, "This must be John the Baptist come back to life again. That is why he can do such miracles." Others thought Jesus was the ancient prophet Elijah. Still others thought he was a prophet like the other great prophets of the past. When Herod heard about Jesus, he said, "John, the man I beheaded, has come back from the dead." For Herod had sent soldiers to arrest and imprison John as a favor to Herodias. She had been his brother Philip's wife, but Herod had married her. John kept telling Herod, "It is illegal for you to marry your brother's wife." Herodias was enraged and wanted John killed in revenge, but without Herod's approval she was powerless. And Herod respected John, knowing that he was a good and holy man, so he kept him under his protection. Herod was disturbed whenever he talked with John, but even so, he liked to listen to him.

Herodias's chance finally came. It was Herod's birthday, and he gave a party for his palace aides, army officers, and the leading citizens of Galilee. Then his daughter, also named Herodias, came in and performed a dance that greatly pleased them all. "Ask me for anything you like," the king said to the girl, "and I will give it to you." Then he promised, "I will give you whatever you ask, up to half of my kingdom!"

She went out and asked her mother, "What should I ask for?"

Her mother told her, "Ask for John the Baptist's head!"

So the girl hurried back to the king and told him, "I want the head of John the Baptist, right now, on a tray!"

Then the king was very sorry, but he was embarrassed to break his oath in front of his guests. So he sent an executioner to the prison to cut off John's head and bring it to him. The soldier beheaded John in the prison, brought his head on a tray, and gave it to the girl, who took it to her mother. When John's disciples heard what had happened, they came for his body and buried it in a tomb. MARK 6:14-29

If you had lived in the days of King Herod, would you have accepted an invitation to his birthday party? Think about it: All the top people were there. The food was the best there could be. It was a chance to check out the king's palace and socialize with the in-crowd.

Sure, it could be a lot of fun. But there is one other thing to consider: these high people had low morals. As the party progressed the king's young daughter pleased them all with a dance. Then things continued downhill—John the Baptist was murdered and his head was brought in for all to see.

Have you noticed that sometimes the world's fun results in spiritual death? Suppose you go to watch a football game with some guys, or attend a party after the prom. The gathering runs its course and you leave feeling inwardly soiled. What looked like fun was murder on your spirit of faith.

Seek the Lord Jesus so your spiritual life will be protected from the spirit of this world.

DAY 2 A Little Lunch Goes a Long Way

After this, Jesus crossed over the Sea of Galilee, also known as the Sea of Tiberias. And a huge crowd kept following him wherever he went, because they saw his miracles as he healed the sick. Then Jesus went up into the hills and sat down with his disciples around him. (It was nearly time for the annual Passover celebration.) Jesus soon saw a great crowd of people climbing the hill, looking for him. Turning to Philip, he asked, "Philip, where can we buy bread to feed all these people?" He was testing Philip, for he already knew what he was going to do.

Philip replied, "It would take a small fortune to feed them!"

Then Andrew, Simon Peter's brother, spoke up. "There's a young boy here with five barley loaves and two fish. But what good is that with this huge crowd?"

"Tell everyone to sit down," Jesus ordered. So all of them—the men alone numbered five thousand—sat down on the grassy slopes. Then Jesus took the loaves, gave thanks to God, and passed them out to the people. Afterward he did the same with the fish. And they all ate until they were full. "Now gather the leftovers," Jesus told his disciples, "so that nothing is wasted." There were only five barley loaves to start with, but twelve baskets were filled with the pieces of bread the people did not eat!

When the people saw this miraculous sign, they exclaimed, "Surely, he is the Prophet we have been expecting!" Jesus saw that they were ready to take him by force and make him king, so he went higher into the hills alone. JOHN 6:1-15

In this familiar passage we see what can result when we entrust our meager resources to the hands of God. When confronted with task of feeding five thousand people far from any town, the disciples were stymied because they focused on what they didn't have. But a young boy offered up the little he *did* have and it was all Jesus needed.

The same is true for us. God doesn't care about how talented we are, how much money we have, or how much time we can offer. If we give nothing,

God will have nothing to use. But if we entrust the little we have to Jesus he can do more than we can imagine. What can you offer to Jesus? Don't delay, the people are hungry!

If Jesus can work a miracle with a couple of fish and a few loaves of bread, imagine what he can do with your gifts.

DAY 3 sink or swim . . . or walk!
WEEK TWENTY

Immediately after this, Jesus made his disciples get back into the boat and cross to the other side of the lake while he sent the people home. Afterward he went up into the hills by himself to pray. Night fell while he was there alone. Meanwhile, the disciples were in trouble far away from land, for a strong wind had risen, and they were fighting heavy waves.

About three o'clock in the morning Jesus came to them, walking on the water. When the disciples saw him, they screamed in terror, thinking he was a ghost. But Jesus spoke to them at once. "It's all right," he said. "I am here! Don't be afraid."

Then Peter called to him, "Lord, if it's really you, tell me to come to you by walking on water."

"All right, come," Jesus said.

So Peter went over the side of the boat and walked on the water toward Jesus. But when he looked around at the high waves, he was terrified and began to sink. "Save me, Lord!" he shouted.

Instantly Jesus reached out his hand and grabbed him. "You don't have much faith," Jesus said. "Why did you doubt me?" And when they climbed back into the boat, the wind stopped.

Then the disciples worshiped him. "You really are the Son of God!" they exclaimed.

MATTHEW 14:22-33

Watch a child jump to her mom in a swimming pool. Over and over again the girl enthusiastically jumps into the waiting arms. She doesn't stop to think, "What if Mom doesn't catch me?" because her trust in her mother is complete.

When Peter stepped out of the boat, he had his eyes on Jesus, so he was able to do the impossible—walk on water! Jesus *told* Peter to get out of the boat so Peter focused on the one who had the power to perform miracles. But as soon as Peter looked at what was going on around him—the high waves, the deep water, and the fact the boat was drifting away—he began to sink.

We may never walk on water, but we will have to walk through difficult situations. If we focus on the difficulties around us, we will falter and begin to sink. But when we keep focused on Jesus and depend on his power, rather than our own, he will bring us through.

Just like Peter, when we trust in Jesus we can do what we thought was impossible.

DAY 4 what Have You Done for Me Lately?

After they had crossed the lake, they landed at Gennesaret. The news of their arrival spread quickly throughout the whole surrounding area, and soon people were bringing all their sick to be healed. The sick begged him to let them touch even the fringe of his robe, and all who touched it were healed.   MATTHEW 14:34-36

Several years ago, a popular song asked the musical question, "What have you done for me lately?" You may have asked this question of your parents, teachers, or even your friends. But are they there just to meet your needs? When a person fails to produce for you, what do you do? Get angry? Walk away?

People flocked to Jesus because of what he could do for them. In this passage the crowd was looking for healing. They wanted Jesus to meet their immediate, physical needs. They didn't even consider his real purpose for being there.

People still come to Jesus in this way. We want Jesus to do our bidding rather than the other way around. Jesus does want to heal us; he does want to give us the best. But he also wants us to come to him because of who he is, not because of what he can do for us.

How do you approach the Lord? With a list of what you want or a list of who he is?

Come to Jesus because he is your Savior and friend.

| DAY 5 | # Two Kinds of Bread

The next morning, back across the lake, crowds began gathering on the shore, waiting to see Jesus. For they knew that he and his disciples had come over together and that the disciples had gone off in their boat, leaving him behind. Several boats from Tiberias landed near the place where the Lord had blessed the bread and the people had eaten. When the crowd saw that Jesus wasn't there, nor his disciples, they got into the boats and went across to Capernaum to look for him. When they arrived and found him, they asked, "Teacher, how did you get here?"

Jesus replied, "The truth is, you want to be with me because I fed you, not because you saw the miraculous sign. But you shouldn't be so concerned about perishable things like food. Spend your energy seeking the eternal life that I, the Son of Man, can give you. For God the Father has sent me for that very purpose."

They replied, "What does God want us to do?"

Jesus told them, "This is what God wants you to do: Believe in the one he has sent."

They replied, "You must show us a miraculous sign if you want us to believe in you. What will you do for us? After all, our ancestors ate manna while they journeyed through the wilderness! As the Scriptures say, 'Moses gave them bread from heaven to eat.'."

Jesus said, "I assure you, Moses didn't give them bread from heaven. My Father did. And now he offers you the true bread from heaven. The true bread of God is the one who comes down from heaven and gives life to the world."

"Sir," they said, "give us that bread every day of our lives."

Jesus replied, "I am the bread of life. No one who comes to me will ever be hungry again. Those who believe in me will never thirst.   JOHN 6.22-35

Imagine that you are walking through a street carnival on your way to work. Along the way many enticements tempt you to stop—games, prizes, food, even your friends ask you to join them for a quick ride. But you know that if you are distracted you won't get to work on time.

Jesus underwent this every day. It was as if a carnival was always swirling around him. Millions would have followed him if he had healed their every disease or performed miracle after miracle. But Jesus knew his purpose for coming to earth was to do the will of the Father. He was not going to let anyone or anything sidetrack him from accomplishing that goal. Likewise, we shouldn't allow anyone or anything to distract us from accomplishing our purpose in Christ.

Do you know your purpose as a Christian? If not, pray that God would reveal this to you.

What did you learn about Jesus from this week's readings?

What reading this week had the most impact on you? Why?

What do you plan to do about what you have learned this week?

Key Verse:

| DAY 1 | **The Tough Stuff**

"I assure you, anyone who believes in me already has eternal life. Yes, I am the bread of life! Your ancestors ate manna in the wilderness, but they all died. However, the bread from heaven gives eternal life to everyone who eats it. I am the living bread that came down out of heaven. Anyone who eats this bread will live forever; this bread is my flesh, offered so the world may live."

Then the people began arguing with each other about what he meant. "How can this man give us his flesh to eat?" they asked.

So Jesus said again, "I assure you, unless you eat the flesh of the Son of Man and drink his blood, you cannot have eternal life within you. But those who eat my flesh and drink my blood have eternal life, and I will raise them at the last day. For my flesh is the true food, and my blood is the true drink. All who eat my flesh and drink my blood remain in me, and I in them. I live by the power of the living Father who sent me; in the same way, those who partake of me will live because of me. I am the true bread from heaven. Anyone who eats this bread will live forever and not die as your ancestors did, even though they ate the manna."

He said these things while he was teaching in the synagogue in Capernaum.

JOHN 6.47-59

There was once a little boy who, when reciting the Lord's Prayer, said, "Our Father, who art in heaven, Howard is thy name." In today's Scripture passage the people were like that little boy. They misunderstood the Lord's words. When Jesus spoke about eating his flesh and drinking his blood, they immediately thought about cannibalism! It was shocking to them.

Jesus was not talking about literally eating his flesh or drinking his blood. He wanted the people to understand that *his* life had to become *their* life if they were to have *eternal* life. But they didn't get it and many left Jesus.

It is true that Jesus' teachings are sometimes difficult to understand. But we must take time to dig a bit deeper, ask questions, and seek answers in order to understand the important truths of the Christian faith.

Don't give up when you can't grasp a Bible truth. Keep digging and ask God to help you understand.

sticking power

Even his disciples said, "This is very hard to understand. How can anyone accept it?"

Jesus knew within himself that his disciples were complaining, so he said to them, "Does this offend you? Then what will you think if you see me, the Son of Man, return to heaven again? It is the Spirit who gives eternal life. Human effort accomplishes nothing. And the very words I have spoken to you are spirit and life. But some of you don't believe me." (For Jesus knew from the beginning who didn't believe, and he knew who would betray him.) Then he said, "That is what I meant when I said that people can't come to me unless the Father brings them to me."

At this point many of his disciples turned away and deserted him. Then Jesus turned to the Twelve and asked, "Are you going to leave, too?"

Simon Peter replied, "Lord, to whom would we go? You alone have the words that give eternal life. We believe them, and we know you are the Holy One of God."

Then Jesus said, "I chose the twelve of you, but one is a devil." He was speaking of Judas, son of Simon Iscariot, one of the Twelve, who would betray him. JOHN 6:60-71

When a team is winning all its games, it's easy to be a fan. Winning may not be everything, but it sure is a lot of fun. It's much tougher to stick with a team that is the doormat of the league. You don't find a lot of hoopla around those kinds of teams.

It was the same with Jesus. At first a lot people were eager to follow him. He was the daring new prophet in town. Many people were excited about being with a man who was doing miracles, healing people, and attracting huge crowds. But this was *before* Jesus' teaching started becoming hard to understand. That's when the crowds began to leave.

Today people react the same way. They embrace the loving Jesus, the forgiving Jesus, the friendly Jesus. But when they encounter a difficult teaching, they decide that Jesus isn't for them. But did we follow everything our parents said when we were children? No, yet we obeyed them at the time. Only later did we understood their reasoning.

Growing up in the faith means sticking with Jesus even when you feel clueless about what is happening to you.

DAY 3   # Going through the Motions

One day some Pharisees and teachers of religious law arrived from Jerusalem to confront Jesus. They noticed that some of Jesus' disciples failed to follow the usual Jewish ritual of hand washing before eating. (The Jews, especially the Pharisees, do not eat until they have poured water over their cupped hands, as required by their ancient traditions. Similarly, they eat nothing bought from the market unless they have immersed their hands in water. This is but one of many traditions they have clung to—such as their ceremony of washing cups, pitchers, and kettles.) So the Pharisees and teachers of religious law asked him, "Why don't your disciples follow our age-old customs? For they eat without first performing the hand-washing ceremony."

Jesus replied, "You hypocrites! Isaiah was prophesying about you when he said,

'These people honor me with their lips, but their hearts are far away. Their worship is a farce, for they replace God's commands with their own man-made teachings.'

For you ignore God's specific laws and substitute your own traditions."   MARK 7:1-8

Here Jesus finds fault with the Pharisees because they ignored God's specific laws and substituted their own traditions. This is a hard lesson to learn. Do you and your Christian friends have your own traditions? These may be certain ways of dressing or patterns of speech. They could include your preference for a certain Bible translation or style of worship. Your traditions could be many little things.

How can you tell if such things are a problem in your Christian life? Look at the Pharisees. They tried to keep many customs and ordinances and criticized others who did not do the same. They thought they were better than everyone else and so they criticized those who were different.

Do you and your friends look askance at Christians who are different than you are? Instead rejoice over the one way that you are the same: You all believe in the Lord Jesus Christ.

Ask God to give you eyes to see Christ in every believer.

Then Jesus left Galilee and went north to the region of Tyre. He tried to keep it secret that he was there, but he couldn't. As usual, the news of his arrival spread fast. Right away a woman came to him whose little girl was possessed by an evil spirit. She had heard about Jesus, and now she came and fell at his feet. She begged him to release her child from the demon's control.

Since she was a Gentile, born in Syrian Phoenicia, Jesus told her, "First I should help my own family, the Jews. It isn't right to take food from the children and throw it to the dogs."

She replied, "That's true, Lord, but even the dogs under the table are given some crumbs from the children's plates."

"Good answer!" he said. "And because you have answered so well, I have healed your daughter." And when she arrived home, her little girl was lying quietly in bed, and the demon was gone.   MARK 7:24-30

The woman in this passage was not about to give up on her only opportunity to see Jesus and get help for her little girl. Think about it: She already had lots of negatives against her—she was a woman, a foreigner, *and* a Gentile. She had to make her way through the crowd and then through the disciples who were probably trying to protect the Lord from the crowd's demands. But the woman succeeded because of her utter desperation.

It is easy to become comfortable and self-satisfied particularly when life is going well. Too often we forget our desperate daily need for Jesus until we hit a difficult situation. What will it take to make you desperate for Jesus?

Seek the knowledge of your daily need for Jesus. Don't let anything prevent you from coming to him every day in prayer.

| DAY 5 what's the story

Jesus left Tyre and went to Sidon, then back to the Sea of Galilee and the region of the Ten Towns. A deaf man with a speech impediment was brought to him, and the people begged Jesus to lay his hands on the man to heal him. Jesus led him to a private place away from the crowd. He put his fingers into the man's ears. Then, spitting onto his own fingers, he touched the man's tongue with the spittle. And looking up to heaven, he sighed and commanded, "Be opened!" Instantly the man could hear perfectly and speak plainly!

Jesus told the crowd not to tell anyone, but the more he told them not to, the more they spread the news, for they were completely amazed. Again and again they said, "Everything he does is wonderful. He even heals those who are deaf and mute." MARK 7:31-37

Each person has a unique way of learning. Some learn best when the information is presented in illustrations or pictures. Others need a more hands-on approach, applying information in a practical way. Jesus understood this. He used the most effective methods to reach people physically, spiritually, and emotionally. Jesus communicated through word-pictures, stories, parables, and lectures, to mention only a few of his methods.

In this passage Jesus used a very different approach to healing the deaf and mute man. He stuck his fingers in the man's ears and touched the man's tongue with his spit. The passage doesn't tell us *why* he took these steps, but we do know that Jesus didn't speak because the man couldn't hear. So he used touch.

Jesus will do the same for you. He will meet you in a way that you will understand, so be ready.

Keep the lines of communication open between you and Jesus, and don't be surprised by how he connects with you.

What did you learn about Jesus from this week's readings?

What reading this week had the most impact on you? Why?

What do you plan to do about what you have learned this week?

Key Verse:

WEEK TWENTY-TWO

| DAY 1 **DON'T FORGET!**

About this time another great crowd had gathered, and the people ran out of food again. Jesus called his disciples and told them, "I feel sorry for these people. They have been here with me for three days, and they have nothing left to eat. And if I send them home without feeding them, they will faint along the road. For some of them have come a long distance."

"How are we supposed to find enough food for them here in the wilderness?" his disciples asked.

"How many loaves of bread do you have?" he asked.

"Seven," they replied. So Jesus told all the people to sit down on the ground. Then he took the seven loaves, thanked God for them, broke them into pieces, and gave them to his disciples, who distributed the bread to the crowd. A few small fish were found, too, so Jesus also blessed these and told the disciples to pass them out.

They ate until they were full, and when the scraps were picked up, there were seven large baskets of food left over! There were about four thousand people in the crowd that day, and he sent them home after they had eaten. Immediately after this, he got into a boat with his disciples and crossed over to the region of Dalmanutha.   MARK 8:1-10

Here Jesus' disciples face a problem they should have been familiar with: They have no food to feed a huge crowd that has gathered to hear Jesus. But they don't seem to remember how, only weeks earlier, Jesus had fed over five thousand people with five loaves of bread and two fish. With seven loaves of bread in their hands, the disciples moan, "How are we supposed to find food for them here in the wilderness?"

You may think, "What's wrong with these guys? How could they forget so soon?" But we're no different. We hear testimonies about God's power, love, and protection; we even experience it sometimes. But in a day or two, we completely forget about it. Then, faced with a similar dilemma we wonder, "Now what will I do?"

When you encounter a difficult situation, stop and remember the Lord. Remember how God has protected you, provided for you, and led you in the past.

When you remember how Jesus has helped you in the past, you will be encouraged in the present.

| DAY 2   # HOW'S YOUR HEART?

When the Pharisees heard that Jesus had arrived, they came to argue with him. Testing him to see if he was from God, they demanded, "Give us a miraculous sign from heaven to prove yourself."

When he heard this, he sighed deeply and said, "Why do you people keep demanding a miraculous sign? I assure you, I will not give this generation any such sign." So he got back into the boat and left them, and he crossed to the other side of the lake.   MARK 8:11-13

Jesus had traveled to many places and the Pharisees may have witnessed or heard about dozens of his miracles. Even so, they asked Jesus to prove himself with yet *another* miraculous sign. But Jesus refused to give them a sign.

Have you ever fallen into that trap? "If he would only show me something spectacular," you think to yourself, "I'll never doubt again." What makes you so sure about this? The disciples saw Jesus' power *firsthand* yet sometimes found faith difficult.

Not only that, but Jesus has *already* proven himself. He died, was buried, and then was resurrected from the dead. This is what finally convinced the disciples. It is enough for us, too. What other sign would you require from Jesus?

Remember, when he was on the cross he said, "It is finished." He had completed the job. Faith means believing in who Jesus is—the resurrected redeemer.

Believe because of what Jesus has done, not for what you hope he might do for you.

| DAY 3   It onLy Takes a LittLe

But the disciples discovered they had forgotten to bring any food, so there was only one loaf of bread with them in the boat. As they were crossing the lake, Jesus warned them, "Beware of the yeast of the Pharisees and of Herod."

They decided he was saying this because they hadn't brought any bread. Jesus knew what they were thinking, so he said, "Why are you so worried about having no food? Won't you ever learn or understand? Are your hearts too hard to take it in? 'You have eyes—can't you see? You have ears—can't you hear?' Don't you remember anything at all? What about the five thousand men I fed with five loaves of bread? How many baskets of leftovers did you pick up afterward?"

"Twelve," they said.

"And when I fed the four thousand with seven loaves, how many large baskets of leftovers did you pick up?"

"Seven," they said.

"Don't you understand even yet?" he asked them.   MARK 8:14-21

Bakers know that only a little yeast will make bread dough double in size in short time. It's amazing what a small amount of yeast can do! Using this example, Jesus was trying to warn his disciples about the influence of the Pharisees' teaching.

Just as a little bit of yeast will make bread rise, small things can negatively effect your life. An off-color joke on a TV show or the disrespectful lyrics of a pop song may seem small, but such small sins can grow and infiltrate your soul. What little sins are you allowing into your life? Maybe it's a little gossip with your friends. Maybe you take pleasure in the daytime soap operas or suggestive rock songs. Beware the power of such "yeast."

Watch out for small sins that can have a big influence in your life.

When they arrived at Bethsaida, some people brought a blind man to Jesus, and they begged him to touch and heal the man. Jesus took the blind man by the hand and led him out of the village. Then, spitting on the man's eyes, he laid his hands on him and asked, "Can you see anything now?"

The man looked around. "Yes," he said, "I see people, but I can't see them very clearly. They look like trees walking around."

Then Jesus placed his hands over the man's eyes again. As the man stared intently, his sight was completely restored, and he could see everything clearly. Jesus sent him home, saying, "Don't go back into the village on your way home."   MARK 8:22-26

If you ever have had your eyes dilated for an eye exam, you know that everything is blurry for a while. Eventually the effects of the eye drops wear off and your normal vision returns. In this situation, when Jesus helped a blind man see, the man at first saw things hazily. Jesus' second touch completely restored his sight.

The Bible doesn't tell us why Jesus healed this man in this way. Maybe he wanted to show the disciples that some healing is gradual. Or Jesus may have used this healing to illustrate that some spiritual truths aren't clearly understood at first.

For example, a Scripture passage may not make sense to us. But as we walk with Jesus, spend time praying and reading the Bible, our spiritual "sight" will become clear and we'll understand the Scripture.

For clearer spiritual eyesight keep studying and stay close to Jesus.

| DAY 5   who Am I?

When Jesus came to the region of Caesarea Philippi, he asked his disciples, "Who do people say that the Son of Man is?"

"Well," they replied, "some say John the Baptist, some say Elijah, and others say Jeremiah or one of the other prophets."

Then he asked them, "Who do you say I am?

Simon Peter answered, "You are the Messiah, the Son of the living God."

Jesus replied, "You are blessed, Simon son of John, because my Father in heaven has revealed this to you. You did not learn this from any human being. Now I say to you that you are Peter, and upon this rock I will build my church, and all the powers of hell will not conquer it. And I will give you the keys of the Kingdom of Heaven. Whatever you lock on earth will be locked in heaven, and whatever you open on earth will be opened in heaven." Then he sternly warned them not to tell anyone that he was the Messiah.   MATTHEW 16:13-20

It's easy to think you have someone figured out because you spend a couple hours in classes with them. But as you get to know them outside class, you see a different person.

Many people thought that they had Jesus figured out. Some thought Jesus was a radical preacher, like John the Baptist. Others considered him to be a sincere religious leader, like Elijah. Still others considered him a great prophet, like Jeremiah.

All those answers contained a little truth but didn't come close to Jesus' true identity. When Peter said that Jesus was the Messiah, the Son of the living God, he gave the right answer even though he didn't completely understand what he was saying. He still had preconceived ideas about the Messiah.

Be watchful about your perceptions of Jesus. Be careful not to confine Jesus to a certain role in your life because of your limited understanding.

Seek Jesus more and more until you truly know him.

What did you learn about Jesus from this week's readings?

What reading this week had the most impact on you? Why?

What do you plan to do about what you have learned this week?

Key Verse:

DAY 1	## Life with God's view

From then on Jesus began to tell his disciples plainly that he had to go to Jerusalem, and he told them what would happen to him there. He would suffer at the hands of the leaders and the leading priests and the teachers of religious law. He would be killed, and he would be raised on the third day.

But Peter took him aside and corrected him. "Heaven forbid, Lord," he said. "This will never happen to you!"

Jesus turned to Peter and said, "Get away from me, Satan! You are a dangerous trap to me. You are seeing things merely from a human point of view, and not from God's."

Then Jesus said to the disciples, "If any of you wants to be my follower, you must put aside your selfish ambition, shoulder your cross, and follow me. If you try to keep your life for yourself, you will lose it. But if you give up your life for me, you will find true life. And how do you benefit if you gain the whole world but lose your own soul in the process? Is anything worth more than your soul? For I, the Son of Man, will come in the glory of my Father with his angels and will judge all people according to their deeds. And I assure you that some of you standing here right now will not die before you see me, the Son of Man, coming in my Kingdom." MATTHEW 16:21-28

Mosaic is an art form that uses small bits of colorful rock or glass to make a beautiful picture. View a mosaic from a distance and you'll see a beautiful landscape or the wonderful expression of a portrait. Stand close and all you can see are the tiny pieces. We get a different view of things depending on our point of view.

This was certainly true in the disciples' case. Jesus clearly explained to them that he would die and be raised from the dead three days later. Yet the disciples didn't really hear what Jesus was saying. They could not understand why Jesus had to die. Even though they had seen Jesus raise others from the dead, they couldn't comprehend how this could happen to him. They couldn't understand because they weren't seeing things from God's perspective.

From a human perspective it's difficult to see beyond what's tangible. We live in the present, physical world and can't imagine anything beyond this.

But just as there is more to this world than meets the eye, Jesus is more than what most people think he is. He is our crucified, resurrected, and ever-present Savior.

Pray that when you tell others about Jesus they'll seem him as he really is, that they'll see him from a heavenly point of view.

| DAY 2 prove it!

Six days later Jesus took Peter and the two brothers, James and John, and led them up a high mountain. As the men watched, Jesus' appearance changed so that his face shone like the sun, and his clothing became dazzling white. Suddenly, Moses and Elijah appeared and began talking with Jesus. Peter blurted out, "Lord, this is wonderful! If you want me to, I'll make three shrines, one for you, one for Moses, and one for Elijah."

But even as he said it, a bright cloud came over them, and a voice from the cloud said, "This is my beloved Son, and I am fully pleased with him. Listen to him." The disciples were terrified and fell face down on the ground.

Jesus came over and touched them. "Get up," he said, "don't be afraid." And when they looked, they saw only Jesus with them. As they descended the mountain, Jesus commanded them, "Don't tell anyone what you have seen until I, the Son of Man, have been raised from the dead."

His disciples asked, "Why do the teachers of religious law insist that Elijah must return before the Messiah comes?"

Jesus replied, "Elijah is indeed coming first to set everything in order. But I tell you, he has already come, but he wasn't recognized, and he was badly mistreated. And soon the Son of Man will also suffer at their hands." Then the disciples realized he had been speaking of John the Baptist.   MATTHEW 17:1-13

"Prove it!" Has anyone ever said that to you when you were trying to tell them about Jesus? You might reply with this question: "What kind of proof will you accept?" The problem is that some people will accept nothing as proof because they already have made up their minds.

The events in today's passage occurred just six days after Jesus told the disciples about his death and resurrection. Here he takes three of his closest associates and gives them proof positive of his claims. Imagine how their view of Jesus' changed after seeing him talking with men who had been dead for centuries!

What will it take for people to realize who Jesus is? It shouldn't take a transfiguration experience. After all, we have the benefit of two thousand years of church history to back up Jesus' claims. Plus, we have the testimony of the entire Bible.

People have all the evidence needed to prove Jesus' case, but they may lack is an open mind to carefully consider that information.

Keep your own mind open to Jesus. This will help others to open up to him.

WEEK TWENTY-THREE | DAY 3 Try Faith First

When they arrived at the foot of the mountain, a huge crowd was waiting for them. A man came and knelt before Jesus and said, "Lord, have mercy on my son, because he has seizures and suffers terribly. He often falls into the fire or into the water. So I brought him to your disciples, but they couldn't heal him."

Jesus replied, "You stubborn, faithless people! How long must I be with you until you believe? How long must I put up with you? Bring the boy to me." Then Jesus rebuked the demon in the boy, and it left him. From that moment the boy was well.

Afterward the disciples asked Jesus privately, "Why couldn't we cast out that demon?"

"You didn't have enough faith," Jesus told them. "I assure you, even if you had faith as small as a mustard seed you could say to this mountain, 'Move from here to there,' and it would move. Nothing would be impossible."   MATTHEW 17:14-21

You probably wouldn't try to to learn to drive without an instructor. You wouldn't attempt to take on a huge task like publishing the school yearbook without a faculty advisor. Some tasks in life are impossible to do on your own.

In this passage the disciples experienced trouble when they tried to perform a miracle without Christ. Maybe they said certain words or laid their hands on the possessed boy. Whatever they tried, they forgot to place their faith in God's ability to perform the task.

Jesus told them that all they needed was a tiny amount of faith and they could move mountains! Instead, the disciples relied on their own strength and forgot to place their faith in God, the true healer.

Do you ever act like the disciples? Have you ever bounced from plan A to plan B all the way to plan Z trying to solve a problem and still fail? That's when you say, "God help me!" Remember the first and most important step: have faith in God's ability to solve your problem.

Next time you feel powerless and frustrated, remember the mustard seed.

Bad News, Good News

One day after they had returned to Galilee, Jesus told them, "The Son of Man is going to be betrayed. He will be killed, but three days later he will be raised from the dead." And the disciples' hearts were filled with grief.   MATTHEW 17:22-23

Imagine that your mom knocks over your audio system and totally wipes it out, and that you get so angry that you don't hear her tell you that she's replaced it with an entirely new system.

This is natural; the disciples were no different. When Jesus told them that he was going to be killed, they were so upset that they didn't even *hear* the next part—three days after his death he would come back to life! Only later did they realize that Jesus *had* to die and that the Resurrection was his triumph.

What does this mean for us? We need to listen to Jesus' entire teaching. For example, he said that we will experience troubles and trials in this world, but he also promised that he will be with us through those troubles. Jesus said plainly that we will die, but he also promised eternal life for those who believe in him. Sometimes the good news included bad news, but Jesus always told the whole story.

Listen for the whole story and then pass it on to others.

| DAY 5   # God Pays Taxes?

On their arrival in Capernaum, the tax collectors for the Temple tax came to Peter and asked him, "Doesn't your teacher pay the Temple tax?"

"Of course he does," Peter replied. Then he went into the house to talk to Jesus about it.

But before he had a chance to speak, Jesus asked him, "What do you think, Peter? Do kings tax their own people or the foreigners they have conquered?"

"They tax the foreigners," Peter replied.

"Well, then," Jesus said, "the citizens are free! However, we don't want to offend them, so go down to the lake and throw in a line. Open the mouth of the first fish you catch, and you will find a coin. Take the coin and pay the tax for both of us."   MATTHEW 17:24-27

Are there things about church that you don't particularly like? Maybe you think the pastor talks too much. Perhaps it's the usher who never smiles. Or maybe you don't like the choice of songs. If so, you basically have two choices: You can either complain to anyone who will listen about long sermons, crabby ushers, or boring songs, or you can overlook these minor issues and hold your fire (and ire) for more important problems.

Even though Jesus had plenty of reasons not to pay the required temple tax, he considered it more important not to offend the religious leaders. So he told Peter to pay the tax. Could Jesus have made this an issue? Could he have demanded his rights as the King of the Jews? Certainly. But Jesus did not consider this a battle worth fighting. More important issues loomed ahead of him.

What minor conflicts do you need to step away from? Remember, Jesus wants you to hold onto the truth of the gospel. The important battle that you may someday face is the good fight of the faith.

Choose your battles carefully and fight for the greater truth.

What did you learn about Jesus from this week's readings?

What reading this week had the most impact on you? Why?

What do you plan to do about what you have learned this week?

Key Verse:

The Top Dog

After they arrived at Capernaum, Jesus and his disciples settled in the house where they would be staying. Jesus asked them, "What were you discussing out on the road?" But they didn't answer, because they had been arguing about which of them was the greatest. He sat down and called the twelve disciples over to him. Then he said, "Anyone who wants to be the first must take last place and be the servant of everyone else."

Then he put a little child among them. Taking the child in his arms, he said to them, "Anyone who welcomes a little child like this on my behalf welcomes me, and anyone who welcomes me welcomes my Father who sent me." MARK 9:33-37

"We're number one! We're number one!" This is a popular cheer among sports fans. The idea of being at the top permeates all our culture. We squabble about which is the best restaurant, who's the most illustrious athlete, who's the greatest recording artist, who's the top dog.

The disciples did this, too. But *they* argued about which among them was the greatest. Each wanted to be singled out as the star disciple. Boy, were they surprised when Jesus announced that the greatest disciple must be the greatest *servant*. How many disciples petitioned to be called the greatest then?

When serving God, it's tempting to draw attention to our good deeds. If our attitude is that we're greater than our brothers and sisters then we have let pride replace service. Jesus on the other hand was willing to be the greatest servant and give up everything, including his life, for others.

How great are you when it comes to serving others? Focus on others, and not on yourself.

Being top dog is good if it means being number one in serving others.

| DAY 2 ## cooperation or competition?

John said to Jesus, "Teacher, we saw a man using your name to cast out demons, but we told him to stop because he isn't one of our group."

"Don't stop him!" Jesus said. "No one who performs miracles in my name will soon be able to speak evil of me. Anyone who is not against us is for us. If anyone gives you even a cup of water because you belong to the Messiah, I assure you, that person will be rewarded."

MARK 9:38-41

Jesus' disciples had just been humiliated. A man had asked them to cast a demon out of his son. All twelve of them together couldn't deliver *one* miracle (see Mark 9:17, 18). Soon the disciples heard that some *outsider* was casting out demons using Jesus' name. Jealousy hit them.

The disciples had lost sight of their goal. Jesus then reminded them that working to further God's Kingdom requires cooperation not competition. When we see others with a successful ministry that clothes the poor or feeds the needy or teaches the gospel, our response should be excitement. We all share the same goal of telling others about Jesus.

How do you feel when other Christians succeed? Jealous? Joyful? Angry? How can you help a fellow believer in his or her ministry?

In the end it won't matter which hands did what; the important thing is that the job was done well.

| DAY 3 ## one Bad Apple

But if anyone causes one of these little ones who trusts in me to lose faith, it would be better for that person to be thrown into the sea with a large millstone tied around the neck. If your hand causes you to sin, cut it off. It is better to enter heaven with only one hand than to go into the unquenchable fires of hell with two hands. If your foot causes you to sin, cut it off. It is better to enter heaven with only one foot than to be thrown into hell with two feet. And if your eye causes you to sin, gouge it out. It is better to enter the Kingdom of God half blind than to have two eyes and be thrown into hell, "where the worm never dies and the fire never goes out."

For everyone will be purified with fire. Salt is good for seasoning. But if it loses its flavor, how do you make it salty again? You must have the qualities of salt among yourselves and live in peace with each other.   MARK 9:42-50

Jesus used hyperbole when he said we should get rid of sin by cutting off parts of our body. God would *never* want us to hurt ourselves. This extravagant exaggeration was used to make a point. Jesus was emphasizing the seriousness of sin. The point is that we shouldn't allow even a small sin to destroy our life.

The saying goes, "One bad apple spoils the whole barrel." And it's true. When shopping for fruit, people pick out only the best pieces. If they find a bad apple when they get home, they throw it away. That rotten fruit would make the good fruit turn bad. If we let sins become habits, then we must go through the painful process of cutting out that sin. It hurts, but it's worth it. Just like the one bad apple in the barrel, sin that's left within us will ultimately rot our soul.

What do you need to cut out of your life in order to follow Jesus more closely?

Don't leave any sin to rot. Open your heart and allow God to remove anything that doesn't glorify him.

DAY 4   caring for the flock

Beware that you don't despise a single one of these little ones. For I tell you that in heaven their angels are always in the presence of my heavenly Father.
If a shepherd has one hundred sheep, and one wanders away and is lost, what will he do? Won't he leave the ninety-nine others and go out into the hills to search for the lost one? And if he finds it, he will surely rejoice over it more than over the ninety-nine that didn't wander away! In the same way, it is not my heavenly Father's will that even one of these little ones should perish.   MATTHEW 18:10-14

You have probably heard about communities that have pulled together to find a lost child. Hundreds of volunteers sacrifice time and comfort to search the countryside for the missing person. Why? Because that one person has meaning; the child is worth looking for.

In this portion of Scripture, Jesus is teaching how important each person is to his Father. Scripture contains ample evidence of God's love for his creation, especially in the way he provides for and protects his believers. Jesus said that his Father knows us intimately, even to the number of hairs on our head.

We must have the same attitude as Jesus, our Shepherd. God wants people to enter into his fold. Understanding this will soften our heart toward others.

We'll see an angry man on the bus and a depressed girl at school as individuals whom God deeply loves, not people to avoid.

Look around you. When you see each person as valuable to God, as lost sheep who need the Shepherd, it will change the way you act toward them.

Make a special attempt to reach out to the lost people in your life. Let them know that their loving Shepherd is looking for them.

| DAY 5 # The uLtimate Fix-it PLan

If another believer sins against you, go privately and point out the fault. If the other person listens and confesses it, you have won that person back. But if you are unsuccessful, take one or two others with you and go back again, so that everything you say may be confirmed by two or three witnesses. If that person still refuses to listen, take your case to the church. If the church decides you are right, but the other person won't accept it, treat that person as a pagan or a corrupt tax collector. I tell you this: Whatever you prohibit on earth is prohibited in heaven, and whatever you allow on earth is allowed in heaven.

I also tell you this: If two of you agree down here on earth concerning anything you ask, my Father in heaven will do it for you. For where two or three gather together because they are mine, I am there among them.   MATTHEW 18:15-20

If your eyeglasses break, you take them to an optical shop. If your car breaks down, you take it to the local auto shop. But what happens when relationships break down? This can even happen in God's family of believers.

Jesus knows about our tendency to hold grudges; that we tend to keep hurts deep inside until we explode with frustration. That's when relationships suffer the most damage. So he offers a solution.

If two people have a problem with each other, they usually talk to *everyone else* about it. But Jesus tells us to go *first* to the person who has hurt us. This usually ends it. If the situation isn't settled, the next step is to find a neutral party to act as mediator. If the problem is still unresolved, a pastor can set up a group meeting.

Do you hold a grudge against a brother or sister? Have you discussed it with him or her yet?

What did you learn about Jesus from this week's readings?

What reading this week had the most impact on you? Why?

What do you plan to do about what you have learned this week?

Key Verse:

| DAY 1 | ## Paying the Debt

Then Peter came to him and asked, "Lord, how often should I forgive someone who sins against me? Seven times?"

"No!" Jesus replied, "seventy times seven!

"For this reason, the Kingdom of Heaven can be compared to a king who decided to bring his accounts up to date with servants who had borrowed money from him. In the process, one of his debtors was brought in who owed him millions of dollars. He couldn't pay, so the king ordered that he, his wife, his children, and everything he had be sold to pay the debt. But the man fell down before the king and begged him, 'Oh, sir, be patient with me, and I will pay it all.' Then the king was filled with pity for him, and he released him and forgave his debt.

"But when the man left the king, he went to a fellow servant who owed him a few thousand dollars. He grabbed him by the throat and demanded instant payment. His fellow servant fell down before him and begged for a little more time. 'Be patient and I will pay it,' he pleaded. But his creditor wouldn't wait. He had the man arrested and jailed until the debt could be paid in full.

"When some of the other servants saw this, they were very upset. They went to the king and told him what had happened. Then the king called in the man he had forgiven and said, 'You evil servant! I forgave you that tremendous debt because you pleaded with me. Shouldn't you have mercy on your fellow servant, just as I had mercy on you?" Then the angry king sent the man to prison until he had paid every penny.

"That's what my heavenly Father will do to you if you refuse to forgive your brothers and sisters in your heart."   MATTHEW 18:21-35

Who is the one person in your life who has hurt you the most? Maybe it's a close friend who revealed a secret about you. Maybe it's a parent who is never around. Maybe it's the bully in class who seems to gain pleasure out of making you miserable.

Here is a tougher question: Have you forgiven that person?

You may find it difficult to forgive. Jesus knows this. He told above parable to illustrate the wonderfully lavish way that we have been forgiven by our great King. Why is this so important? Because this is where your forgiveness of others begins. When you understand how you have been forgiven a debt that you could never repay, it will overflow into an attitude of forgiveness for others.

Who do you need to forgive today?

Pray for the strength to forgive.

| DAY 2 # timing is everything

After this, Jesus stayed in Galilee, going from village to village. He wanted to stay out of Judea where the Jewish leaders were plotting his death. But soon it was time for the Festival of Shelters, and Jesus' brothers urged him to go to Judea for the celebration. "Go where your followers can see your miracles!" they scoffed. "You can't become a public figure if you hide like this! If you can do such wonderful things, prove it to the world!" For even his brothers didn't believe in him.

Jesus replied, "Now is not the right time for me to go. But you can go anytime, and it will make no difference. The world can't hate you, but it does hate me because I accuse it of sin and evil. You go on. I am not yet ready to go to this festival, because my time has not yet come." So Jesus remained in Galilee.   JOHN 7:1-9

The Bible often tells the story of God's perfect timing. Joseph languished for three long years in prison until, *at the right time*, he was brought to Pharaoh and made the second in command in all Egypt. The Israelites waited for hundreds of years for the Messiah until, *at the right time*, God sent his Son to save the entire world.

In this passage, we see Jesus' brothers mocking him, urging him to attend the big festival in Jerusalem and put on a show for the people there. "If you're so great, prove it," they taunted. It must have been tempting to Jesus show his brothers a few miracles and prove to them who he *really* was.

But Jesus had a strong sense of his mission. He knew his Father's timing and he knew that to go to Jerusalem at that particularly time was not in the plan. "My time has not yet come" was Jesus' response. He had to wait for God's timing, not his own.

Timing is everything. It was for Jesus during his mission on earth, and it is for us now. When God tells you to wait, either through your circumstances or the people he has put into your life, then you need to wait. When he tells you to go, then it's time to get moving.

Seek to understand God's timing. He will open doors for you at just the right time.

| DAY 3 **NO EXCUSES**

As the time drew near for his return to heaven, Jesus resolutely set out for Jerusalem. He sent messengers ahead to a Samaritan village to prepare for his arrival. But they were turned away. The people of the village refused to have anything to do with Jesus because he had re-solved to go to Jerusalem. When James and John heard about it, they said to Jesus, "Lord, should we order down fire from heaven to burn them up?" But Jesus turned and rebuked them. So they went on to another village.

As they were walking along someone said to Jesus, "I will follow you no matter where you go."

But Jesus replied, "Foxes have dens to live in, and birds have nests, but I, the Son of Man, have no home of my own, not even a place to lay my head."

He said to another person, "Come, be my disciple."

The man agreed, but he said, "Lord, first let me return home and bury my father."

Jesus replied, "Let those who are spiritually dead care for their own dead. Your duty is to go and preach the coming of the Kingdom of God."

Another said, "Yes, Lord, I will follow you, but first let me say good-bye to my family."

But Jesus told him, "Anyone who puts a hand to the plow and then looks back is not fit for the Kingdom of God." LUKE 9:51-62

Suppose you ask someone out for a date or invite a friend from school over to watch videos. The first time you ask, your friend declines because of other plans. But if you ask a second or third time and he or she still has other plans, that person is simply making excuses.

That's what's happening in these verses. When Jesus asked these three individuals to come and join him, they come up with reasonable responses: "First let me return home and bury my father;" "First let me say good-bye to my family." Jesus knew these were simply excuses to avoid making a commitment.

These people were presented with a life-changing choice. But they each decided to put other things before Jesus. When we let possessions, concerns, or people take precedence over Jesus, we do not have correct priorities. Jesus is not concerned with our excuses. Either we're with him all the way, or we're not.

What excuses do you give to avoid serving others, reading the Bible, or making a commitment to Jesus? To follow Christ, it's vital that you put him before anything else in the world.

Don't let lame excuses prevent you from placing your full faith in Jesus.

| DAY 4 # speaking out

But after his brothers had left for the festival, Jesus also went, though secretly, staying out of public view. The Jewish leaders tried to find him at the festival and kept asking if anyone had seen him. There was a lot of discussion about him among the crowds. Some said, "He's a wonderful man," while others said, "He's nothing but a fraud, deceiving the people." But no one had the courage to speak favorably about him in public, for they were afraid of getting in trouble with the Jewish leaders.   JOHN 7:10-13

Imagine you're at a basketball game. The only seats you can get are on the opposing team's side. There you sit in the middle of fans for the other team. Your team is winning but you don't risk standing up and cheering because the people around you wouldn't appreciate your enthusiasm.

During this festival in Jerusalem, Jesus was the hot topic of the day. In private some people said he was a fraud, others said he was a wonderful man. But "no one had the courage to speak favorably about him in public." No one. Not one person in that crowd had the courage to stand up in faith and speak for the Lord.

Many Christians don't have a problem talking about their faith when surrounded by believers. But ask them to make the same statements outside the safe confines of the church and they suddenly lose their voice.

Jesus wants us to speak out for him no matter where we are or who we are with. He promises all who acknowledge him on earth that he will acknowledge them before God (Matthew 10:32). What more do you need to motivate you to speak out?

Don't let the crowd keep you from standing up for Christ.

DAY 5 Risky Business

On the last day, the climax of the festival, Jesus stood and shouted to the crowds, "If you are thirsty, come to me! If you believe in me, come and drink! For the Scriptures declare that rivers of living water will flow out from within." (When he said "living water," he was speaking of the Spirit, who would be given to everyone believing in him. But the Spirit had not yet been given, because Jesus had not yet entered into his glory.)

When the crowds heard him say this, some of them declared, "This man surely is the Prophet." Others said, "He is the Messiah." Still others said, "But he can't be! Will the Messiah come from Galilee? For the Scriptures clearly state that the Messiah will be born of the royal line of David, in Bethlehem, the village where King David was born." So the crowd was divided in their opinion about him. And some wanted him arrested, but no one touched him.

The Temple guards who had been sent to arrest him returned to the leading priests and Pharisees. "Why didn't you bring him in?" they demanded.

"We have never heard anyone talk like this!" the guards responded.

"Have you been led astray, too?" the Pharisees mocked. "Is there a single one of us rulers or Pharisees who believes in him? These ignorant crowds do, but what do they know about it? A curse on them anyway!"

Nicodemus, the leader who had met with Jesus earlier, then spoke up. "Is it legal to convict a man before he is given a hearing?" he asked.

They replied, "Are you from Galilee, too? Search the Scriptures and see for yourself—no prophet ever comes from Galilee!" JOHN 7:37-52

What are you willing to risk for your convictions? Obviously, if it's an opinion about a movie, not a lot is at stake. But what if your convictions caused people to avoid you or even put you down? What do you risk by standing up for your faith in Jesus Christ?

In this passage people continue to debate about Jesus' identity. In the previous passage no one stood up to publicly support Jesus. But here we see one man with the courage to speak in defense of the Lord.

That man was Nicodemus, a well-respected religious leader who earlier had come to Jesus in the secrecy of the night to hear what he had to say (John 3:2-21). Apparently, Nicodemus was impressed with what he heard because here he risks his reputation and challenges the Pharisees. Right away he is mocked by his peers.

It's easy to keep silent when we suspect that we might be ridiculed for what we believe. In those situations remember Nicodemus and what he was willing to risk for Jesus.

Pray that God will give you the courage of your convictions no matter what the risk.

What did you learn about Jesus from this week's readings?

What reading this week had the most impact on you? Why?

What do you plan to do about what you have learned this week?

Key Verse:

| DAY 1 | jury, judge, and jailer

Then the meeting broke up and everybody went home.

Jesus returned to the Mount of Olives, but early the next morning he was back again at the Temple. A crowd soon gathered, and he sat down and taught them. As he was speaking, the teachers of religious law and Pharisees brought a woman they had caught in the act of adultery. They put her in front of the crowd.

"Teacher," they said to Jesus, "this woman was caught in the very act of adultery The law of Moses says to stone her. What do you say?"

They were trying to trap him into saying something they could use against him, but Jesus stooped down and wrote in the dust with his finger. They kept demanding an answer, so he stood up again and said, "All right, stone her. But let those who have never sinned throw the first stones!" Then he stooped down again and wrote in the dust.

When the accusers heard this, they slipped away one by one, beginning with the oldest, until only Jesus was left in the middle of the crowd with the woman. Then Jesus stood up again and said to her, "Where are your accusers? Didn't even one of them condemn you?"

"No, Lord," she said.

And Jesus said, "Neither do I. Go and sin no more."   JOHN 7:53—8:11

You know the boy who consistently cheats on his schoolwork. You know the gossip queen at the lunch table. And it wouldn't take you long to write down a list of your brother's or sister's faults. It's easy to see the sins in other people, but we all have a blind spot when it comes to our own faults.

The Pharisees in this passage certainly did. They brought to Jesus a woman caught in the act of adultery expecting that he would condemn her. Instead Jesus said, "Let those who have never sinned throw the first stones!" That cleared the area fast!

It's easy to condemn the Pharisees for being self-righteous. But have you ever been quick to judge, condemn, and even punish others for their sins? In doing this you act like you have never sinned.

Make sure you check out your own sins before pointing out the sins in others.

| DAY 2 | judgment caLL

Jesus said to the people, "I am the light of the world. If you follow me, you won't be stumbling through the darkness, because you will have the light that leads to life."

The Pharisees replied, "You are making false claims about yourself!"

Jesus told them, "These claims are valid even though I make them about myself. For I know where I came from and where I am going, but you don't know this about me. You judge me with all your human limitations, but I am not judging anyone. And if I did, my judgment would be correct in every respect because I am not alone—I have with me the Father who sent me. Your own law says that if two people agree about something, their witness is accepted as fact. I am one witness, and my Father who sent me is the other."

"Where is your father?" they asked.

Jesus answered, "Since you don't know who I am, you don't know who my Father is. If you knew me, then you would know my Father, too." Jesus made these statements while he was teaching in the section of the Temple known as the Treasury. But he was not arrested, because his time had not yet come. JOHN 8:12-20

Whether it's an art contest, a music competition, or a gymnastics match, it's critical to have the proper judges. It wouldn't make sense to have an expert in gymnastics judge art, or someone who is tone deaf judge a music contest. The Pharisees thought Jesus was an out-and-out liar, a lunatic, demon-possessed. The only problem with their verdict was that they had no business judging him at all.

Here is what Jesus said to them, "You judge me with all your human limitations." In other words, they didn't have a clue what they were talking about. Only Jesus has the qualifications of a judge because he alone was sinless.

Leave judgment to Jesus, the only one qualified for the job.

| DAY 3 # The Hard Evidence

Later Jesus said to them again, "I am going away. You will search for me and die in your sin. You cannot come where I am going."

The Jewish leaders asked, "Is he planning to commit suicide? What does he mean, 'You cannot come where I am going'?"

Then he said to them, "You are from below; I am from above. You are of this world; I am not. That is why I said that you will die in your sins; for unless you believe that I am who I say I am, you will die in your sins."

"Tell us who you are," they demanded.

Jesus replied, "I am the one I have always claimed to be. I have much to say about you and much to condemn, but I won't. For I say only what I have heard from the one who sent me, and he is true." But they still didn't understand that he was talking to them about his Father.

So Jesus said, "When you have lifted up the Son of Man on the cross, then you will realize that I am he and that I do nothing on my own, but I speak what the Father taught me. And the one who sent me is with me—he has not deserted me. For I always do those things that are pleasing to him." Then many who heard him say these things believed in him.

JOHN 8:21-30

Say a boy from down the street walked into school and announced that he had just signed a multimillion dollar deal to play professional football. Most likely, you wouldn't believe him until you saw him in the lineup. Some claims cannot be believed without hard evidence.

Jesus made many claims about his identity. In this passage he says that he and God the Father are one. "I am from above . . . I am not of this world . . . and the one who sent me is with me." Jesus is God.

People say Jesus was a good teacher, a righteous man, or a revolutionary leader, but not God. Yet Jesus said, "When you have lifted up the Son of Man on the cross, then you will realize that I am he." We have seen Jesus on the cross. We have seen the resurrection. This hard evidence supports Christ's claims.

Make sure you examine the evidence so you can fully believe in Jesus.

ReaL Truth, ReaL Freedom

Jesus said to the people who believed in him, "You are truly my disciples if you keep obeying my teachings. And you will know the truth, and the truth will set you free."

"But we are descendants of Abraham," they said. "We have never been slaves to anyone on earth. What do you mean, 'set free'?"

Jesus replied, "I assure you that everyone who sins is a slave of sin. A slave is not a permanent member of the family, but a son is part of the family forever. So if the Son sets you free, you will indeed be free." JOHN 8:31-36

A sign at the Central Intelligence Agency in Langley, Virginia, reads: *And ye shall know the truth, and the truth shall make you free.* These are the words of John 8:32, an oft-quoted verse that means different things to different people. Typically it means that we should look for the truth.

But this is not even close to what Jesus was talking about. The truth is Jesus. Period. If you know Jesus the Son of God you will be truly be free. This came as big news to the Jews. They thought that they were free. After all, they weren't slaves to anyone. So what was all this talk about being set free? Free from what?

Jesus was talking about freedom from the deadly trap of sin. As the truth, Jesus can free us from sin and all its consequences. That's real freedom.

Look for the real truth that leads to real freedom. Look for Jesus.

| DAY 5 conflict avoidance

The people retorted, "You Samaritan devil! Didn't we say all along that you were possessed by a demon?"

"No," Jesus said, "I have no demon in me. For I honor my Father—and you dishonor me. And though I have no wish to glorify myself, God wants to glorify me. Let him be the judge. I assure you, anyone who obeys my teaching will never die!"

The people said, "Now we know you are possessed by a demon. Even Abraham and the prophets died, but you say that those who obey your teaching will never die! Are you greater than our father Abraham, who died? Are you greater than the prophets, who died? Who do you think you are?"

Jesus answered, "If I am merely boasting about myself, it doesn't count. But it is my Father who says these glorious things about me. You say, 'He is our God,' but you do not even know him. I know him. If I said otherwise, I would be as great a liar as you! But it is true—I know him and obey him. Your ancestor Abraham rejoiced as he looked forward to my coming. He saw it and was glad."

The people said, "You aren't even fifty years old. How can you say you have seen Abraham?"

Jesus answered, "The truth is, I existed before Abraham was even born!" At that point they picked up stones to kill him. But Jesus hid himself from them and left the Temple.
JOHN 8:48-59

You probably think that your school is in some way the best. But what do you do when your claims are challenged? If your critics start insulting your school, do you try to out-yell them? Do you attack *their* school? Do you back off your claim and say, "Sorry, I made a mistake"?

Jesus never backed away from his critics. In this passage, we see him going head-to-head with a group of people who, among other things, claimed that he was demon-possessed and a liar. Those are fighting words!

How did Jesus handle this? Simply by stating the truth. He was not afraid of conflicts but he was always prepared to give an answer. His intent wasn't to upset people, although his opponents didn't like his answers. In fact, they were so angry that they wanted to kill him. Still, Jesus did not back away simply because it was the easy thing to do.

We can learn from Jesus' example. Standing up for what you believe may not win you friends. It often may gain you some enemies. But if you prepare yourself with the truth, you won't have to fear the conflict.

Prepare for opposition by understanding the truth of the gospel.

What did you learn about Jesus from this week's readings?

What reading this week had the most impact on you? Why?

What do you plan to do about what you have learned this week?

Key Verse:

WEEK TWENTY-SEVEN

DAY 1 ## Harvest Time

The Lord now chose seventy-two other disciples and sent them on ahead in pairs to all the towns and villages he planned to visit. These were his instructions to them: "The harvest is so great, but the workers are so few. Pray to the Lord who is in charge of the harvest, and ask him to send out more workers for his fields. Go now, and remember that I am sending you out as lambs among wolves. Don't take along any money, or a traveler's bag, or even an extra pair of sandals. And don't stop to greet anyone on the road.

"Whenever you enter a home, give it your blessing. If those who live there are worthy, the blessing will stand; if they are not, the blessing will return to you. When you enter a town, don't move around from home to home. Stay in one place, eating and drinking what they provide you. Don't hesitate to accept hospitality, because those who work deserve their pay.

"If a town welcomes you, eat whatever is set before you and heal the sick. As you heal them, say, 'The Kingdom of God is near you now.' But if a town refuses to welcome you, go out into its streets and say, 'We wipe the dust of your town from our feet as a public announcement of your doom. And don't forget the Kingdom of God is near!' The truth is, even wicked Sodom will be better off than such a town on the Judgment day.

"What horrors await you, Korazin and Bethsaida! For if the miracles I did in you had been done in wicked Tyre and Sidon, their people would have sat in deep repentance long ago, clothed in sackcloth and throwing ashes on their heads to show their remorse. Yes, Tyre and Sidon will be better off on the judgment day than you. And you people of Capernaum, will you be exalted to heaven? No, you will be brought down to the place of the dead."

Then he said to the disciples, "Anyone who accepts your message is also accepting me. And anyone who rejects you is rejecting me. And anyone who rejects me is rejecting God who sent me."   LUKE 10:1-16

Imagine receiving a phone call from someone really important—the mayor, the governor, or even the president—that goes something like this: "I want you to be my personal emissary on an urgent mission. You will represent me. When you speak, you will speak with all the authority of my office."

You might be surprised, flattered, honored, or even overwhelmed, but you would *not* yawn and say, "Naaah, I'm just not interested. Call back some other time."

That's what happened when Jesus sent out his disciples to announce the coming of God's Kingdom, saying that however the people of those towns responded to them (the disciples), he would take it personally. The same commands and promises apply to those who seek to be his disciples today. We are to be involved in the harvest of souls. When we share the gospel with others, we speak with the authority of Jesus himself. If they respect what we say, they respect him; if they mock and scoff or simply ignore us, they do so to Jesus as well.

With that as our assurance and our authority, we can be about the business of announcing the coming of the kingdom with confidence and joy.

You are not responsible for the outcome, but you are responsible to come out and share the Good News with others.

DAY 2 The privileged few

When the seventy-two disciples returned, they joyfully reported to him, "Lord, even the demons obey us when we use your name!"

"Yes," he told them, "I saw Satan falling from heaven as a flash of lightning! And I have given you authority over all the power of the enemy, and you can walk among snakes and scorpions and crush them. Nothing will injure you. But don't rejoice just because evil spirits obey you; rejoice because your names are registered as citizens of heaven."

Then Jesus was filled with the joy of the Holy Spirit and said, "O Father, Lord of heaven and earth, thank you for hiding the truth from those who think themselves so wise and clever, and for revealing it to the childlike. Yes, Father, it pleased you to do it this way.

"My Father has given me authority over everything. No one really knows the Son except the Father, and no one really knows the Father except the Son and those to whom the Son chooses to reveal him."

Then when they were alone, he turned to the disciples and said, "How privileged you are to see what you have seen. I tell you, many prophets and kings have longed to see and hear what you have seen and heard, but they could not." LUKE 10:17-24

It must have been exciting to witness some of the great miracles and acts of God recorded in the Old Testament: the parting of the Red Sea, the collapse of the walls of Jericho, Elijah's defeat of the prophets of Baal on Mt. Carmel, and so many others. Then consider the incredible opportunity that the disciples had to walk alongside Jesus! What a privilege!

Sometimes it's easy to think that the disciples had it all—firsthand knowledge of the living, breathing Christ; eyewitnesses to his many miracles and healings; opportunities to ask Jesus whatever questions were on their minds. The disciples were indeed privileged, but that didn't always translate into a vibrant, confident faith.

It would have been great to have walked with Jesus, no doubt about that. But we also need to consider what we have as his followers today—the entire Bible, a multitude of translations and commentaries to help us understand God's Word, the history and work of the church, and of course, the Holy Spirit at work in our lives.

Just like the disciples, however, with these privileges come responsibility. We need to make use of the knowledge and the resources available to us not only to grow in our own faith, but also to share what we have with others.

Remember it is a privilege to know Jesus and share your faith with others!

| WEEK TWENTY-SEVEN | DAY 3 | # The ReaL DeaL |

One day an expert in religious law stood up to test Jesus by asking him this question: "Teacher, what must I do to receive eternal life?"

Jesus replied, "What does the law of Moses say? How do you read it?"

The man answered, "'You must love the Lord your God with all your heart, all your soul, all your strength, and all your mind.' And, 'Love your neighbor as yourself.'"

"Right!" Jesus told him. "Do this and you will live!"

The man wanted to justify his actions, so he asked Jesus, "And who is my neighbor?"

Jesus replied with an illustration: "A Jewish man was traveling on a trip from Jerusalem to Jericho, and he was attacked by bandits. They stripped him of his clothes and money, beat him up, and left him half dead beside the road.

"By chance a Jewish priest came along; but when he saw the man lying there, he crossed to the other side of the road and passed him by. A Temple assistant walked over and looked at him lying there, but he also passed by on the other side.

"Then a despised Samaritan came along, and when he saw the man, he felt deep pity. Kneeling beside him, the Samaritan soothed his wounds with medicine and bandaged them. Then he put the man on his own donkey and took him to an inn, where he took care of him. The next day he handed the innkeeper two pieces of silver and told him to take care of the man. 'If his bill runs higher than that,' he said, "I'll pay the difference the next time I am here.'

"Now which of these three would you say was a neighbor to the man who was attacked by bandits?" Jesus asked.

The man replied, "The one who showed him mercy."

Then Jesus said, "Yes, now go and do the same." LUKE 10:25-37

Finish this sentence: The last person on earth I would look to for a good example is _____.

The view you have of that person is probably about the same as the way the Jews thought of the Samaritans. To the Jews, Samaritans were half-breeds, turncoats, and outcasts—complete losers. And that's who Jesus uses as the model for extending love and compassion to those in need!

Jesus loves to lift up the most unexpected and unlikely people as examples of faithfulness. This Samaritan, so looked down upon by the Jews, was the one who demonstrated Christlike, sacrificial love—not the respectable and religious ones. They *talked* a good game and put on a good show, but they didn't live out their faith.

Talk is cheap, especially religious talk. Being Jesus' disciple means going beyond words and extending a compassionate hand to others in his name, no matter what the cost. After all, some good Samaritan went out of his way for us.

Make sure your Christlike compassion is more than just show.

| WEEK TWENTY-SEVEN | DAY 4 | QUALITY TIME |

As Jesus and the disciples continued on their way to Jerusalem, they came to a village where a woman named Martha welcomed them into her home. Her sister, Mary, sat at the Lord's feet, listening to what he taught. But Martha was worrying over the big dinner she was preparing. She came to Jesus and said, "Lord, doesn't it seem unfair to you that my sister just sits here while I do all the work? Tell her to come and help me."

But the Lord said to her, "My dear Martha, you are so upset over all these details! There is really only one thing worth being concerned about. Mary has discovered it—and I won't take it away from her." LUKE 10:38-42

There are some activities that are just more important than others. No one would argue that it's more important to eat good, nutritious meals than to munch on snack food all day. It's clear that it's more important to get your homework done than to watch the latest episode of your favorite TV show.

So, what is the most important thing for a Christian to do? Witness, tithe, go to Bible studies, or serve as a foreign missionary? How about . . . *spending time with Jesus?*

It doesn't sound as glamorous as preaching to stadiums full of people or building hospitals for lepers, but according to Luke 10:38-42, just being with the Lord is priority number one for the Christian, or it should be. Those other aspects of the Christian life—like serving others and church involvement—are also important and should not be neglected. But getting to know Jesus is the foundation for everything else a Christian thinks, says, and does.

It's easy to get so caught up in Christian activities that we neglect this basic necessity. We can spend so much time working in the kingdom that we have no time or energy left for the King. That's a formula for spiritual burnout. Learn from these two sisters, and remember what is truly important.

Reading these passages and devotionals is one great way to spend time with your King!

DAY 5   Teach Me!
WEEK TWENTY SEVEN

Once when Jesus had been out praying, one of his disciples came to him as he finished and said, "Lord, teach us to pray, just as John taught his disciples."

He said, "This is how you should pray."

"Father, may your name be honored. May your Kingdom come soon. Give us our food day by day. And forgive us our sins—just as we forgive those who have sinned against us. And don't let us yield to temptation."

Then, teaching them more about prayer, he used this illustration: "Suppose you went to a friend's house at midnight, wanting to borrow three loaves of bread. You would say to him, 'A friend of mine has just arrived for a visit, and I have nothing for him to eat.' He would call out from his bedroom, 'Don't bother me. The door is locked for the night, and we are all in bed. I can't help you this time.' But I tell you this—though he won't do it as a friend, if you keep knocking long enough, he will get up and give you what you want so his reputation won't be damaged.

"And so I tell you, keep on asking, and you will be given what you ask for. Keep on looking, and you will find. Keep on knocking, and the door will be opened. For everyone who asks, receives. Everyone who seeks, finds. And the door is opened to everyone who knocks.

"You fathers—if your children ask for a fish, do you give them a snake instead? Or if they ask for an egg, do you give them a scorpion? Of course not! If you sinful people know how to give good gifts to your children, how much more will your heavenly Father give the Holy Spirit to those who ask him."   LUKE 11:1-13

Most of us have had a person in our life—whether it's a favorite teacher, an older sibling, or a coach—whom we have admired and wanted to emulate. Maybe we copied the way they organized their desk, or we dressed like they did, or we worked hard to acquire the same skills they had. Whatever it was, these people were key role models for us.

It was much the same for the disciples. In Jesus' day it was quite common for rabbis to teach their students how to pray, and the students' prayers would then resemble the rabbi's. Naturally enough, the disciples wanted to learn to pray like Jesus.

It's noteworthy that Jesus' answer in verses 2-4 (and the parallel passage in Matthew 6:9-13) and the story that follows assumes that we are in the practice of praying. It's also important to note that Jesus doesn't say we should pray these words as meaningless repetition, as sometimes happens in church services and other places of group prayer. Prayer is not just reciting a list of wants or repeating key words and phrases in some magical order.

Rather, Jesus was teaching his disciples a model for communion between our heavenly Father and his children. It was to be the framework for spending time with God, not the completed package.

Following a pattern or order is fine. But just as you would not want to spend much time talking with someone who said the same words in the same order every time you saw him or her, prayer needs to be honest and meaningful. Keep it fresh; keep it real.

Let Jesus' model direct you, but not dictate to you, how you spend time with God.

What did you learn about Jesus from this week's readings?

What reading this week had the most impact on you? Why?

What do you plan to do about what you have learned this week?

Key Verse:

WEEK TWENTY-EIGHT

DAY 1   He's for Real!

One day Jesus cast a demon out of a man who couldn't speak, and the man's voice returned to him. The crowd was amazed, but some said, "No wonder he can cast out demons. He gets his power from Satan, the prince of demons!" Trying to test Jesus, others asked for a miraculous sign from heaven to see if he was from God.

He knew their thoughts, so he said, "Any kingdom at war with itself is doomed. A divided home is also doomed. You say I am empowered by the prince of demons. But if Satan is fighting against himself by empowering me to cast out his demons, how can his kingdom survive? And if I am empowered by the prince of demons, what about your own followers? They cast out demons, too, so they will judge you for what you have said. But if I am casting out demons by the power of God, then the Kingdom of God has arrived among you. For when Satan, who is completely armed, guards his palace, it is safe—until someone who is stronger attacks and overpowers him, strips him of his weapons, and carries off his belongings.

"Anyone who isn't helping me opposes me, and anyone who isn't working with me is actually working against me.

"When an evil spirit leaves a person, it goes into the desert, searching for rest. But when it finds none, it says, 'I will return to the person I came from.' So it returns and finds that its former home is all swept and clean. Then the spirit finds seven other spirits more evil than itself, and they all enter the person and live there. And so that person is worse off than before."

As he was speaking, a woman in the crowd called out, "God bless your mother—the womb from which you came, and the breasts that nursed you!"

He replied, "But even more blessed are all who hear the word of God and put it into practice."   LUKE 11:14-28

Check out any number of sports teams, both college and professional, and you can find someone dressed up like the devil, strolling along the sidelines with pitchfork in hand, exhorting his or her team to defeat the opposition. It's just a mascot, and another cute, harmless depiction of a mythical character, right?

Seriously, when you consider Satan, demons, demon possession, can an enlightened, educated, modern person believe in such things? Yes, and for a number of compelling reasons.

First, if you accept that there is a holy, loving, all-knowing, and all-powerful Being—God—and his good angels, why would you doubt the existence of an unholy, destructive creature—Satan—and his evil companions? You may not like the thought; it may make you uncomfortable; but it is not inconsistent.

Second, the Bible clearly teaches the existence of Satan, demons, and demonic activity. The Gospels alone make reference to the devil by one name or another over 35 times and demons more than 50, plus many more instances in the rest of the Scriptures. If you take the Bible seriously, you can hardly escape the conclusion that it takes the subject seriously.

Third, it's abundantly clear that Jesus believed in a real devil and demons. He clashed with them, took authority over them, scared them, and generally rocked their world. Ultimately he triumphed over them at the cross and an empty tomb (Colossians 2:13-15).

Satan, demons, and demon possession are real. So be careful not to fall into the trap of thinking that he's just a cute mascot walking along the sidelines.

Satan is no cute, mythical character. He is for real, and he is the enemy!

DAY 2 warning signs

As the crowd pressed in on Jesus, he said, "These are evil times, and this evil generation keeps asking me to show them a miraculous sign. But the only sign I will give them is the sign of the prophet Jonah. What happened to him was a sign to the people of Nineveh that God had sent him. What happens to me will be a sign that God has sent me, the Son of Man, to these people.

"The queen of Sheba will rise up against this generation on judgment day and condemn it, because she came from a distant land to hear the wisdom of Solomon. And now someone greater than Solomon is here—and you refuse to listen to him. The people of Nineveh, too, will rise up against this generation on judgment day and condemn it, because they repented at the preaching of Jonah. And now someone greater than Jonah is here—and you refuse to repent." LUKE 11:29-32

Imagine taking a drive in a convertible on a clear, sunny day. After a while, however, you notice ominous-looking clouds in the distance. Soon, you begin to see cars coming toward you with their lights on; then some that have their windshield wipers on. The sky gets darker by the minute, and the air gets cooler. You think about pulling over and putting the top up, but decide not to. "It won't rain on me!" When you get drenched, as you inevitably will, you'll have no one to blame but yourself. All the warning signs were there.

Jesus gave essentially the same message to the people of his time. All the signs were there for them to turn from their sins and accept him as Savior. Yet many refused to believe.

We're not that much different today. Our culture, founded on biblical principles, has been moving away from those values for many years. During that time:

- crime rates have skyrocketed;
- divorce and family breakdown have reached epidemic proportions;
- teen suicide, alcoholism, drug abuse, pregnancy, and abortion have increased astronomically;
- school violence and gang involvement have risen to unprecedented levels; and so forth.

And still we drive on, or many young people do, ignoring all the warning signals. "It won't rain on me!" Jesus' message is as timely and relevant today as ever: Repent!

The signs are clear—turn from your sins and turn to Jesus.

| WEEK TWENTY-EIGHT | DAY 3 # Let the Light shine

"No one lights a lamp and then hides it or puts it under a basket. Instead, it is put on a lampstand to give light to all who enter the room. Your eye is a lamp for your body. A pure eye lets sunshine into your soul. But an evil eye shuts out the light and plunges you into darkness. Make sure that the light you think you have is not really darkness. If you are filled with light, with no dark corners, then your whole life will be radiant, as though a floodlight is shining on you." LUKE 11:33-36

Cable TV. Movies. Magazines. Catalogues. The Internet. DVDs. Videos and video games. Our world is a non-stop, 24/7/365 smorgasbord of sensory input, and much of it is incredibly ungodly. The popular media's treatment of sexuality, violence, family, male-female relationships, the value of human life, and morality in general, is a direct, non-subtle, in-your-face repudiation of the Christian life and worldview.

It's very difficult to avoid being exposed to all these corrupting influences, and indeed, they are not all completely, utterly, irredeemably evil. But there is more than enough negative and sinful content in them to cause us to handle them with great care. After all, if a swimming pool only had a couple of great white sharks in it—would you jump in and splash around for awhile and take your chances?

Jesus' message here is clear. What we spend our time looking at and filling our minds with has tremendous impact on how we live. (See Philippians 4:8-9.) In a world like ours, we need God's grace to desire him and his holiness more than we desire the incredibly well-packaged, attractive toxic waste for our souls so readily available.

With what are you filling your mind throughout the day? Take an inventory of the TV shows you watch, the music you listen to, and the books and magazines you read.

Fill your mind with light and let Jesus' goodness shine through you.

Membership Rules

As Jesus was speaking, one of the Pharisees invited him home for a meal. So he went in and took his place at the table. His host was amazed to see that he sat down to eat without first performing the ceremonial washing required by Jewish custom. Then the Lord said to him, "You Pharisees are so careful to clean the outside of the cup and the dish, but inside you are still filthy—full of greed and wickedness! Fools! Didn't God make the inside as well as the outside? So give to the needy what you greedily possess, and you will be clean all over.

'But how terrible it will be for you Pharisees! For you are careful to tithe even the tiniest part of your income, but you completely forget about justice and the love of God. You should tithe, yes, but you should not leave undone the more important things.

'How terrible it will be for you Pharisees! For how you love the seats of honor in the synagogues and the respectful greetings from everyone as you walk through the markets! Yes, how terrible it will be for you. For you are like hidden graves in a field. People walk over them without knowing the corruption they are stepping on.'

"Teacher," said an expert in religious law, "you have insulted us, too, in what you just said."

"Yes," said Jesus, "how terrible it will be for you experts in religious law! For you crush people beneath impossible religious demands, and you never lift a finger to help ease the burden. How terrible it will be for you! For you build tombs for the very prophets your ancestors killed long ago. Murderers! You agree with your ancestors that what they did was right. You would have done the same yourselves. This is what God in his wisdom said about you: 'I will send prophets and apostles to them, and they will kill some and persecute the others.'

"And you of this generation will be held responsible for the murder of all God's prophets from the creation of the world—from the murder of Abel to the murder of Zechariah, who was killed between the altar and the sanctuary. Yes, it will surely be charged against you.

"How terrible it will be for you experts in religious law! For you hide the key to knowledge from the people. You don't enter the Kingdom yourselves, and you prevent others from entering."

As Jesus finished speaking, the Pharisees and teachers of religious law were furious. From that time on they grilled him with many hostile questions, trying to trap him into saying something they could use against him.   LUKE 11:37-54

If you have ever joined an organization or club, you know certain membership rules apply: attend the meetings, pay dues, work or join a committee, and so forth. While the rules are there to help keep order and keep the organization going, sometimes those same rules can be used to exclude others from the group.

This passage records Jesus addressing this very situation among the Pharisees. God's commandments and laws were given to us to act as guardrails and signposts along the path: guardrails to keep us out of the ditches morally and ethically, and signposts to point the way to the Messiah (Galatians 3:23-25). What the Pharisees and experts in religious law had done was to take those guardrails and signposts and build a fence with them to keep other people out of the Kingdom of God.

Trying to impress God and other people with our obedience to a list of dos and don'ts is called *legalism*. Legalism looks enough like real Christianity to pass as a counterfeit in many people's eyes. But legalism is driven by fear and arrogance: fear of God's punishment, and pride in our own goodness. Christianity on the other hand is fueled by love and humility: love for God and people (see Matthew 22:35-40) and humble recognition of our own sinfulness and need for God's grace (see Ephesians 2:8-10).

Jesus reserved his harshest criticism for the spiritually proud and those who sought to exclude others from God's love. Ask God to help you avoid those pitfalls *and* the sin of legalism.

God's kingdom is not an exclusive club. Look for ways to include others in God's love.

what God Thinks

Meanwhile, the crowds grew until thousands were milling about and crushing each other. Jesus turned first to his disciples and warned them, "Beware of the yeast of the Pharisees— beware of their hypocrisy. The time is coming when everything will be revealed; all that is secret will be made public. Whatever you have said in the dark will be heard in the light, and what you have whispered behind closed doors will be shouted from the housetops for all to hear!

"Dear friends, don't be afraid of those who want to kill you. They can only kill the body; they cannot do any more to you. But I'll tell you whom to fear. Fear God, who has the power to kill people and then throw them into hell.

"What is the price of five sparrows? A couple of pennies? Yet God does not forget a single one of them. And the very hairs on your head are all numbered. So don't be afraid; you are more valuable to him than a whole flock of sparrows.

"And I assure you of this: If anyone acknowledges me publicly here on earth, I, the Son of Man, will openly acknowledge that person in the presence of God's angels. But if anyone denies me here on earth, I will deny that person before God's angels. Yet those who speak against the Son of Man may be forgiven, but anyone who speaks blasphemies against the Holy Spirit will never be forgiven.

"And when you are brought to trial in the synagogues and before rulers and authorities, don't worry about what to say in your defense, for the Holy Spirit will teach you what needs to be said even as you are standing there."   LUKE 12:1-12

Job interviews can be nerve-wracking. You want to make a good first impression, so you wear your best clothes, prepare for the expected (and unexpected) questions, and hope you don't make any mistakes. When it's all over, you walk out the door and immediately begin wondering, "What did that person think about me?"

Do you ever wonder what God thinks about you—or if he even thinks about you at all?

Jesus addresses these questions, among others, in this passage. He compares the value God places on a handful of sparrows with how he looks at us. Those sparrows, inexpensive and inconsequential then as they are now, *are continually on the mind of God*. He never stops thinking about them! And, Jesus goes on to say that God places a much higher value on us than many, many sparrows.

This is a source of great comfort to the Christian—regardless of where you are, the time of day, or the circumstances, God is with you. It also carries with it a certain measure of admonition. God thinks of us constantly, and he thinks of us lovingly, but he also thinks of us *honestly*. Others may be fooled by an outward show of religiosity, but God knows our hearts. He doesn't expect perfection of us by any means, but he does expect sincerity and humility. We may not always feel we can open and honest with other people, but we can be with the Father who thinks of us so much.

Take heart! God knows you completely and loves you.

What did you learn about Jesus from this week's readings?

What reading this week had the most impact on you? Why?

What do you plan to do about what you have learned this week?

Key Verse:

WEEKTWENTY-NINE

DAY 1 Heavenly Payoffs

WEEK TWENTY-NINE

Then someone called from the crowd, "Teacher, please tell my brother to divide our father's estate with me."

Jesus replied, "Friend, who made me a judge over you to decide such things as that?" Then he said, "Beware! Don't be greedy for what you don't have. Real life is not measured by how much we own."

And he gave an illustration: "A rich man had a fertile farm that produced fine crops. In fact, his barns were full to overflowing. So he said, 'I know! I'll tear down my barns and build bigger ones. Then I'll have room enough to store everything. And I'll sit back and say to myself, My friend, you have enough stored away for years to come. Now take it easy! Eat, drink, and be merry!'

"But God said to him, 'You fool! You will die this very night. Then who will get it all?'

"Yes, a person is a fool to store up earthly wealth but not have a rich relationship with God." LUKE 12:13-21

If a visitor from another planet observed our society for a while, he or she or it, might well conclude that our highest goal in life is to make money and acquire possessions. We spend a phenomenal amount of time and energy in the pursuit of both of those.

Nothing is inherently wrong with having wealth and the things it brings. Money is great to have, but it makes a lousy god. Jesus admonishes this man not to get so caught up in *things* that he misses out on what is of ultimate importance. This stands as a warning for us as well. As someone has put it, there is a big difference between making a living and making a life.

You don't need to feel guilty if God blesses you with some measure of affluence. Just don't get so wrapped up in the gifts that you forget who gave them to you. Of all people, Christians need to remember that this life, though important, is just the launching pad for our eternal destination.

Invest in earthly pursuits now that will have a heavenly payoff later.

consider the Lilies

Then turning to his disciples, Jesus said, "So I tell you, don't worry about everyday life—whether you have enough food to eat or clothes to wear. For life consists of far more than food and clothing. Look at the ravens. They don't need to plant or harvest or put food in barns because God feeds them. And you are far more valuable to him than any birds! Can all your worries add a single moment to your life? Of course not! And if worry can't do little things like that, what's the use of worrying over bigger things?

"Look at the lilies and how they grow. They don't work or make their clothing, yet Solomon in all his glory was not dressed as beautifully as they are. And if God cares so wonderfully for flowers that are here today and gone tomorrow, won't he more surely care for you? You have so little faith! And don't worry about food—what to eat and drink. Don't worry whether God will provide it for you. These things dominate the thoughts of most people, but your Father already knows your needs. He will give you all you need from day to day if you make the Kingdom of God your primary concern.

"So don't be afraid, little flock. For it gives your Father great happiness to give you the Kingdom.

"Sell what you have and give to those in need. This will store up treasure for you in heaven! And the purses of heaven have no holes in them. Your treasure will be safe—no thief can steal it and no moth can destroy it. Wherever your treasure is, there your heart and thoughts will also be."   LUKE 12:22-34

What's your goal in life? To have a family and a satisfying career? To go to college and to pursue a certain profession, such as medicine or law? To perform on Broadway or play professional sports? To gather as much food, clothing, and other possessions as humanly possible? Not many people would list that last item as a personal goal, but we sometimes live as though it is one.

Following the story of the rich fool (vv.16-21), Jesus directly addressed that very subject of *materialism*—the belief that the goal of life is to accumulate possessions.

"Look at the ravens," Jesus said. God provides food for them. "Look at the lilies," he added. God takes care of their clothing. Neither ravens nor lilies have to work hard or worry about the future—God simply provides for them. And he cares much more about us than he does the birds and the flowers!

Food and clothing are two of our most basic needs. If God meets those needs for his other creatures, he can be trusted to meet them for us. This doesn't mean we are to sit idly and do nothing while God parachutes care packages into our laps; the Bible has a lot to say about the importance of a good work ethic as well. (See, for example, Genesis 1:26-28; Proverbs 14:23,

18:9, 21:25, 22:29, 31:10-31; Colossians 3:23; 1 Thessalonians 5:12-13; 2 Thessalonians 3:10-13.) But it does mean we're not to worry and wring our hands about such things.

Someone has said, "A man may worry himself to death, but he cannot worry himself into a longer span of life." Work hard; do your part, and remember how God takes care of the flowers and the wild creatures.

Trust your heavenly Father to give you what you truly need.

DAY 3 ReTURN TRIP
WEEK TWENTY-NINE

"Be dressed for service and well prepared, as though you were waiting for your master to return from the wedding feast. Then you will be ready to open the door and let him in the moment he arrives and knocks. There will be special favor for those who are ready and waiting for his return. I tell you, he himself will seat them, put on an apron, and serve them as they sit and eat! He may come in the middle of the night or just before dawn. But whenever he comes, there will be special favor for his servants who are ready!

"Know this: A homeowner who knew exactly when a burglar was coming would not permit the house to be broken into. You must be ready all the time, for the Son of Man will come when least expected."

Peter asked, "Lord, is this illustration just for us or for everyone?"

And the Lord replied, "I'm talking to any faithful, sensible servant to whom the master gives the responsibility of managing his household and feeding his family. If the master returns and finds that the servant has done a good job, there will be a reward. I assure you, the master will put that servant in charge of all he owns. But if the servant thinks, 'My master won't be back for a while,' and begins oppressing the other servants, partying, and getting drunk—well, the master will return unannounced and unexpected. He will tear the servant apart and banish him with the unfaithful. The servant will be severely punished, for though he knew his duty, he refused to do it."

"But people who are not aware that they are doing wrong will be punished only lightly. Much is required from those to whom much is given, and much more is required from those to whom much more is given."   LUKE 12:35-48

The teacher leaves the classroom for a few minutes and tells everyone to continue working quietly at his or her desk. Oh sure—that's going to happen.

You know what goes on! Some students do as they're told, some—maybe even most—*don't*. They see the opportunity for some serious goofing off, and they grab it. Sooner or later, though, the teacher does return . . . and woe to the student caught standing on the teacher's desk with the teacher's notebook in his hands. He wishes he had exercised a bit more restraint and maturity.

Jesus is coming back some day. Until then, he has left us plenty of work to do and an enormous task to accomplish: bringing the kingdoms of this world under the authority of the Kingdom of God and its rightful Ruler. Christians are not to obey God simply to avoid being caught and punished if we're unruly; we're to seek to honor him and bring glory to him because we love him. And we are to never forget: Jesus *is* coming back. We don't know when, but we know he's coming. He promised.

So, don't get caught up in some sinful behavior or get involved in activities that do nothing to promote God's kingdom. Be ready with a life that radiates generosity, diligence, purpose, and love.

Live each day as if Jesus will return that very minute.

WEEK TWENTY-NINE | DAY 4 ## NO MiddLe Ground

"I have come to bring fire to the earth, and I wish that my task were already completed! There is a terrible baptism ahead of me, and I am under a heavy burden until it is accomplished. Do you think I have come to bring peace to the earth? No, I have come to bring strife and division! From now on families will be split apart, three in favor of me, and two against— or the other way around. There will be a division between father and son, mother and daughter, mother-in-law and daughter-in-law." LUKE 12:49-53

Christians love to talk about the unifying power of the gospel, and it is true. The good news of God's love is available to men, women, rich, poor, young, old, black, white, yellow, brown, red and every other skin tone and ethnic and racial makeup. The call to come to Jesus goes out to all who will receive it, and it commands us to become one in him.

But that same gospel message also *divides*. It divides not on the basis of gender, race, or age, but on the basis of who is willing to hear it, embrace it, and build a life on it. Obviously, not everyone is . . . and hence the division.

Some people hear the claims of Jesus and believe them, submitting to him as Lord and Savior. Some reject him outright; still others shrug their shoulders and remain noncommittal. In the end, however, the Bible is clear that only two choices are open to us: to spend an eternity with the One we call

Savior, Master, Lord, and Friend; or to spend that eternity separated from the One we refused to give proper honor and respect.

The gospel does unify as no other message can. It also divides as none other will, forever.

There is no middle ground, no sitting on the fence, when it comes to what you believe about Jesus.

DAY 5 check the signs

Then Jesus turned to the crowd and said, "When you see clouds beginning to form in the west, you say, 'Here comes a shower.' And you are right. When the south wind blows, you say, 'Today will be a scorcher.' And it is. You hypocrites! You know how to interpret the appearance of the earth and the sky, but you can't interpret these present times.

"Why can't you decide for yourselves what is right? If you are on the way to court and you meet your accuser, try to settle the matter before it reaches the judge, or you may be sentenced and handed over to an officer and thrown in jail. And if that happens, you won't be free again until you have paid the last penny."   LUKE 12:54-59

If a batter misses a hit-and-run sign, that's bad, but it's not that big a deal. Same with a marching band missing the "cutoff" sign from the drum major or majorette. Nobody's life depends on it. But if a driver misses a stop sign, that's a lot more serious. He could get a ticket, or worse, somebody could get hurt or even killed as a result. Simply put, some signs are a lot more important than others.

Jesus' language about the signs of the times and the coming judgment is rather ominous. Again, this Jesus sounds very different from the politically correct Jesus presented in many churches and youth ministries today. This one calls people hypocrites and speaks of courtrooms, judgment, and penalties.

It's important to say again that we don't know *when* Jesus is coming back, only that one day he *will*. He has told us the signs are there for us to see, if we want to. Or we could end up like his listeners did, refusing to recognize what was going on right in front of their faces and missing out on the biggest event to hit earth since Adam.

Check out the signs pointing to Jesus. Your life **does** depend upon it.

What did you learn about Jesus from this week's readings?

What reading this week had the most impact on you? Why?

What do you plan to do about what you have learned this week?

Key Verse:

	DAY 1	**Production Time**

About this time Jesus was informed that Pilate had murdered some people from Galilee as they were sacrificing at the Temple in Jerusalem. "Do you think those Galileans were worse sinners than other people from Galilee?" he asked. "Is that why they suffered? Not at all! And you will also perish unless you turn from your evil ways and turn to God. And what about the eighteen men who died when the Tower of Siloam fell on them? Were they the worst sinners in Jerusalem? No, and I tell you again that unless you repent, you will also perish."

Then Jesus used this illustration: "A man planted a fig tree in his garden and came again and again to see if there was any fruit on it, but he was always disappointed. Finally, he said to his gardener, 'I've waited three years, and there hasn't been a single fig! Cut it down. It's taking up space we can use for something else.'

"The gardener answered, 'Give it one more chance. Leave it another year, and I'll give it special attention and plenty of fertilizer. If we get figs next year, fine. If not, you can cut it down.'"   LUKE 13:1-9

When we hear news of a calamity, such as a young teen killed in a car accident, we have a tendency to try and explain what went wrong: the driver was out late; he ran a stop sign; she was drinking at a party right before it happened; he wasn't wearing a seatbelt. Our human inclination is to assume that if something bad happens to you, God must have known that you deserved it.

Jesus puts that notion to rest in this passage, saying that *everyone* is a sinner who needs to repent. To repent means to turn *away* from your sins and turn *toward* God. Not just with pseudo-spiritual lip service, but really and sincerely.

In the story of the fig tree, the tree seems to be the nation of Israel, and the fruit is repentance. Notice the disappointment of the vineyard owner, his efforts to make the tree fruitful, and his willingness to be patient and give it one more chance. Notice one last aspect of the story, too: there does come a point comes where his patience is exhausted, and he says, "Cut it down."

For those who are discouraged, who feel like no matter what they do, it's never good enough—God has lots of patience, and he is always ready to give another chance.

For those who are apathetic and unappreciative—God reaches a point where he says, "Enough." Have you been enjoying the benefits of having a relationship with Jesus but have given nothing in return? If so, now's the time to produce.

Look for ways you can be "fruitful" for Jesus.

DAY 2 Healing Touch

One Sabbath day as Jesus was teaching in a synagogue, he saw a woman who had been crippled by an evil spirit. She had been bent double for eighteen years and was unable to stand up straight. When Jesus saw her, he called her over and said, "Woman, you are healed of your sickness!" Then he touched her, and instantly she could stand straight. How she praised and thanked God!

But the leader in charge of the synagogue was indignant that Jesus had healed her on the Sabbath day. "There are six days of the week for working," he said to the crowd. "Come on those days to be healed, not on the Sabbath."

But the Lord replied, "You hypocrite! You work on the Sabbath day! Don't you untie your ox or your donkey from their stalls on the Sabbath and lead them out for water? Wasn't it necessary for me, even on the Sabbath day, to free this dear woman from the bondage in which Satan has held her for eighteen years?" This shamed his enemies. And all the people rejoiced at the wonderful things he did.   LUKE 13:10-17

How do you react when you see a person who is crippled, disabled, physically, mentally or otherwise handicapped? Most of us probably turn away; after all, we've been told not to stare at people who are "different."

Here was a woman who had been ravaged by an evil spirit for eighteen years, her body so twisted that she couldn't straighten up. We can only imagine the days and nights of pain and terror she must have endured, the social ostracism, and what all this must have done to her appearance. How would you have reacted if you had seen her?

Jesus saw her not as a freak show, not as someone to avoid, but as a person in desperate need of his healing touch. Where others saw an unwanted distraction, and the Pharisees saw a violation of Sabbath protocols, Jesus saw this woman and her need.

Jesus wants you to do the same. When you look beyond the surface and see the needs of the individual, you bring his healing touch to that person.

The next time you see someone "different," ask God for the grace to see that person as Jesus does.

DAY 3 transformations

Then Jesus said, "What is the Kingdom of God like? How can I illustrate it? It is like a tiny mustard seed planted in a garden; it grows and becomes a tree, and the birds come and find shelter among its branches."

He also asked, "What else is the Kingdom of God like? It is like yeast used by a woman making bread. Even though she used a large amount of flour, the yeast permeated every part of the dough." LUKE 13:18-21

One of the reasons Jesus' preaching was and is so memorable and so compelling is his use of images. He takes spiritual truths and explains them in terms of other, more readily understandable life situations.

The first story, comparing the kingdom of God to a tiny mustard seed, tells us that Christianity would start small but eventually grow very large. That of course is exactly what has happened: from an initial group of twelve not-so-faithful followers Christianity has grown into the largest religion the world has ever seen. Well over one billion people today profess to be Christians. (Of course, only God knows whether anyone *truly* trusts in Jesus as Lord, but the point remains that Christians comprise the largest faith-group in history.) And Christianity is growing today the world over faster than ever before!

The second story, comparing the kingdom to yeast, is about the other side of the coin—*inner transformation.* Christianity has not only penetrated every corner of the planet; it changes individual men, women, and young people in every aspect of their lives. Following Jesus is not merely a Sunday-only event or a half-hearted assent to a nice moral and ethical code. *It is a way of life that transforms a person completely, heart, soul, body, and mind.*

Global transformation and personal conversion: that's what happens in the kingdom of God.

The gospel of Jesus Christ alone has the power to change the world—and you!

As Jesus was walking along, he saw a man who had been blind from birth. "Teacher," his disciples asked him, "why was this man born blind? Was it a result of his own sins or those of his parents?"

"It was not because of his sins or his parents' sins," Jesus answered. "He was born blind so the power of God could be seen in him. All of us must quickly carry out the tasks assigned us by the one who sent me, because there is little time left before the night falls and all work comes to an end. But while I am still here in the world, I am the light of the world."

Then he spit on the ground, made mud with the saliva, and smoothed the mud over the blind man's eyes. He told him, "Go and wash in the pool of Siloam" (Siloam means Sent). So the man went and washed, and came back seeing!

His neighbors and others who knew him as a blind beggar asked each other, "Is this the same man—that beggar?" Some said he was, and others said, "No, but he surely looks like him!"

And the beggar kept saying, "I am the same man!"

They asked, "Who healed you? What happened?"

He told them, "The man they call Jesus made mud and smoothed it over my eyes and told me, 'Go to the pool of Siloam and wash off the mud.' I went and washed, and now I can see!"

"Where is he now?" they asked.

"I don't know," he replied.   JOHN 9:1-12

Sometimes in our life, a person comes along who really drives us and pushes us to achieve. It may be a coach or a teacher, a private instructor or a parent. At times, their constant pushing feels as though they are picking on us and making life miserable for no particular reason.

Sometimes we feel the same way about God when difficulties or suffering hits. We feel as though God is picking on us or taking it out on us for no particular reason. This is a common response to suffering, pain, and loss. But John 9:1-12 gives another perspective: sometimes we suffer "so the power of God can be seen in us." In other words, *our suffering can be a platform from which God can be glorified.*

Have you ever heard someone who has been through a tragic accident, catastrophic illness, or loss of a loved one but who still professes belief in God and his goodness? That person's testimony is incredibly powerful. The pain is still just as real, the loss just as profound—nothing in the Bible or Christian theology is intended to minimize or trivialize that. But knowing that the pain has a purpose can make the difference between hope and despair when we go through the tough times.

The gospel message is unique among all the world's religious teachings because it tells of a God who left heaven, became one of us, suffered, and died for his ruined creation. For the Christian, suffering never needs to be meaningless because Jesus himself has suffered and given meaning to our afflictions. Through them, God may be bringing glory to himself in a way we could never do if we never went through the pain.

When suffering is part of your life, remember the One who suffered for you, and who will suffer with you.

DAY 5 # Thought Police

Then they took the man to the Pharisees. Now as it happened, Jesus had healed the man on a Sabbath. The Pharisees asked the man all about it. So he told them, "He smoothed the mud over my eyes, and when it was washed away, I could see!"

Some of the Pharisees said, "This man Jesus is not from God, for he is working on the Sabbath." Others said, "But how could an ordinary sinner do such miraculous signs?" So there was a deep division of opinion among them.

Then the Pharisees once again questioned the man who had been blind and demanded, "This man who opened your eyes—who do you say he is?"

The man replied, "I think he must be a prophet."

The Jewish leaders wouldn't believe he had been blind, so they called in his parents. They asked them, "Is this your son? Was he born blind? If so, how can he see?"

His parents replied, "We know this is our son and that he was born blind, but we don't know how he can see or who healed him. He is old enough to speak for himself. Ask him." They said this because they were afraid of the Jewish leaders, who had announced that anyone saying Jesus was the Messiah would be expelled from the synagogue. That's why they said, "He is old enough to speak for himself. Ask him."

So for the second time they called in the man who had been blind and told him, "Give glory to God by telling the truth, because we know Jesus is a sinner."

"I don't know whether he is a sinner," the man replied. "But I know this: I was blind, and now I can see!"

"But what did he do?" they asked. "How did he heal you?"

"Look!" the man exclaimed. "I told you once. Didn't you listen? Why do you want to hear it again? Do you want to become his disciples, too?"

Then they cursed him and said, "You are his disciple, but we are disciples of Moses. We know God spoke to Moses, but as for this man, we don't know anything about him."

"Why, that's very strange!" the man replied. "He healed my eyes, and yet you don't know anything about him! Well, God doesn't listen to sinners, but he is ready to hear those who worship him and do his will. Never since the world began has anyone been able to open the eyes of someone born blind. If this man were not from God, he couldn't do it."

"You were born in sin!" they answered. "Are you trying to teach us?" And they threw him out of the synagogue.   JOHN 9:13-34

An old saying states that you can't teach an old dog new tricks. Basically, it's talking about people who are entrenched in thinking about something a certain way or doing something the same way as it always has been done. When a new idea comes along, these people immediately shut down and are unwilling to consider any other possibilities.

Jesus encountered that attitude among the religious leaders of his day. He had just given a blind man back his sight, but instead of celebrating the miracle, the Pharisees turn into religious thought police. When they asked the former blind man, "This man who opened your eyes—who do you say he is?"—what they really meant was, "Say what we want you to say about him." They couldn't accept the fact that there might be a new idea, a new possibility, a new teaching that might help people.

It's okay to have a healthy skepticism about someone's claims to spiritual truth (or anything else, for that matter). Such reservation will keep you from foolishly falling for religious con men and frauds who love to prey on the gullible. But when the truth is presented and the evidence is on the table for all to see, only fools and Pharisees refuse to believe.

The Bible's claims about Jesus as the Son of God and Savior of lost men and women are open for any amount of fair and open-minded examination. In fact, God welcomes our questions!

Whether it's you or a friend that needs further convincing, keep yourself open to the possibility of Christ and his claim on your life.

What did you learn about Jesus from this week's readings?

What reading this week had the most impact on you? Why?

What do you plan to do about what you have learned this week?

Key Verse:

| DAY 1 | ## seeing is believing

When Jesus heard what had happened, he found the man and said, "Do you believe in the Son of Man?"

The man answered, "Who is he, sir, because I would like to."

"You have seen him," Jesus said, "and he is speaking to you!"

"Yes, Lord," the man said, "I believe!" And he worshiped Jesus.

Then Jesus told him, "I have come to judge the world. I have come to give sight to the blind and to show those who think they see that they are blind."

The Pharisees who were standing there heard him and asked, "Are you saying we are blind?"

"If you were blind, you wouldn't be guilty," Jesus replied. "But you remain guilty because you claim you can see." JOHN 9:35-41

You've heard the expression, "Seeing is believing." This is doubly true in this encounter between Jesus and a blind man.

The man had been born blind, and Jesus had healed him, restoring his vision. When he learned who it was that had done this, he believed in Jesus and *worshiped* him. Others around were *spiritually* blind, and when given the same opportunity—*to believe and worship*—they chose to stay blind. How tragic!

From time to time, you will be faced with a choice between embracing belief or disbelief, and it's often easier not to believe. Our culture elevates skepticism and cynicism to the place of admirable qualities. Many young people think such detachment is cool. If you begin to think that way, remember who gave you your sight in the first place.

Seeing Jesus spiritually is believing.

sacrificial sheep

"I assure you, anyone who sneaks over the wall of a sheepfold, rather than going through the gate, must surely be a thief and a robber! For a shepherd enters through the gate. The gate-keeper opens the gate for him, and the sheep hear his voice and come to him. He calls his own sheep by name and leads them out. After he has gathered his own flock, he walks ahead of them, and they follow him because they recognize his voice. They won't follow a stranger; they will run from him because they don't recognize his voice."

Those who heard Jesus use this illustration didn't understand what he meant, so he explained it to them. "I assure you, I am the gate for the sheep," he said. "All others who came before me were thieves and robbers. But the true sheep did not listen to them. Yes, I am the gate. Those who come in through me will be saved. Wherever they go, they will find green pastures. The thief's purpose is to steal and kill and destroy. My purpose is to give life in all its fullness.

"I am the good shepherd. The good shepherd lays down his life for the sheep. A hired hand will run when he sees a wolf coming. He will leave the sheep because they aren't his and he isn't their shepherd. And so the wolf attacks them and scatters the flock. The hired hand runs away because he is merely hired and has no real concern for the sheep.

"I am the good shepherd; I know my own sheep, and they know me, just as my Father knows me and I know the Father. And I lay down my life for the sheep. I have other sheep, too, that are not in this sheepfold. I must bring them also, and they will listen to my voice; and there will be one flock with one shepherd.

"The Father loves me because I lay down my life that I may have it back again. No one can take my life from me. I lay down my life voluntarily. For I have the right to lay it down when I want to and also the power to take it again. For my Father has given me this command."

When he said these things, the people were again divided in their opinions about him. Some of them said, "He has a demon, or he's crazy. Why listen to a man like that?" Others said, "This doesn't sound like a man possessed by a demon! Can a demon open the eyes of the blind?" JOHN 10:1-21

When you received presents as a young child at Christmas or on your birthday, you probably tore through the wrapping paper to open the present—and then you couldn't wait for the next one! As you got older, however, watching others open their presents, particularly the ones you bought, was just as enjoyable as *getting* them. You realized that gifts were not just about getting, but about giving as well.

The Christian life is much the same. At first, when we were told about becoming a Christian, we were told about the great things God offers those who receive Jesus as Lord: forgiveness, mercy, joy, peace, a family of brothers and sisters all over the world, eternal life with him forever. All those things are true, and more besides.

Yet the Christian life is not a one-way street wherein we only *receive* good things from God. The heart of the gospel is that Jesus loved us enough to lay down his life for us in an act of incomparable sacrifice and selflessness: *"I lay down my life for the sheep."* If we are to follow him, we have to take seriously our opportunities and our responsibilities to lay down our lives for others as well. No, our sacrifices will not compare with the one Jesus made; nor will they pay for anyone's sins, including our own. But they will honor our Lord, and fulfill his commands that we love God and one another sacrificially and selflessly.

What sacrifices can you make for others as part of your response to Jesus?

DAY 3 It Makes a Difference

It was now winter, and Jesus was in Jerusalem at the time of Hanukkah. He was at the Temple, walking through the section known as Solomon's Colonnade. The Jewish leaders surrounded him and asked, "How long are you going to keep us in suspense? If you are the Messiah, tell us plainly."

Jesus replied, "I have already told you, and you don't believe me. The proof is what I do in the name of my Father. But you don't believe me because you are not part of my flock. My sheep recognize my voice; I know them, and they follow me. I give them eternal life, and they will never perish. No one will snatch them away from me, for my Father has given them to me, and he is more powerful than anyone else. So no one can take them from me. The Father and I are one."

Once again the Jewish leaders picked up stones to kill him. Jesus said, "At my Father's direction I have done many things to help the people. For which one of these good deeds are you killing me?"

They replied, "Not for any good work, but for blasphemy, because you, a mere man, have made yourself God."

Jesus replied, "It is written in your own law that God said to certain leaders of the people, 'I say, you are gods!' And you know that the Scriptures cannot be altered. So if those people, who received God's message, were called 'gods,' why do you call it blasphemy when the Holy One who was sent into the world by the Father says, 'I am the Son of God'? Don't believe me unless I carry out my Father's work. But if I do his work, believe in what I have done, even if you don't believe me. Then you will realize that the Father is in me, and I am in the Father."

Once again they tried to arrest him, but he got away and left them. He went beyond the

Jordan River to stay near the place where John was first baptizing. And many followed him. "John didn't do miracles," they remarked to one another, "but all his predictions about this man have come true." And many believed in him there.   JOHN 10:22-42

Who is Jesus?

If you ask 100 people that question, you may very well get 100 different answers. Opinions about Jesus vary widely. Some say he is an important historical figure, the founder of the largest religious faith the world has ever seen. Others see him as mostly legendary or mythical, the equivalent of a King Arthur, an historical figure who was transformed into a larger-than-life figure. Still others seem to resent him and the unattainable moral and ethical standards he embodies. And many more barely stifle a yawn when asked about Jesus, or anything remotely "religious."

Jesus' opponents had various ideas about him, too, none positive. They called him crazy, a drunk, and a glutton and even demon-possessed. In this passage they also called him a blasphemer for claiming to be God. And they were absolutely right—unless he was, and is, in fact, *God.*

That's the glaring choice we must make about Jesus. Either he is who he claimed to be—God Almighty—and therefore deserving of our utmost devotion and worship; or else he is who his enemies said: a liar, a phony, a false messiah, and even a devil.

Who is Jesus? The biblical answer is clear. He is the unique God-man, the only Son of the Father, Savior and Lord, and the *only* way to salvation and eternal life. How you answer the question makes all the difference in the world and the world to come.

What's your final answer to the question: **who is Jesus?**

The Narrow Door

Jesus went through the towns and villages, teaching as he went, always pressing on toward Jerusalem. Someone asked him, "Lord, will only a few be saved?"

He replied, "The door to heaven is narrow. Work hard to get in, because many will try to enter, but when the head of the house has locked the door, it will be too late. Then you will stand outside knocking and pleading, 'Lord, open the door for us!' But he will reply, 'I do not know you.' You will say, 'But we ate and drank with you, and you taught in our streets.' And he will reply, 'I tell you, I don't know you. Go away, all you who do evil.'

"And there will be great weeping and gnashing of teeth, for you will see Abraham, Isaac, Jacob, and all the prophets within the Kingdom of God, but you will be thrown out. Then people will come from all over the world to take their places in the Kingdom of God. And note this: Some who are despised now will be greatly honored then; and some who are greatly honored now will be despised then."   LUKE 13:22-30

You and your family are going on a long-awaited vacation to a small island off the coastline. The only way to get to the island, however, is over a narrow, one-way bridge. Does that prevent you from going? Does anyone argue that there ought to be another way to the island? Of course not. Your family is just grateful there is a way on to the island!

Yet for some reason, when we tell others that there is only one way to God—through Jesus Christ—people often respond that can't be right. There has to be more than one way.

A great folk-religion today says that everyone—or almost everyone, with a few glaring exceptions—goes to heaven when they die. To say otherwise violates the one great commandment still agreed upon in our culture: *Thou shalt be tolerant.*

But Jesus says something quite different in this passage: "The door to heaven is narrow." He also says that many who think they should be allowed to enter won't, and that others who seem the most unlikely will be given great honor in heaven. Clearly, God operates with a different set of values and priorities than we do.

When reading a passage like this, we can focus on the exclusive, restrictive aspects of the gospel, such as that the door is narrow. Or we can center in on the gracious, inclusive aspects: that God has offered us a way *at all*, and that that way runs through a cross.

Let God's overflowing grace take you through the narrow door.

A few minutes later some Pharisees said to him, "Get out of here if you want to live, because Herod Antipas wants to kill you!"

Jesus replied, "Go tell that fox that I will keep on casting out demons and doing miracles of healing today and tomorrow; and the third day I will accomplish my purpose. Yes, today, tomorrow, and the next day I must proceed on my way. For it wouldn't do for a prophet of God to be killed except in Jerusalem!

"O Jerusalem, Jerusalem, the city that kills the prophets and stones God's messengers! How often I have wanted to gather your children together as a hen protects her chicks beneath her wings, but you wouldn't let me. And now look, your house is left to you empty. And you will never see me again until you say, 'Bless the one who comes in the name of the Lord!'" LUKE 13:31-35

Suppose your best friend started staying after school each day to help a teacher you know that your friend has had difficulty with in the past. Your friend doesn't say anything about it to you, but it's the number one topic at lunch: Why is your friend doing this? You don't really know, but you suspect that your friend might be trying to get a better grade, or get in good with the teacher, or even make up for a failing grade.

A person's motivations are often difficult to understand. In this passage it's hard to understand what motivated the Pharisees who told Jesus to flee from Herod. They may have been trying to get him out of their "home turf" in order to more effectively silence him. They may have given up on trying to strong-arm him, and this was a more subtle way of getting him to move on. They may have genuinely had his best interests at heart, as Nicodemus and Joseph of Arimathea did.

In any group, whatever else members have in common, they will hold many different views of or opinions about Jesus. The Pharisees, usually depicted as Jesus' enemies, also had divided attitudes toward him. While many if not most of them clearly disliked him and felt threatened by him, some had more positive regard.

We may not be sure what motivated them, nor anyone else for that matter, in their relationship with Jesus. What we need to do is focus on our motives for our relationship with Jesus—and that it is not based on our needs, but in extending his love to others.

Make sure your motives are pure when it comes to following Jesus.

What did you learn about Jesus from this week's readings?

What reading this week had the most impact on you? Why?

What do you plan to do about what you have learned this week?

Key Verse:

DAY 1 The Heart of the Matter

One Sabbath day Jesus was in the home of a leader of the Pharisees. The people were watching him closely, because there was a man there whose arms and legs were swollen. Jesus asked the Pharisees and experts in religious law, "Well, is it permitted in the law to heal people on the Sabbath day, or not?" When they refused to answer, Jesus touched the sick man and healed him and sent him away. Then he turned to them and asked, "Which of you doesn't work on the Sabbath? If your son or your cow falls into a pit, don't you proceed at once to get him out?" Again they had no answer.   LUKE 14:1-6

There's a pond with a "No Swimming" sign posted. As you're walking by, you notice a youngster flailing in the water. Even though it is against the rules, you jump in and swim over to help the youngster and pull him to safety. No one would even argue that it was wrong for you to ignore that sign, and certainly no one would punish you for breaking that rule.

In this passage, the Pharisees couldn't see beyond the rules they had made regarding the Sabbath and to the greater need that Jesus addressed in healing a sick man.

God gave mankind a Sabbath—a day to rest, play, and worship—for our benefit. It was meant for our good, not as an excuse to set up unnecessary and detrimental rules and requirements. And yet, how often we lose sight of the original purpose!

The Pharisees gathered in the house on this occasion were guilty of the same thing. They had forgotten what the Sabbath was for, and instead were merely using it as a platform from which to watch for "lawbreakers"—sort of like setting a speed trap along the road of religious obedience. They were looking for some infraction, some excuse to criticize, like some Christians and churches do even today. When Jesus healed this poor man, obviously a wonderful thing, they could not (or would not) see the miracle or the tremendous blessing it was for him. All they saw was that a "rule" had been broken, and they frankly didn't much care why.

Obedience and faithfulness to God's commands are important. So are people. When the two conflict with one another, keep your eyes on what is truly important. When in doubt, consider what Jesus did, and lean toward showing compassion.

Look beyond the letter of the law to Jesus' heart.

DAY 2 check your ego at the door

When Jesus noticed that all who had come to the dinner were trying to sit near the head of the table, he gave them this advice: "If you are invited to a wedding feast, don't always head for the best seat. What if someone more respected than you has also been invited? The host will say, 'Let this person sit here instead.' Then you will be embarrassed and will have to take whatever seat is left at the foot of the table!

"Do this instead—sit at the foot of the table. Then when your host sees you, he will come and say, 'Friend, we have a better place than this for you!' Then you will be honored in front of all the other guests. For the proud will be humbled, but the humble will be honored."

Then he turned to his host. "When you put on a luncheon or a dinner," he said, "don't invite your friends, brothers, relatives, and rich neighbors. For they will repay you by inviting you back. Instead, invite the poor, the crippled, the lame, and the blind. Then at the resurrection of the godly, God will reward you for inviting those who could not repay you." LUKE 14:7-14

Some athletes—at all levels of the game—have perfected the art of celebration. A basketball player dunks on the defender and hangs on the basket a second longer than necessary to emphasize the point. A hitter crosses home plate after crushing a ball into the upper deck with both fists pumping in the air. A receiver catches a touchdown pass over the head of the cornerback and performs a special dance.

Our culture not only tolerates but positively promotes the celebration of self and personal achievement. Humility seems to be a relic of a bygone era.

Yet this passage, like many others in the Bible, turns such thinking upside-down, elevating humility and denigrating selfish pride. Indeed, Jesus reserved his harshest words for the spiritually proud, those whose opinions of their own holiness were overblown. Passages like Luke 14:7-14 serve as a pin puncturing a balloon to deflate their over-inflated self-images.

Over and over in the Scriptures, God offers men and women a choice: *humble* yourself, and I will *exalt* you; exalt *yourself*, and *I* will humble you. The choice is ours.

Make sure your ego is in check when you come before God.

| DAY 3 **NOT NOW!**

Hearing this, a man sitting at the table with Jesus exclaimed, "What a privilege it would be to have a share in the Kingdom of God!"

Jesus replied with this illustration: "A man prepared a great feast and sent out many invitations. When all was ready, he sent his servant around to notify the guests that it was time for them to come. But they all began making excuses. One said he had just bought a field and wanted to inspect it, so he asked to be excused. Another said he had just bought five pair of oxen and wanted to try them out. Another had just been married, so he said he couldn't come.

"The servant returned and told his master what they had said. His master was angry and said, 'Go quickly into the streets and alleys of the city and invite the poor, the crippled, the lame, and the blind.' After the servant had done this, he reported, 'There is still room for more.' So his master said, 'Go out into the country lanes and behind the hedges and urge anyone you find to come, so that the house will be full. For none of those I invited first will get even the smallest taste of what I had prepared for them.'"   LUKE 14:15-24

You receive an invitation to attend a party from a classmate that you know only casually. This particular person is not one of the most popular kids in school, but since nothing else is happening that weekend, you agree to go. When the day rolls around, however, you have a ton of homework to get done, your mom's been after you to clean your room, and you really don't have the time to spend at this party. So you try to find an excuse for not going.

For the people in this passage, time was critical. On the surface, their reasons for backing out were legitimate: one wanted to inspect a field, another to test a new team of oxen, a third to be with his new bride. Simply put, the time of the party was inconvenient for them. So they find an excuse and missed the most important event of all—entrance into God's kingdom.

When God calls, *answer*. You don't want to miss out on your opportunity. Every day someone who thought he had plenty of time runs out. If you have not yet accepted Jesus' invitation to join him at his feast—why not? And if you have sent in your RSVP, think of those you know who need a personal invitation—from you.

Don't miss out on your opportunity to join be God's eternal feast.

count the cost

Great crowds were following Jesus. He turned around and said to them, "If you want to be my follower you must love me more than your own father and mother, wife and children, brothers and sisters—yes, more than your own life. Otherwise, you cannot be my disciple. And you cannot be my disciple if you do not carry your own cross and follow me.

"But don't begin until you count the cost. For who would begin construction of a building without first getting estimates and then checking to see if there is enough money to pay the bills? Otherwise, you might complete only the foundation before running out of funds. And then how everyone would laugh at you! They would say, 'There's the person who started that building and ran out of money before it was finished!'

"Or what king would ever dream of going to war without first sitting down with his counselors and discussing whether his army of ten thousand is strong enough to defeat the twenty thousand soldiers who are marching against him? If he is not able, then while the enemy is still far away, he will send a delegation to discuss terms of peace. So no one can become my disciple without giving up everything for me.

"Salt is good for seasoning. But if it loses its flavor, how do you make it salty again? Flavorless salt is good neither for the soil nor for fertilizer. It is thrown away. Anyone who is willing to hear should listen and understand!" LUKE 14:25-35

Every Sunday morning, churches are filled with people who have made a decision to follow Jesus. Unfortunately, so are many golf courses, restaurants, living rooms and bedrooms. Why? Why do some people who make that decision live it out, while others don't? It is, of course, quite possible to be involved in a church without being serious about your Christian commitment, but it is a start. Conversely, it is hardly possible to be committed to Jesus if you are not committed to the church.

Part of the answer is found in this passage. If we're going to follow Christ, we must be prepared to pay the cost. What that cost will be exactly varies from person to person. Some Christians are called upon to make great sacrifices, some losing even their lives for the sake of their Lord, while others lead lives of comparative ease and affluence. Only God knows what he will ask of each person. The question for each of us is, are we willing to pay that price, whatever it is?

The message of Luke 14:25-35 seems plain enough: before we set off on the journey of Christian discipleship, we need to count the cost and decide whether we're willing to pay it.

No matter what it will cost you to follow Jesus, he promises it will be worth it!

|DAY 5 # Risky Love

Tax collectors and other notorious sinners often came to listen to Jesus teach. This made the Pharisees and teachers of religious law complain that he was associating with such despicable people—even eating with them!

So Jesus used this illustration: "If you had one hundred sheep, and one of them strayed away and was lost in the wilderness, wouldn't you leave the ninety-nine others to go and search for the lost one until you found it? And then you would joyfully carry it home on your shoulders. When you arrived, you would call together your friends and neighbors to rejoice with you because your lost sheep was found. In the same way, heaven will be happier over one lost sinner who returns to God than over ninety-nine others who are righteous and haven't strayed away!" LUKE 15:1-7

When people talk about this story from Luke's Gospel, they usually picture it as though the shepherd put the ninety-nine non-straying sheep somewhere safe and then went out to find the lost one. (There is even an old hymn that describes it just that way.) But that's not what this text says. It says the shepherd left the ninety-nine right where they were and went in search of the one who strayed. That's risky . . . and it says something important about the love of God for lost people.

It illustrates for us the risky nature of God's love. What possible risk does an omnipotent God expose himself to? Just this: the all-powerful, immortal, invincible God took the form of a weak, helpless, vulnerable human baby. He did this knowing that he put himself in peril of undergoing the same sicknesses, pain, suffering and even death that his creatures are subject to.

What a foolish, dangerous thing to do! Only a God who loves beyond reason, beyond measure, would do such a thing. That's the God who came to earth as one of us.

When you get discouraged or feel far from God, remember the risk he took just to find you!

What did you learn about Jesus from this week's readings?

What reading this week had the most impact on you? Why?

What do you plan to do about what you have learned this week?

Key Verse:

| DAY 1 | ## Lost and Found

"Or suppose a woman has ten valuable silver coins and loses one. Won't she light a lamp and look in every corner of the house and sweep every nook and cranny until she finds it? And when she finds it, she will call in her friends and neighbors to rejoice with her because she has found her lost coin. In the same way, there is joy in the presence of God's angels when even one sinner repents." LUKE 15:8-10

This is the second story in Luke 15 in which a person loses something of value and goes to look for it; this time, a coin. Again, the person does not sit back passively and say, "Oh well—I sure will miss that coin." No, she lights a lamp, sweeps the house and searches until she finds it. And once again, it illustrates something very important about God's love.

Just as the lost coin was important to the woman, Jesus wanted his listeners to know that each and every person is valuable to God. In the same way that we celebrate finding our lost wallet or missing ring, God and his angels celebrate over every single person that turns from sin and believes in Christ. (Just think of it, the angels rejoiced over you one day!)

The point is that God is intensely and personally involved in the lives of each of his children. He is not neutral or indifferent to our condition. God grieves over the lost and rejoices over the found. He delights in each and every child that is brought into his kingdom.

Imagine what would happen if Jesus' church shared this same intense concern for lost people.

To whom in your circle of friends or family can you extend Jesus' care and concern?

DAY 2 # the wanderer

To illustrate the point further, Jesus told them this story: "A man had two sons. The younger son told his father, 'I want my share of your estate now, instead of waiting until you die.' So his father agreed to divide his wealth between his sons.

"A few days later this younger son packed all his belongings and took a trip to a distant land, and there he wasted all his money on wild living. About the time his money ran out, a great famine swept over the land, and he began to starve. He persuaded a local farmer to hire him to feed his pigs. The boy became so hungry that even the pods he was feeding the pigs looked good to him. But no one gave him anything.

"When he finally came to his senses, he said to himself, 'At home even the hired men have food enough to spare, and here I am, dying of hunger! I will go home to my father and say, "Father, I have sinned against both heaven and you, and I am no longer worthy of being called your son. Please take me on as a hired man."'

"So he returned home to his father. And while he was still a long distance away, his father saw him coming. Filled with love and compassion, he ran to his son, embraced him, and kissed him. His son said to him, 'Father, I have sinned against both heaven and you, and I am no longer worthy of being called your son.'"

"But his father said to the servants, 'Quick! Bring the finest robe in the house and put it on him. Get a ring for his finger, and sandals for his feet. And kill the calf we have been fattening in the pen. We must celebrate with a feast, for this son of mine was dead and has now returned to life. He was lost, but now he is found.' So the party began.

"Meanwhile, the older son was in the fields working. When he returned home, he heard music and dancing in the house, and he asked one of the servants what was going on. 'Your brother is back,' he was told, 'and your father has killed the calf we were fattening and has prepared a great feast. We are celebrating because of his safe return.'

"The older brother was angry and wouldn't go in. His father came out and begged him, but he replied, 'All these years I've worked hard for you and never once refused to do a single thing you told me to. And in all that time you never gave me even one young goat for a feast with my friends. Yet when this son of yours comes back after squandering your money on prostitutes, you celebrate by killing the finest calf we have.'

"His father said to him, 'Look, dear son, you and I are very close, and everything I have is yours. We had to celebrate this happy day. For your brother was dead and has come back to life! He was lost, but now he is found!'" LUKE 15:11-32

This is the third story in Luke 15 of something lost and found. This time the lost object is a son, infinitely more valuable than a sheep or a coin. And even so, it's interesting that, unlike the shepherd or the woman, the father does not run off to find his son. No, instead, he lets him go "get lost."

Why? If a son is indeed more precious than a sheep or coin, why doesn't the father go after him, or just refuse to let him go in the first place?

Because people, unlike sheep or coins, have been given a measure of free will by our Creator. He has designed us so that we are able to choose right from wrong, to know truth from error and to decide whether or not to return his love for us. We can, like this young man, wander off in pursuit of our own pleasures; indeed, Isaiah 53:6 says we all do to some degree. But we can also, like this young prodigal, realize the error of our ways in time, and return to the only One who can help us turn from our sins: Jesus Christ. Like the prodigal we can return to the Father who loves us so faithfully and waits for us so patiently.

Jesus wanted his listeners to know the heart of his Father. Whatever we have done, however far we have wandered from our home, isn't it comforting—even compelling—to know that God waits, watching down the road and longing for his lost child to return?

When you wander from God, remember the One who is waiting patiently for you with open arms.

| DAY 3 ## Master of your Life

Jesus told this story to his disciples: "A rich man hired a manager to handle his affairs, but soon a rumor went around that the manager was thoroughly dishonest. So his employer called him in and said, 'What's this I hear about your stealing from me? Get your report in order, because you are going to be dismissed.'

"The manager thought to himself, 'Now what? I'm through here, and I don't have the strength to go out and dig ditches, and I'm too proud to beg. I know just the thing! And then I'll have plenty of friends to take care of me when I leave!'

"So he invited each person who owed money to his employer to come and discuss the situation. He asked the first one, 'How much do you owe him?' The man replied, 'I owe him eight hundred gallons of olive oil.' So the manager told him, 'Tear up that bill and write another one for four hundred gallons.'

"'And how much do you owe my employer?' he asked the next man. 'A thousand bushels of wheat,' was the reply. 'Here,' the manager said, 'take your bill and replace it with one for only eight hundred bushels.'

"The rich man had to admire the dishonest rascal for being so shrewd. And it is true that the citizens of this world are more shrewd than the godly are. I tell you, use your worldly resources to benefit others and make friends. In this way, your generosity stores up a reward for you in heaven.

"Unless you are faithful in small matters, you won't be faithful in large ones. If you cheat even a little, you won't be honest with greater responsibilities. And if you are untrustworthy about worldly wealth, who will trust you with the true riches of heaven? And if you are not faithful with other people's money, why should you be trusted with money of your own?

"No one can serve two masters. For you will hate one and love the other, or be devoted to one and despise the other. You cannot serve both God and money."

The Pharisees, who dearly loved their money, naturally scoffed at all this. Then he said to them, "You like to look good in public, but God knows your evil hearts. What this world honors is an abomination in the sight of God.

"Until John the Baptist began to preach, the laws of Moses and the messages of the prophets were your guides. But now the Good News of the Kingdom of God is preached, and eager multitudes are forcing their way in. But that doesn't mean that the law has lost its force in even the smallest point. It is stronger and more permanent than heaven and earth.

"Anyone who divorces his wife and marries someone else commits adultery, and anyone who marries a divorced woman commits adultery."   LUKE 16:1-18

Imagine standing on a dock and stepping onto a high-powered speedboat. Just as you place your left foot in the boat, with your right one still on the dock, the boat begins to pull away, quickly. You're going to have to make a decision, and *fast*, or else the decision will be made for you, and it will be one you won't enjoy very much.

That's the kind of tension you experience when you try to live the Christian life and still hang on to the world's values, attitudes and behaviors. The two lifestyles cannot peacefully coexist in the same person—they are as opposite as a photograph and its negative. You have to choose one or the other, and *fast*, or you'll find yourself in the position of the guy with one foot on the dock and the other in the boat.

Jesus said, "No one can serve two masters. For you will hate one and love the other, or be devoted to one and despise the other." The specific conflict he spoke about involved money—still a very tempting and *demanding* false god—but it could just as easily been sex, popularity, power, or any number of other idols.

Consider your own life. What do you devote your time, energy, and abilities to serving?

No one can serve two masters. Who will you serve?

| DAY 4   # what wiLL it Take?

Jesus said, "There was a certain rich man who was splendidly clothed and who lived each day in luxury. At his door lay a diseased beggar named Lazarus. As Lazarus lay there longing for scraps from the rich man's table, the dogs would come and lick his open sores. Finally, the beggar died and was carried by the angels to be with Abraham. The rich man also died and was buried, and his soul went to the place of the dead. There, in torment, he saw Lazarus in the far distance with Abraham.

"The rich man shouted, 'Father Abraham, have some pity! Send Lazarus over here to dip the tip of his finger in water and cool my tongue, because I am in anguish in these flames.'

"But Abraham said to him, 'Son, remember that during your lifetime you had everything you wanted, and Lazarus had nothing. So now he is here being comforted, and you are in anguish. And besides, there is a great chasm separating us. Anyone who wanted to cross over to you from here is stopped at its edge, and no one there can cross over to us.'

"Then the rich man said, 'Please, Father Abraham, send him to my father's home. For I have five brothers, and I want him to warn them about this place of torment so they won't have to come here when they die.'

"But Abraham said, 'Moses and the prophets have warned them. Your brothers can read their writings anytime they want to.'

"The rich man replied, 'No, Father Abraham! But if someone is sent to them from the dead, then they will turn from their sins.'

"But Abraham said, 'If they won't listen to Moses and the prophets, they won't listen even if someone rises from the dead.'"   LUKE 16:19-31

It's frustrating when you try to communicate what you believe about Jesus to someone who will not listen to anything you have to say. Your personal experience with Christ, the Old Testament prophecies that point to Christ, the witness of church history and countless changed lives . . . none of it seemed to get through the fog. Maybe you wanted to say to your friend, "What will it take to convince you?"

Maybe you *should* ask that question. Luke 16:19-31 is a story Jesus told about a rich man who died and went to hell, and wanted to warn his brothers not to make the same mistake. Abraham tells this man that they have the testimony of the Old Testament, and that should be enough. And if that's not enough, Abraham says, they won't listen even to someone who rises from the dead . . . a chilling prediction and rebuke rolled into one.

When you share your faith with someone who seems to shoot down everything you have to say before you've even finished your sentences, maybe you ought to ask, "What amount of evidence would convince you

Jesus is who he says he is?" If the answer is, "*None*," save your breath and pray that God will open your friend's eyes, mind, and heart before the rich man in the story did.

The time is now to make your case for Christ. Pray that it will be heard.

DAY 5 The Easy Life?

One day Jesus said to his disciples, "There will always be temptations to sin, but how terrible it will be for the person who does the tempting. It would be better to be thrown into the sea with a large millstone tied around the neck than to face the punishment in store for harming one of these little ones. I am warning you! If another believer sins, rebuke him; then if he repents, forgive him. Even if he wrongs you seven times a day and each time turns again and asks forgiveness, forgive him."

One day the apostles said to the Lord, "We need more faith; tell us how to get it."

"Even if you had faith as small as a mustard seed," the Lord answered, "you could say to this mulberry tree, 'May God uproot you and throw you into the sea,' and it would obey you!

"When a servant comes in from plowing or taking care of sheep, he doesn't just sit down and eat. He must first prepare his master's meal and serve him his supper before eating his own. And the servant is not even thanked, because he is merely doing what he is supposed to do. In the same way, when you obey me you should say, 'We are not worthy of praise. We are servants who have simply done our duty.'"   LUKE 17:1-10

Get rich . . . be popular . . . earn respect and power . . . live a life free of illness and worry. If the gospel promised any of the above, there probably wouldn't be enough pews in the churches to hold all the people. So why does the Bible offer instead of the easy life, a more difficult path? Consider what believers are advised:

Steer clear of sin; make sure you avoid participating in anyone else's temptation; practice repentance and forgiveness; have faith; put the needs of others before your own; This stuff is hard! Didn't somebody tell us that being a Christian would solve our problems? It seems as though these kinds of demands are the problem.

If it were easy, everyone would follow Jesus. Well, not everyone; there will always be those who will not submit themselves to anyone. But more people would undoubtedly embrace Christ as Lord if the bar were set a little lower. But these ethical and moral standards are, frankly, impossible.

That's precisely the point. If we could do this stuff on our own, we wouldn't need God's grace. If we really did completely avoid sin, we wouldn't need forgiveness. If we could save ourselves, we wouldn't need a Savior. But we cannot, and we do, which is something to thank Jesus for as we go to him in worship and prayer.

Follow Christ because he is the Truth—not because the way is easy!

What did you learn about Jesus from this week's readings?

What reading this week had the most impact on you? Why?

What do you plan to do about what you have learned this week?

Key Verse:

DAY 1 The Good in the Bad

A man named Lazarus was sick. He lived in Bethany with his sisters, Mary and Martha. This is the Mary who poured the expensive perfume on the Lord's feet and wiped them with her hair. Her brother, Lazarus, was sick. So the two sisters sent a message to Jesus telling him, "Lord, the one you love is very sick."

But when Jesus heard about it he said, "Lazarus's sickness will not end in death. No, it is for the glory of God. I, the Son of God, will receive glory from this." Although Jesus loved Martha, Mary, and Lazarus, he stayed where he was for the next two days and did not go to them. Finally after two days, he said to his disciples, "Let's go to Judea again."

But his disciples objected. "Teacher," they said, "only a few days ago the Jewish leaders in Judea were trying to kill you. Are you going there again?"

Jesus replied, "There are twelve hours of daylight every day. As long as it is light, people can walk safely. They can see because they have the light of this world. Only at night is there danger of stumbling because there is no light." Then he said, "Our friend Lazarus has fallen asleep, but now I will go and wake him up."

The disciples said, "Lord, if he is sleeping, that means he is getting better!" They thought Jesus meant Lazarus was having a good night's rest, but Jesus meant Lazarus had died.

Then he told them plainly, "Lazarus is dead. And for your sake, I am glad I wasn't there, because this will give you another opportunity to believe in me. Come, let's go see him."

Thomas, nicknamed the Twin, said to his fellow disciples, "Let's go, too—and die with Jesus."   JOHN 11:1-16

The first time we fail a test, are cut from the team, or say good-bye to a friend who is moving, we are hit with the reality that life is tough. Disappointment, deep sorrow, and grief are part of life.

When we go through difficult times—times of illness, suffering, sadness, or even death of a loved one—our first impulse is to cry out, "Why, God? Why did this happen to me [or my loved one]? What is your purpose in all this?"

Frankly, we may never know the reasons for such suffering. It may never seem to make sense in our lives. Or it may be that God is working on a different agenda altogether.

If you had asked him, Lazarus would undoubtedly have preferred not to undergo death. Mary and Martha would not have wanted to be bereft of their brother, even for four days. No one who knew this family would have signed up for this course if it were an elective! But God had other priorities beyond the comfort and momentary happiness of Lazarus, Mary, Martha, and their friends. Jesus spells it out in verse 4, saying that Lazarus's death "is for the glory of God. I, the Son of God, will receive glory from this."

No one wants to suffer. No one wants to lose friends and loved ones. But when a believer faces trials, there is a clear promise in the Bible: God can bring good out of any bad situation. (See Genesis 50:20 and Romans 8:28.) Through these difficulties, we can honor Christ and bring him glory.

Look at your difficulties as opportunities to honor Jesus.

WEEK THIRTY-FOUR | DAY 2 tears of compassion

When Jesus arrived at Bethany, he was told that Lazarus had already been in his grave for four days. Bethany was only a few miles down the road from Jerusalem, and many of the people had come to pay their respects and console Martha and Mary on their loss. When Martha got word that Jesus was coming, she went to meet him. But Mary stayed at home. Martha said to Jesus, "Lord, if you had been here, my brother would not have died. But even now I know that God will give you whatever you ask."

Jesus told her, "Your brother will rise again."

"Yes," Martha said, "when everyone else rises, on resurrection day."

Jesus told her, "I am the resurrection and the life. Those who believe in me, even though they die like everyone else, will live again. They are given eternal life for believing in me and will never perish. Do you believe this, Martha?"

"Yes, Lord," she told him. "I have always believed you are the Messiah, the Son of God, the one who has come into the world from God." Then she left him and returned to Mary. She called Mary aside from the mourners and told her, "The Teacher is here and wants to see you." So Mary immediately went to him.

Now Jesus had stayed outside the village, at the place where Martha met him. When the people who were at the house trying to console Mary saw her leave so hastily, they assumed she was going to Lazarus's grave to weep. So they followed her there. When Mary arrived and saw Jesus, she fell down at his feet and said, "Lord, if you had been here, my brother would not have died."

When Jesus saw her weeping and saw the other people wailing with her, he was moved with indignation and was deeply troubled. "Where have you put him?" he asked them.

They told him, "Lord, come and see." Then Jesus wept. The people who were standing nearby said, "See how much he loved him." But some said, "This man healed a blind man. Why couldn't he keep Lazarus from dying?" JOHN 11:17-37

What makes you cry? Sad movies, cutting onions, bad news? Extreme pain, anger, or frustration?

In many cultures, it's not considered acceptable for adults or young adults, especially men, to cry. It is seen as a sign of weakness or emotional immaturity to express strong feelings in this way. Moreover, many Christians believe it is somehow "unspiritual" to grieve to the point of weeping over the death of a loved one, thinking that it somehow indicates a lack of trust in God.

And yet here in this passage we read of Jesus weeping at the grave of his dear friend Lazarus. Scholars disagree over what exactly caused him to weep: whether it was grief, compassion for Mary and Martha, anger at the lack of faith he saw in the other mourners there at the tomb, or something else. Whatever the cause—*Jesus wept*. He cried real tears, tasted real salt, felt real emotion.

God gave you your ability to feel emotion, even sadness, sorrow, anger, and grief. The Bible describes God as experiencing the full range of emotions that humans experience. It's part of what it means to be made in his image. So while it is possible to be *overly* emotional or even *ruled* by your feelings, the fact that you *have* those feelings is perfectly normal. Just ask Jesus.

Next time you need to cry, remember that Jesus weeps with you.

| DAY 3 **BeLieve It!**

And again Jesus was deeply troubled. Then they came to the grave. It was a cave with a stone rolled across its entrance. "Roll the stone aside," Jesus told them.

But Martha, the dead man's sister, said, "Lord, by now the smell will be terrible because he has been dead for four days."

Jesus responded, "Didn't I tell you that you will see God's glory if you believe?" So they rolled the stone aside. Then Jesus looked up to heaven and said, "Father, thank you for hearing me. You always hear me, but I said it out loud for the sake of all these people standing here, so they will believe you sent me." Then Jesus shouted, "Lazarus, come out!" And Lazarus came out, bound in graveclothes, his face wrapped in a headcloth. Jesus told them, "Unwrap him and let him go!" JOHN 11:38-44

"If you *think you can, or you think you can't, you're probably right."* This old saying makes a very succinct yet accurate statement about the power of *belief*.

Belief is an incredibly powerful force, one of the most potent in the world. Civilizations are built upon and wars are fought over systems of belief. Belief causes one person to fly an airplane into a skyscraper full of people, and another person to run into that building at the risk of his own life to try to save others. Jesus tells Martha that her faith will even determine whether or not she sees the glory of God.

We have a natural tendency to think that our standing with God is determined by our good works or lack thereof. *If you are a good person, God will love you and you will go to heaven. If you are not, he doesn't and you won't.* But the Bible's message is totally contrary to that: you *aren't* good enough, and you never will be, to *earn* God's love. That's why Jesus came—to do for us what we cannot do for ourselves; to perfectly obey his Father and fulfill his requirements of holiness; and to die in our place to make the payment for our sins we could never make.

The question is not whether we're good enough; we're not. The only question is, do we truly believe in Jesus, who alone has power over life and death?

Faith in Jesus is the only solution to a sinful world.

| DAY 4 | worLdLy sacrifice

Many of the people who were with Mary believed in Jesus when they saw this happen. But some went to the Pharisees and told them what Jesus had done. Then the leading priests and Pharisees called the high council together to discuss the situation. "What are we going to do?" they asked each other. "This man certainly performs many miraculous signs. If we leave him alone, the whole nation will follow him, and then the Roman army will come and destroy both our Temple and our nation."

And one of them, Caiaphas, who was high priest that year, said, "How can you be so stupid? Why should the whole nation be destroyed? Let this one man die for the people."

This prophecy that Jesus should die for the entire nation came from Caiaphas in his position as high priest. He didn't think of it himself; he was inspired to say it. It was a prediction that Jesus' death would be not for Israel only, but for the gathering together of all the children of God scattered around the world.

So from that time on the Jewish leaders began to plot Jesus' death. As a result, Jesus stopped his public ministry among the people and left Jerusalem. He went to a place near the wilderness, to the village of Ephraim, and stayed there with his disciples.

It was now almost time for the celebration of Passover, and many people from the country arrived in Jerusalem several days early so they could go through the cleansing ceremony before the Passover began. They wanted to see Jesus, and as they talked in the Temple, they asked each other, "What do you think? Will he come for the Passover?" Meanwhile, the leading priests and Pharisees had publicly announced that anyone seeing Jesus must report him immediately so they could arrest him.   JOHN 11:45-57

Every day you probably run into someone—the secretary in the school office, the clerk at the grocery store, or the teller at the bank—who chirps, "Have a nice day!" The words just roll off their tongues without any real meaning, but imagine when you *actually have* a nice day! All of a sudden that phrase takes on new meaning.

When Caiaphas said, "Why should the whole nation be destroyed? Let this one man die for the people," he had no idea how prophetic his words were. He only meant that it would be better for him and his political allies for Jesus to die rather than continue to threaten their power and influence.

But the truth is that Jesus' death benefits people everywhere, from different tribes, nations, language groups, and cultures the world over. Through him—and only through him—is it possible for men, women, and young people in all parts of the globe to experience the love, joy, forgiveness, peace, and eternal life a relationship with God offers.

As is so often the case throughout the Bible and beyond, what people meant for evil, God used for good. Caiaphas and his associates thought that by killing Jesus they could put an end to him and his influence over people. Instead, they were used by God in plotting the murder of Jesus of Nazareth, thereby opening up a way of salvation that has changed more lives than any other event in history.

When difficult events occur in your life, remember that God's promise extends to you: He will work out *everything* for good for those who love him (see Romans 8:28).

How have you benefited from the one event that has changed the world?

| DAY 5 **DON'T FORGET TO SAY THANKS!**

As Jesus continued on toward Jerusalem, he reached the border between Galilee and Samaria. As he entered a village there, ten lepers stood at a distance, crying out, "Jesus, Master, have mercy on us!"

He looked at them and said, "Go show yourselves to the priests." And as they went, their leprosy disappeared.

One of them, when he saw that he was healed, came back to Jesus, shouting, "Praise God, I'm healed!" He fell face down on the ground at Jesus' feet, thanking him for what he had done. This man was a Samaritan.

Jesus asked, "Didn't I heal ten men? Where are the other nine? Does only this foreigner return to give glory to God?" And Jesus said to the man, "Stand up and go. Your faith has made you well." LUKE 17:11-19

The elevator is out of service; the person at the drive-thru is unclear on the concept of *fast* food; the cable goes out for several hours . . . and we go ballistic! Such inconvenience! Don't they know we're in a hurry? Don't they know we need it *right now*?

All too often we focus on the minor inconveniences of life without realizing how blessed we are to live in a society that has elevators, fast-food restaurants, and vending machines. Most people in the world can only *dream* of having access to elevators, fast food, and cable TV. Instead of going crazy over the irritations we face, we should instead be grateful to God for all his goodness and kindness to us. Gratitude is one of the most endearing qualities anyone can possess, and unfortunately, it seems to be increasingly rare among young people. It is also an essential mark of Christian maturity.

Only one of the ten lepers Jesus healed bothered to say, "Thank you." You may not have been healed of anything as dramatic as leprosy, but Jesus did die for you to forgive your sins and give you eternal life.

Have you said "Thank you" lately?

What did you learn about Jesus from this week's readings?

What reading this week had the most impact on you? Why?

What do you plan to do about what you have learned this week?

Key Verse:

| DAY 1 | Future shock

One day the Pharisees asked Jesus, "When will the Kingdom of God come?"

Jesus replied, "The Kingdom of God isn't ushered in with visible signs. You won't be able to say, 'Here it is!' or 'It's over there!' For the Kingdom of God is among you."

Later he talked again about this with his disciples. "The time is coming when you will long to share in the days of the Son of Man, but you won't be able to," he said. "Reports will reach you that the Son of Man has returned and that he is in this place or that. Don't believe such reports or go out to look for him. For when the Son of Man returns, you will know it beyond all doubt. It will be as evident as the lightning that flashes across the sky. But first the Son of Man must suffer terribly and be rejected by this generation.

"When the Son of Man returns, the world will be like the people were in Noah's day. In those days before the flood, the people enjoyed banquets and parties and weddings right up to the time Noah entered his boat and the flood came to destroy them all.

"And the world will be as it was in the days of Lot. People went about their daily business— eating and drinking, buying and selling, farming and building— until the morning Lot left Sodom. Then fire and burning sulfur rained down from heaven and destroyed them all. Yes, it will be 'business as usual' right up to the hour when the Son of Man returns. On that day a person outside the house must not go into the house to pack. A person in the field must not return to town. Remember what happened to Lot's wife! Whoever clings to this life will lose it, and whoever loses this life will save it. That night two people will be asleep in one bed; one will be taken away, and the other will be left. Two women will be grinding flour together at the mill; one will be taken, the other left."

"Lord, where will this happen?" the disciples asked.

Jesus replied, "Just as the gathering of vultures shows there is a carcass nearby, so these signs indicate that the end is near."   LUKE 17:20-37

You may have seen the TV ads for psychic readers. The camera zooms in on an exotically dressed woman who confidently makes pronouncements about a person's life, such as "You will meet a tall and handsome stranger." Those ads may be laughable, but, in reality, everyone wants to know about the future.

In the Christian community, many books and studies have been written about the future and, in particular, the end times. "When will Jesus return? What will it be like? Do you think he's coming back in our life-time?"

People have lots of questions like these about what will happen in the end times. You may have had similar thoughts. The truth is, however, is that no one knows the exact time, the exact day, or the exact way that everything will unfold. Jesus described the events leading up to the end as "business as usual." In other words, the last day will begin like any other day; nothing unusual will mark it as anything significant.

So how are Christians supposed to respond? Jesus made that answer quite clear—we are to be spiritually and morally ready. We need to live each day as if Jesus were coming back that very hour and be diligent in doing the work he has given us to do.

So don't get caught up in the whys and the hows and the whens. Despite how some Christians talk, no one knows how long it will be until Jesus returns. Until that day, *be ready.*

Make sure you are ready for Jesus' return even as you watch and wait.

| WEEK THIRTY-FIVE | DAY 2 | persistent prayer

One day Jesus told his disciples a story to illustrate their need for constant prayer and to show them that they must never give up. "There was a judge in a certain city," he said, "who was a godless man with great contempt for everyone. A widow of that city came to him repeatedly, appealing for justice against someone who had harmed her. The judge ignored her for a while, but eventually she wore him out. 'I fear neither God nor man,' he said to himself, 'but this woman is driving me crazy. I'm going to see that she gets justice, because she is wearing me out with her constant requests!'"

Then the Lord said, "Learn a lesson from this evil judge. Even he rendered a just decision in the end, so don't you think God will surely give justice to his chosen people who plead with him day and night? Will he keep putting them off? I tell you, he will grant justice to them quickly! But when I, the Son of Man, return, how many will I find who have faith?"

LUKE 18:1-8

You have probably witnessed the following scene at the grocery store: A mom and her toddler are waiting in the checkout line. It's not long before the tot notices the alluring display of candy and begins whining in a loud voice, "I want some candy." The child continues this lament until

232

the mother finally wears down and hands the child some candy, just to get some peace! (Maybe you have even lived this experience at one time or another!)

In this passage Jesus was commending a woman in the parable who was as persistent in her pursuit as was the child asking for candy. The key theme in this parable is persistent prayer, prayer that is tenacious, resolute, dogged, and enduring. Why was the woman finally answered in the parable? Not because of the eloquence of her request. Not because of the urgency of her request. No, Jesus taught that it was because of the persistence of her prayer.

That doesn't mean endlessly repeating your prayer, nor is Jesus suggesting that long prayers are the key to being heard by God. What Jesus is talking about is keeping our requests constantly before the Father, keeping the lines of communication open at all times, and never giving up in bringing our prayers before God.

As we persist in prayer, believing that God will answer us, we can't help but grow in faith, in character, and in hope.

Keep your requests constantly before God in prayer, believing that he will answer you!

WEEK THIRTY-FIVE | DAY 3 ## NO PLace for pride

Then Jesus told this story to some who had great self-confidence and scorned everyone else: "Two men went to the Temple to pray. One was a Pharisee, and the other was a dishonest tax collector. The proud Pharisee stood by himself and prayed this prayer: 'I thank you, God, that I am not a sinner like everyone else, especially like that tax collector over there! For I never cheat, I don't sin, I don't commit adultery, I fast twice a week, and I give you a tenth of my income.'

"But the tax collector stood at a distance and dared not even lift his eyes to heaven as he prayed. Instead, he beat his chest in sorrow, saying, 'O God, be merciful to me, for I am a sinner.' I tell you, this sinner, not the Pharisee, returned home justified before God. For the proud will be humbled, but the humble will be honored." LUKE 18:9-14

Who would you rather hang out with—the know-it-all who constantly reminds everyone of his or her intelligence, or the person who is able to admit to being less than perfect? We all know people like the former, and, quite frankly, those people aren't fun to be around.

Jesus informed his listeners that God rejects people who are spiritually arrogant. In this parable, these two men, different as they are, share common traits. They are both Jews. They both go to the Temple to pray. And they both present themselves to God for his consideration. That's where the similarities end.

The Pharisee wanted to impress God with his personal righteousness, especially in comparison with others. He wasn't interested in getting closer to God—his prayer had no hint of confession or repentance, no sense of reverence or awe in God's presence. In the Scriptures, whenever people *really* come into the presence of God, they experience fear, trembling, bowing, and a keen sense of their own unworthiness (see, for example, Luke 5:8 and Isaiah 6:1-5).

In contrast, the tax collector cried out to God to forgive him for his *lack* of righteousness, and *he* was the one who was made right before God.

This is one of the biggest stumbling blocks people have about becoming Christians: *having to acknowledge their own unworthiness.* But that's where knowing God begins. God gives a choice: humble yourself, and he will exalt you; exalt yourself, and he will humble you.

Avoid singing your own praises; let God lead the chorus!

DAY 4 HOLY Matrimony

Then Jesus left Capernaum and went southward to the region of Judea and into the area east of the Jordan River. As always there were the crowds, and as usual he taught them.

Some Pharisees came and tried to trap him with this question: "Should a man be allowed to divorce his wife?"

"What did Moses say about divorce?" Jesus asked them.

"Well, he permitted it," they replied. "He said a man merely has to write his wife an official letter of divorce and send her away."

But Jesus responded, "He wrote those instructions only as a concession to your hard-hearted wickedness. But God's plan was seen from the beginning of creation, for 'He made them male and female.' 'This explains why a man leaves his father and mother and is joined to his wife, and the two are united into one.' Since they are no longer two but one, let no one separate them, for God has joined them together."

Later, when he was alone with his disciples in the house, they brought up the subject again. He told them, "Whoever divorces his wife and marries someone else commits adultery against her. And if a woman divorces her husband and remarries, she commits adultery." MARK 10:1-12

In the movies, falling in love and getting married looks so *easy*. Or if not easy, at least *funny*. With problems neatly resolved by the end of the film, the happy couple walks off hand-in-hand into the sunset.

Real life is not that simple. In fact, many of your friends—and maybe you—have lived through their parents' divorce. Divorce has become an epidemic that has affected millions of lives and caused deep pain and distress.

Divorce was a fact of life back in Jesus' time as well. The Bible teaches that marriage is God's idea (see Genesis 2:18-25). God instituted marriage, but he *allows* divorce in some circumstances (see Matthew 19:3-10; 1 Corinthians 7:10-16). Marriage, like anything else worthwhile, takes a lot of hard work. We should never enter into it lightly, and we must never leave it lightly, either.

While marriage may seem to you too far off in the future to be thinking about it, it's not. Now is the time to understand how God views marriage and to make a personal commitment to enter into marriage with that same mindset. God regards marriage as a lifelong partnership—we should, too.

Regard marriage as a permanent condition, not just a passing fancy.

| WEEK THIRTY-FIVE | DAY 5 | childLike Faith |

One day some parents brought their children to Jesus so he could touch them and bless them, but the disciples told them not to bother him. But when Jesus saw what was happening, he was very displeased with his disciples. He said to them, "Let the children come to me. Don't stop them! For the Kingdom of God belongs to such as these. I assure you, anyone who doesn't have their kind of faith will never get into the Kingdom of God." Then he took the children into his arms and placed his hands on their heads and blessed them.

MARK 10:13-16

When you see a young child with his or her parents, it is the very picture of trust. A baby doesn't question his mother when she puts him in the car seat and buckles him in. He doesn't ask, "Why are you taking me there? What if I don't want to go? Why don't we go another route?" No, the child sits back and goes wherever the parent takes him.

It's this type of complete trust that Jesus was pointing out to his disciples—the total security that a child has in someone who cares about them.

We are called to have that same kind of trust in our heavenly Father, Jesus said, to trust him completely and totally no matter what the circumstances.

We may never understand all the mysteries on this side of heaven. We may never be able to answer satisfactorily all the whys in our lives. It should be enough for us to know, however, that God loves us so much that he provided a way for the complete forgiveness of our sins through his Son, Jesus Christ.

When we can say with simplicity that we trust God with our very lives, then we can approach him with the childlike faith that Jesus described to his disciples.

Come to the kingdom with the joy and faith of a child—God's child!

What did you learn about Jesus from this week's readings?

What reading this week had the most impact on you? Why?

What do you plan to do about what you have learned this week?

Key Verse:

WEEK THIRTY-SIX

| DAY 1 | ## Good Enough?

As he was starting out on a trip, a man came running up to Jesus, knelt down, and asked, "Good Teacher, what should I do to get eternal life?"

"Why do you call me good?" Jesus asked. "Only God is truly good. But as for your question, you know the commandments: 'Do not murder. Do not commit adultery. Do not steal. Do not testify falsely. Do not cheat. Honor your father and mother.'"

"Teacher," the man replied, "I've obeyed all these commandments since I was a child."

Jesus felt genuine love for this man as he looked at him. "You lack only one thing," he told him. "Go and sell all you have and give the money to the poor, and you will have treasure in heaven. Then come, follow me." At this, the man's face fell, and he went sadly away because he had many possessions.

Jesus looked around and said to his disciples, "How hard it is for rich people to get into the Kingdom of God!" This amazed them. But Jesus said again, "Dear children, it is very hard to get into the Kingdom of God. It is easier for a camel to go through the eye of a needle than for a rich person to enter the Kingdom of God!"

The disciples were astounded. "Then who in the world can be saved?" they asked.

Jesus looked at them intently and said, "Humanly speaking, it is impossible. But not with God. Everything is possible with God."

Then Peter began to mention all that he and the other disciples had left behind. "We've given up everything to follow you," he said.

And Jesus replied, "I assure you that everyone who has given up house or brothers or sisters or mother or father or children or property, for my sake and for the Good News, will receive now in return, a hundred times over, houses, brothers, sisters, mothers, children, and property—with persecutions. And in the world to come they will have eternal life. But many who seem to be important now will be the least important then, and those who are considered least here will be the greatest then." MARK 10:17-31

Who is the person you know who would be the most difficult to reach with the gospel, the guy or girl you can least picture becoming a Christian? Maybe it's some leather-wearing headbanger, the all-state athlete, or the hardest partying kid in your school. Or maybe it's the person who leads the most morally upright, respectable life of anyone around.

Wait a minute. That can't be right . . . can it? Why would a good person be resistant to receiving Jesus as Lord? Precisely because he or she *is* such a good person (humanly speaking). Such people often have real difficulty accepting that they are sinners who really need the salvation purchased on a cross by a real, bleeding, dying Savior. "That's for other people, those who have done really bad things, like murder or robbing banks. I'm good enough on my own," they seem to think.

This rich man was apparently a very good person. Jesus accepted his statement that he had kept the commandments. But there is a difference between external obedience and internal love and devotion, so Jesus cut the heart of the issue: his love for his money. The point was clear and compelling—*your heart only has room for one God.* Who will yours be?

What in your life may be preventing you from wholehearted commitment to Christ?

| DAY 2 | # God's Payment Plan

"For the Kingdom of Heaven is like the owner of an estate who went out early one morning to hire workers for his vineyard. He agreed to pay the normal daily wage and sent them out to work.

"At nine o'clock in the morning he was passing through the marketplace and saw some people standing around doing nothing. So he hired them, telling them he would pay them whatever was right at the end of the day. At noon and again around three o'clock he did the same thing. At five o'clock that evening he was in town again and saw some more people standing around. He asked them, 'Why haven't you been working today?'

"They replied, 'Because no one hired us.'

"The owner of the estate told them, 'Then go on out and join the others in my vineyard.'

"That evening he told the foreman to call the workers in and pay them, beginning with the last workers first. When those hired at five o'clock were paid, each received a full day's wage. When those hired earlier came to get their pay, they assumed they would receive more. But they, too, were paid a day's wage. When they received their pay, they protested, 'Those people worked only one hour, and yet you've paid them just as much as you paid us who worked all day in the scorching heat.'

"He answered one of them, 'Friend, I haven't been unfair! Didn't you agree to work all day for the usual wage? Take it and go. I wanted to pay this last worker the same as you. Is it against the law for me to do what I want with my money? Should you be angry because I am kind?'

"And so it is, that many who are first now will be last then; and those who are last now will be first then." MATTHEW 20:1-16

Suppose you had been hired to paint your neighbor's fence. You agree to the payment and spend one entire Saturday working from morning until dusk to finish the job. Half-way through the day, your neighbor brings in another person to help get the job done. As you're finishing up, the neighbor hires yet *another* painter to touch up the "welcome" sign. No big deals until you discover that the other two each receive the *same* pay as you!

Now put yourself into Jesus' parable. How do you think you would have reacted to the payment scale if you had been one of the first people hired? One of the ones in the middle group? One of the last?

We probably would have felt cheated had we been in the first group hired, had mixed feelings if we were one of the middle bunch, and had some guilt if we were in the last. It goes against our human sense of fairness to see the last workers hired paid equally with the first. And therein lies the problem.

God does not work along the same grid of reward and punishment as we do. *Good thing!* The Bible is clear that if God gave us what we deserved, we would all perish. God deals with us on the basis of *grace*, not *justice*. So whether a person serves Christ faithfully for 80 years or comes to him on his or her deathbed, salvation is the free gift of God. We don't *earn* it; we just *receive* it.

Keep your focus on God's gracious gifts to you and off what he has given to others.

DAY 3 A Role to Play

They were now on the way to Jerusalem, and Jesus was walking ahead of them. The disciples were filled with dread and the people following behind were overwhelmed with fear. Taking the twelve disciples aside, Jesus once more began to describe everything that was about to happen to him in Jerusalem. "When we get to Jerusalem," he told them, "the Son of Man will be betrayed to the leading priests and the teachers of religious law. They will sentence him to die and hand him over to the Romans. They will mock him, spit on him, beat him with their whips, and kill him, but after three days he will rise again." MARK 10:32-34

Suppose you know with absolute certainty that if you visit the neighboring town, a group of thugs is waiting to beat you up. In fact, the probability is quite high that you may even be killed. What would you do? The answer is obvious, isn't it? You wouldn't go near that town, or if you did, you would be with lots of protection.

Jesus knew exactly what was waiting for him in Jerusalem. He knew that he was going to be betrayed. He knew that he would be arrested, tried, and sentenced to die. Before dying a horrible death on the cross, he knew he was going to be ridiculed, beaten, whipped nearly to death. He *knew*. Yet he kept walking.

There were no surprises for Jesus in Jerusalem. He didn't have any false ideas that it was going to be a big celebration and the crowning moment of his ministry. He wasn't hoping that maybe there were some mixed signals from heaven and that God had gotten it all wrong. He *knew*.

So why did he go? Jesus went because he was obedient to his Father. He went because of his great love for us. Christ went because he knew that three days beyond the grave he would rise victorious and defeat Satan and death and sin forever.

It makes no sense to our human way of thinking. In fact, we may never understand this side of heaven the why behind God's plan. But we can thank him that he willingly and lovingly choose to die for us that we may live.

Thank God today for the sacrifice he made for you!

Life with a purpose

Then James and John, the sons of Zebedee, came over and spoke to him. "Teacher," they said, "we want you to do us a favor."

"What is it?" he asked.

"In your glorious Kingdom, we want to sit in places of honor next to you," they said, "one at your right and the other at your left."

But Jesus answered, "You don't know what you are asking! Are you able to drink from the bitter cup of sorrow I am about to drink? Are you able to be baptized with the baptism of suffering I must be baptized with?"

"Oh yes," they said, "we are able!"

And Jesus said, "You will indeed drink from my cup and be baptized with my baptism, but I have no right to say who will sit on the thrones next to mine. God has prepared those places for the ones he has chosen."

When the ten other disciples discovered what James and John had asked, they were indignant. So Jesus called them together and said, "You know that in this world kings are tyrants, and officials lord it over the people beneath them. But among you it should be quite different. Whoever wants to be a leader among you must be your servant, and whoever wants to be first must be the slave of all. For even I, the Son of Man, came here not to be served but to serve others, and to give my life as a ransom for many." MARK 10:35-45

The guidance department at any high school offers a battery of tests to help students discover their interests, their potential, and even pinpoint future careers. The underlying question that accompanies all this test-taking is to help students discover their purpose in life.?

Most people answer that question in terms of what kind of job or career they hope to have, or perhaps goals they have set for themselves. Nothing is wrong with those answers, but they fall short. Your life's purpose should be bigger, deeper, and more profound than any job or career goal.

Jesus' statement to his disciples must have stunned them: *I came here not to be served but to serve others, and to give my life as a ransom for many.* His purpose was not to amass wealth and honors for himself but to give his life way and even die for others, which is the opposite of our all-too-common preoccupation with our own wants and desires!

Jesus came to liberate us from our need to be in control, from our self-centeredness, and our petty little grievances and power struggles. Those tendencies won't go easily; they won't die without a struggle. We have to bring them back to him, to the foot of his cross daily and leave them there. That is why he came, that is why he lived and why he died: to liberate us and set us free from our bondage to sin. His purpose was to die so that we might live.

What is your purpose in life?

| WEEK THIRTY-SIX | DAY 5 | point of view

And so they reached Jericho. Later, as Jesus and his disciples left town, a great crowd was following. A blind beggar named Bartimaeus (son of Timaeus) was sitting beside the road as Jesus was going by. When Bartimaeus heard that Jesus from Nazareth was nearby, he began to shout out, "Jesus, Son of David, have mercy on me!"

"Be quiet!" some of the people yelled at him.

But he only shouted louder, "Son of David, have mercy on me!"

When Jesus heard him, he stopped and said, "Tell him to come here."

So they called the blind man. "Cheer up," they said. "Come on, he's calling you!" Bartimaeus threw aside his coat, jumped up, and came to Jesus.

"What do you want me to do for you?" Jesus asked.

"Teacher," the blind man said, "I want to see!"

And Jesus said to him, "Go your way. Your faith has healed you." And instantly the blind man could see! Then he followed Jesus down the road. MARK 10:46-52

You and a large group of your friends enter a crowded restaurant for lunch. From your point of view, you are a group of hungry people wanting to eat. To the waitress who has to serve you, your group represents a potential tip. To the businessman seeking a quiet lunch, you and your friends may represent a noisy nuisance. It all depends upon your point of view!

The story of blind Bartimaeus is all about point of view. He was a beggar who desperately wanted to be able to see again. He wanted it so much that he was willing to make a nuisance of himself in order to get the attention of Jesus of Nazareth. The multitude saw him as a distraction. The disciples apparently didn't notice him at all. Bartimaeus probably thought of himself as a failure and a burden to others. But Jesus saw him as a broken man in need of healing.

Who were the truly blind people in this story? Where everyone else saw just one more broken down vestige of humanity, Jesus saw a person created in the image of God, a person of worth, dignity, and value.

Jesus always sees the worth of the individual—young or old, dull or intelligent, rich or poor, healthy or diseased. He saw the worth of a blind beggar named Bartimaeus and changed his life.

When you meet a person who is poor, mentally or physically challenged, a social misfit, or just different, what do you see? Someone to avoid or pity, or someone to reach out to in the grace and mercy of our Lord? In God's eyes, we are all like Bartimaeus: blind, broken-down beggars in need of healing. The only difference is, some of us have cried out, "Jesus, Son of David, have mercy on me!"

Try looking at others—and yourself—from Jesus' point of view.

What did you learn about Jesus from this week's readings?

What reading this week had the most impact on you? Why?

What do you plan to do about what you have learned this week?

Key Verse:

DAY 1 The untouchables

Jesus entered Jericho and made his way through the town. There was a man there named Zacchaeus. He was one of the most influential Jews in the Roman tax-collecting business, and he had become very rich. He tried to get a look at Jesus, but he was too short to see over the crowds. So he ran ahead and climbed a sycamore tree beside the road, so he could watch from there.

When Jesus came by, he looked up at Zacchaeus and called him by name. "Zacchaeus!" he said. "Quick, come down! For I must be a guest in your home today."

Zacchaeus quickly climbed down and took Jesus to his house in great excitement and joy. But the crowds were displeased. "He has gone to be the guest of a notorious sinner," they grumbled.

Meanwhile, Zacchaeus stood there and said to the Lord, "I will give half my wealth to the poor, Lord, and if I have overcharged people on their taxes, I will give them back four times as much!"

Jesus responded, "Salvation has come to this home today, for this man has shown himself to be a son of Abraham. And I, the Son of Man, have come to seek and save those like him who are lost." LUKE 19:1-10

Who is the most despised, disliked person you know? What would you think if Jesus came to your school one day (or your job, your neighborhood, etc.) and picked that person out from everyone else and said, "*You!* Come with me"?

That's what happened when Jesus came to Jericho and called out Zacchaeus. Zacchaeus, whose name means "righteous one," was anything but. He was a tax collector, never a popular occupation, and worse, he was a Jew who worked for the hated Romans. He made his living by swindling his countrymen. We probably couldn't find a more despised person in Jericho. And that's who Jesus picked out, even going to his home!

Jesus loves to call the most unlikely people to himself. Maybe because they are more likely to accept his invitation. Maybe because they realize better than others that they have nothing to lose. That person whose face popped into you mind when you read that first question—how might he or she respond if presented with the message of God's love? Could you be the one to present it?

The person others exclude may be the one Jesus wants you to include.

| DAY 2 Playing it safe

The crowd was listening to everything Jesus said. And because he was nearing Jerusalem, he told a story to correct the impression that the Kingdom of God would begin right away. He said, "A nobleman was called away to a distant empire to be crowned king and then return. Before he left, he called together ten servants and gave them ten pounds of silver to invest for him while he was gone. But his people hated him and sent a delegation after him to say they did not want him to be their king.

"When he returned, the king called in the servants to whom he had given the money. He wanted to find out what they had done with the money and what their profits were. The first servant reported a tremendous gain—ten times as much as the original amount! 'Well done!' the king exclaimed. 'You are a trustworthy servant. You have been faithful with the little I entrusted to you, so you will be governor of ten cities as your reward.'

"The next servant also reported a good gain—five times the original amount. 'Well done!' the king said. 'You can be governor over five cities.'

"But the third servant brought back only the original amount of money and said, 'I hid it and kept it safe. I was afraid because you are a hard man to deal with, taking what isn't yours and harvesting crops you didn't plant.'

"'You wicked servant!' the king roared. 'Hard, am I? If you knew so much about me and how tough I am, why didn't you deposit the money in the bank so I could at least get some interest on it?' Then turning to the others standing nearby, the king ordered, 'Take the money from this servant, and give it to the one who earned the most.'

"'But, master,' they said, 'that servant has enough already!'

"'Yes,' the king replied, 'but to those who use well what they are given, even more will be given. But from those who are unfaithful, even what little they have will be taken away. And now about these enemies of mine who didn't want me to be their king—bring them in and execute them right here in my presence.'"   LUKE 19:11-27

The family garden plot is your dad's particular pride and joy. Every year he spends hours planning and buying seeds, working the soil, and caring for the plants as the garden grows. You know how important the garden is to him, so when he asks you to plant some seeds for him one weekend, you take the seeds and put them safely in the top drawer of your desk.

Later in the summer, your dad notices that none of those seeds have come up and he asks you what happened. You tell him, "I know how much you care about your garden and I didn't want any of the seeds to die. So I decided to keep them safe in my desk drawer."

That doesn't make much sense, does it? But that's exactly what the third servant in Jesus' parable did—he played it safe. He knew his master was a tough-minded businessman who didn't like to lose money, so the servant protected himself by burying the master's money and keeping it "safe."

The only problem was that the servant had a job to do—his job was to invest his master's money, like the other two servants did. But he didn't do his job because he was thinking only about himself rather than what his master wanted him to do.

In the same way, Jesus gives each one of us certain talents, abilities, and resources to do his work. We are to use what God has given us for his purposes and not our own. We should be willing to risk everything for his kingdom and not play it safe.

Be willing to risk all you have for the kingdom and not be caught playing it safe.

DAY 3 the cost of worship

WEEK THIRTY-SEVEN

Six days before the Passover ceremonies began, Jesus arrived in Bethany, the home of Lazarus—the man he had raised from the dead. A dinner was prepared in Jesus' honor. Martha served, and Lazarus sat at the table with him. Then Mary took a twelve-ounce jar of expensive perfume made from essence of nard, and she anointed Jesus' feet with it and wiped his feet with her hair. And the house was filled with fragrance.

But Judas Iscariot, one of his disciples—the one who would betray him—said, "That perfume was worth a small fortune. It should have been sold and the money given to the poor." Not that he cared for the poor—he was a thief who was in charge of the disciples' funds, and he often took some for his own use.

Jesus replied, "Leave her alone. She did it in preparation for my burial. You will always have the poor among you, but I will not be here with you much longer."

When all the people heard of Jesus' arrival, they flocked to see him and also to see Lazarus, the man Jesus had raised from the dead. Then the leading priests decided to kill Lazarus, too, for it was because of him that many of the people had deserted them and believed in Jesus. JOHN 12:1-11

"How much did this cost you?"

That's a question you would never ask someone who just gave you a birthday or Christmas present. In one context such a question is appropriate—and that is *worship.*

We often think of worship in terms of what's in it for us: Do we like the music? Are the seats comfortable? Is the sermon interesting? Those questions are legitimate, but they are secondary. The most important issue in worship isn't what we get but what we give. Mary poured out a very expensive jar of perfume and wiped Jesus' feet with her hair, an expensive act or servanthood, humility, and adoration. In so doing, she set an excellent example for all who worship.

When we worship, the issue is not as much about us and what we take from a worship service as what we put into it. In worship, do we sing exuberantly, pray fervently, give sacrificially, and listen intently? Or do we simply go through the motions, putting as little effort into it as possible? When you leave the worship service this Sunday, don't ask, "What did I get out of it?" Instead, ask: "What did it cost me?"

God deserves your personal best when it comes to worship.

WEEK THIRTY-SEVEN | DAY 4 | # A worthy King

As Jesus and the disciples approached Jerusalem, they came to the town of Bethphage on the Mount of Olives. Jesus sent two of them on ahead. "Go into the village over there," he said, "and you will see a donkey tied there, with its colt beside it. Untie them and bring them here. If anyone asks what you are doing, just say, 'The Lord needs them,' and he will immediately send them." This was done to fulfill the prophecy,

"Tell the people of Israel, 'Look, your King is coming to you. He is humble, riding on a donkey—even on a donkey's colt.'"

The two disciples did as Jesus said. They brought the animals to him and threw their garments over the colt, and he sat on it.

Most of the crowd spread their coats on the road ahead of Jesus, and others cut branches from the trees and spread them on the road. He was in the center of the procession, and the crowds all around him were shouting,

"Praise God for the Son of David! Bless the one who comes in the name of the Lord! Praise God in highest heaven!"

The entire city of Jerusalem was stirred as he entered. "Who is this?" they asked.

And the crowds replied, "It's Jesus, the prophet from Nazareth in Galilee."

MATTHEW 21:1-11

Throughout high school, your town has cheered on and supported the hometown football star. Even when he went away to the state college, many in the town followed his career and supported him. Now the hometown hero is playing semipro football and is returning to play—this time for the opposing team. As he takes the field against the town favorites, the cheers suddenly have turned to boos.

Jesus knew what that felt like. At the beginning of the week, the crowds stretched along the dusty road, waving their palm branches, and cheering Jesus as he rode past them on a donkey. A few days later, another crowd gathered and yelled just as loudly—for Jesus to be put to death. Where had all of Jesus' so-called fans go?

When it became apparent that Jesus was not going to be crowned the next king of Israel, and in fact, had become Public Enemy Number One, the crowds deserted him. They switched allegiance and ran away as fast as they could when they realized that Jesus was not going to be the type of king they wanted.

It's easy to say we are for Jesus when life is going well for us or when we are with the "crowd" that is cheering Jesus on. But what happens when difficulties enter our life and Jesus doesn't meet our expectations? Are we really for Jesus then?

Don't let the crowds or your circumstances sway you from sticking with Jesus.

Stay in his cheering section, and stay true to the King.

| DAY 5 # the ReaL jesus

Jesus entered the Temple and began to drive out the merchants and their customers. He knocked over the tables of the money changers and the stalls of those selling doves. He said, "The Scriptures declare, 'My Temple will be called a place of prayer,' but you have turned it into a den of thieves!"

The blind and the lame came to him, and he healed them there in the Temple. The leading priests and the teachers of religious law saw these wonderful miracles and heard even the little children in the Temple shouting, "Praise God for the Son of David." But they were indignant and asked Jesus, "Do you hear what these children are saying?"

"Yes," Jesus replied. "Haven't you ever read the Scriptures? For they say, 'You have taught children and infants to give you praise.'" Then he returned to Bethany, where he stayed overnight.   MATTHEW 21:12-17

If you attended Sunday school classes as a child, then you probably had a distinct image of Jesus as the loving, kindly Good Shepherd. Singing songs like "Jesus Loves Me," and "Jesus Loves the Little Children" depict a kind, gentle Jesus who welcomes little kids with open arms.

So this passage comes as a rather jarring picture of that same Jesus. Why would Jesus do things like that—knocking over tables and chasing people out of the temple? Maybe he wasn't so meek and mild after all.

By now, if you've really been paying attention, you've discovered that the Jesus we meet in the Bible isn't quite the tame, mild-mannered, politically correct person you may have heard about in church and at Christmastime. The real Jesus was strong and courageous, a man of great passions who would shake things up. His primary concern was not to win popularity contests (although at times he enjoyed tremendous public support), but to honor and glorify his Father in heaven.

The merchants and moneychangers were abusing the people who came to the temple to worship. They exploited their need to bring sacrificial animals, and the noise of their business transactions made it impossible for the Gentiles to worship. (The merchants' and money changers' tables were set up in the Court of the Gentiles.) No wonder Jesus was furious!

We also face choices over whether to seek the approval of people or the glory of God. When those challenges come, we need to ask God for grace to stand with Jesus and be courageous about what we believe.

Help others to see the bold, passionate nature of Jesus in you.

What did you learn about Jesus from this week's readings?

What reading this week had the most impact on you? Why?

What do you plan to do about what you have learned this week?

Key Verse:

| DAY 1 | ## MY way?

Some Greeks who had come to Jerusalem to attend the Passover paid a visit to Philip, who was from Bethsaida in Galilee. They said, "Sir, we want to meet Jesus." Philip told Andrew about it, and they went together to ask Jesus.

Jesus replied, "The time has come for the Son of Man to enter into his glory. The truth is, a kernel of wheat must be planted in the soil. Unless it dies it will be alone—a single seed. But its death will produce many new kernels—a plentiful harvest of new lives. Those who love their life in this world will lose it. Those who despise their life in this world will keep it for eternal life. All those who want to be my disciples must come and follow me, because my servants must be where I am. And if they follow me, the Father will honor them. Now my soul is deeply troubled. Should I pray, 'Father, save me from what lies ahead'? But that is the very reason why I came! Father, bring glory to your name.'

Then a voice spoke from heaven, saying, "I have already brought it glory, and I will do it again." When the crowd heard the voice, some thought it was thunder, while others declared an angel had spoken to him.

Then Jesus told them, "The voice was for your benefit, not mine. The time of judgment for the world has come, when the prince of this world will be cast out. And when I am lifted up on the cross, I will draw everyone to myself." He said this to indicate how he was going to die.

"Die? asked the crowd. "We understood from Scripture that the Messiah would live forever. Why are you saying the Son of Man will die? Who is this Son of Man you are talking about?"

Jesus replied, "My light will shine out for you just a little while longer. Walk in it while you can, so you will not stumble when the darkness falls. If you walk in the darkness, you cannot see where you are going. Believe in the light while there is still time; then you will become children of the light." After saying these things, Jesus went away and was hidden from them.   JOHN 12:20-36

When we receive Christ as Lord, we receive great things from God: forgiveness, peace, assurance, the Holy Spirit to guide and comfort, heaven when we die, and many other wonderful gifts. In exchange, we give up the right to run our own lives however we see fit. That's part of what it means to acknowledge Jesus as Lord: *he's in charge now.*

This is one of the main reasons following Jesus often seems difficult—it involves dying to self, and that can be very painful. We all like to get our own way. When we face situations where we have to submit our wills to God's, we need to be willing to say "Lord, I give you this time, this thought, this desire, this will, in honor of the moment that you died for me."

Dying to self can also be very liberating. It frees us from the tyranny of always having to get our own way. Whether it seems painful or painless, it is the way of the cross, the way of the disciple. "Those who love their life in this world will lose it. Those who despise their life in this world will keep it for eternal life."

What dreams, desires, and plans in your life do you need to die to today for the sake of Jesus?

| DAY 2 Hidden Faith

But despite all the miraculous signs he had done, most of the people did not believe in him. This is exactly what Isaiah the prophet had predicted:
  "Lord, who has believed our message? To whom will the Lord reveal his saving power?"
  But the people couldn't believe, for as Isaiah also said,
  "The Lord has blinded their eyes and hardened their hearts—so their eyes cannot see, and their hearts cannot understand, and they cannot turn to me and let me heal them."
  Isaiah was referring to Jesus when he made this prediction, because he was given a vision of the Messiah's glory. Many people, including some of the Jewish leaders, believed in him. But they wouldn't admit it to anyone because of their fear that the Pharisees would expel them from the synagogue. For they loved human praise more than the praise of God.

JOHN 12:37-43

Imagine being in a situation where everyone in science class believes one theory about the creation of the world, and you believe another. That's not difficult to imagine, is it? If you are a Christian, and serious about your relationship with Jesus, you will undoubtedly find yourself in situations when you are in the minority—maybe even a minority of one.

By this point in Jesus' earthly ministry many people, including some of the Jewish leaders, were convinced that he was indeed the promised Messiah. But they also knew making that belief known would be dangerous, putting them at risk of public ridicule and even excommunication from the synagogue. Rather than risk it, they kept their faith in Jesus to themselves.

How sad! And yet, how typical. All Christians face situations when we have to choose which means more: *the acceptance of people* or *the approval of God.* Peer pressure is for a moment. God's approval is for eternity.

Let others know where you stand on issues of faith—even if it means standing alone.

| DAY 3 | # walk on the light side

Jesus shouted to the crowds, "If you trust me, you are really trusting God who sent me. For when you see me, you are seeing the one who sent me. I have come as a light to shine in this dark world, so that all who put their trust in me will no longer remain in the darkness. If anyone hears me and doesn't obey me, I am not his judge—for I have come to save the world and not to judge it. But all who reject me and my message will be judged at the day of judgment by the truth I have spoken. I don't speak on my own authority. The Father who sent me gave me his own instructions as to what I should say. And I know his instructions lead to eternal life; so I say whatever the Father tells me to say!"   JOHN 12:44-50

If you have ever been camping, at one time or another you probably had to pitch your tent in the dark. You fumble around in the limited light cast by a lantern to find a level piece of ground, and you have to work mainly by feel to put the tent up. You have a vague sense of your surroundings, and it's only in the bright light of day that you can truly and clearly see where you are.

In this passage, Jesus was addressing the spiritual condition of those who trust in him versus those who do not—light versus darkness. Without Jesus in our lives, we are spiritually in the dark. We fumble through our lives with only a vague sense of our true spiritual condition.

Jesus has come "as a light to shine in this dark world," and only in his light, can we truly and clearly see ourselves as we really are—sinners in desperate need of a Savior. When we choose to follow Jesus and trust in him, Christ will light the way before us and show us how to live. His light exposes the sin in our lives and guides us out of the darkness.

Have you allowed Jesus' light to shine in your life? Trust in Jesus and live in the true light.

Let Jesus' light guide you out of the darkness.

| DAY 4 **just for show**

In the morning, as Jesus was returning to Jerusalem, he was hungry, and he noticed a fig tree beside the road. He went over to see if there were any figs on it, but there were only leaves. Then he said to it, "May you never bear fruit again!" And immediately the fig tree withered up.

The disciples were amazed when they saw this and asked, "How did the fig tree wither so quickly?"

Then Jesus told them, "I assure you, if you have faith and don't doubt, you can do things like this and much more. You can even say to this mountain, 'May God lift you up and throw you into the sea,' and it will happen. If you believe, you will receive whatever you ask for in prayer." MATTHEW 21:18-22

Imagine a beautiful box of chocolates—all different shapes and flavors, dark chocolate, white chocolate, sweet-smelling milk chocolate. You carefully select a delectable piece; your mouth waters as you anticipate that first burst of chocolate flavor. You take a bite—and immediately spit it out! Yuck! The chocolate was filled with a liver and spinach paste!

Appearances often can be deceiving. What you see often is not what you get. Jesus was addressing this very issue when he came upon the fruitless fig tree on his way to Jerusalem.

When Jesus cursed the fig tree, he actually was acting out a parable about fruitless religion, or religion without substance. Just as the fig tree looked good from a distance, so did the temple with its impressive building and many activities. On closer inspection, however, the temple, like the tree, was unproductive. Worship in the temple was hollow because it was carried out without meaning or sincerity.

The point is clear. If we just go through the motions of faith—attend church, go to a Bible study, and have a prayer time—without it meaning anything, we will be just like the fig tree. Real faith means being productive for God, working and serving others to advance his kingdom.

Make sure your faith is producing fruit for the kingdom.

| DAY 5 # The Best offense

When Jesus returned to the Temple and began teaching, the leading priests and other leaders came up to him. They demanded, "By whose authority did you drive out the merchants from the Temple? Who gave you such authority?"

"I'll tell you who gave me the authority to do these things if you answer one question," Jesus replied. "Did John's baptism come from heaven or was it merely human?"

They talked it over among themselves. "If we say it was from heaven, he will ask why we didn't believe him. But if we say it was merely human, we'll be mobbed, because the people think he was a prophet." So they finally replied, "We don't know."

And Jesus responded, "Then I won't answer your question either."   MATTHEW 21:23-27

Everyone knows the old expression, "The best defense is a good offense." When someone challenges your Christian faith, answer his questions as best you can . . . *and then ask some questions of your own.*

Believing that Jesus is Lord does pose some intellectual challenges. When people have legitimate questions about what we believe we need to answer those questions honestly, directly, patiently, and compassionately. Blatant unbelief has serious intellectual problems of its own, and Christians need to be willing to lovingly "go on the offensive" in challenging the skeptic. We do this not merely to win the argument but to *win over the person.*

Jesus was a master at taking a question and turning it around on the questioner. In a world increasingly hostile toward the Christian faith, God's people need to learn to do this as well. First Peter 3:15-16 says in part, "Instead, you must worship Christ as Lord of your life. And if you are asked about your Christian hope, always be ready to explain it. But you must do this in a gentle and respectful way."

If you only play defense, the best you can hope for is a 0–0 tie. If we want to win the battle and ultimately the person, we have to play offense like Jesus did.

Go on the offensive for Christ and win others for him.

What did you learn about Jesus from this week's readings?

What reading this week had the most impact on you? Why?

What do you plan to do about what you have learned this week?

Key Verse:

WEEK THIRTY-NINE

| DAY 1 ## what's your track record?

"But what do you think about this? A man with two sons told the older boy, 'Son, go out and work in the vineyard today.' The son answered, 'No, I won't go,' but later he changed his mind and went anyway. Then the father told the other son, 'You go,' and he said, 'Yes, sir, I will.' But he didn't go. Which of the two was obeying his father?"

They replied, "The first, of course."

Then Jesus explained his meaning: "I assure you, corrupt tax collectors and prostitutes will get into the Kingdom of God before you do. For John the Baptist came and showed you the way to life, and you didn't believe him, while tax collectors and prostitutes did. And even when you saw this happening, you refused to turn from your sins and believe him."

MATTHEW 21:28-32

Do you always do everything your parents tell you to do? People who answer yes to that question will probably lie about other things as well.

If we're honest, no one obeys his or her parents 100 percent of the time, first time, all the time. But is your overall track record one that is characterized by obedience, disobedience, total indifference, or what?

Obeying your parents is one key indicator of spiritual maturity. (It is also commanded in Exodus 20:12, the Fifth Commandment.) But it is only one indicator among many that comprise obedience to your heavenly Father, which is the goal of *all* the Commandments.

Do you always do everything God tells you to do, first time, every time? Of course not. No one obeys God 100 percent of the time either. But the same question applies here: is your overall track record one that is characterized by obedience, disobedience, total indifference, or what?

Check your obedience track record and work towards improving it.

Then Jesus began telling them stories: "A man planted a vineyard, built a wall around it, dug a pit for pressing out the grape juice, and built a lookout tower. Then he leased the vineyard to tenant farmers and moved to another country. At grape-picking time he sent one of his servants to collect his share of the crop. But the farmers grabbed the servant, beat him up, and sent him back empty-handed.

"The owner then sent another servant, but they beat him over the head and treated him shamefully. The next servant he sent was killed. Others who were sent were either beaten or killed, until there was only one left—his son whom he loved dearly. The owner finally sent him, thinking, 'Surely they will respect my son.'

"But the farmers said to one another, 'Here comes the heir to this estate. Let's kill him and get the estate for ourselves!' So they grabbed him and murdered him and threw his body out of the vineyard.

"What do you suppose the owner of the vineyard will do?" Jesus asked. "I'll tell you—he will come and kill them all and lease the vineyard to others. Didn't you ever read this in the Scriptures?

'The stone rejected by the builders has now become the cornerstone. This is the Lord's doing, and it is marvelous to see.'"

The Jewish leaders wanted to arrest him for using this illustration because they realized he was pointing at them—they were the wicked farmers in his story. But they were afraid to touch him because of the crowds. So they left him and went away.   MARK 12:1-12

You may have heard some versions of good news/bad news jokes, like the golfing buddies who wonder whether there'll be golf in heaven. One dies, comes back and says to his friend, "The good news is, there's golf in heaven. The bad news is, you're in our foursome tomorrow morning."

This parable is a good news/bad news story. The good news is, God (the owner) has graciously provided a fruitful vineyard in which his people are to work. Notice that it is *his* vineyard, not *ours*. That's a lesson all churches, ministries, their leaders, and all individual Christians should take to heart. The further good news is that God is very patient with those who work in his vineyard. He has sent his servants (the prophets) time after time to remind us who the owner is and what he expects of us. Finally, he sent his Son to make the ultimate amnesty offer, and he ended up on Golgotha's cross.

Hence the bad news. God's patience and longsuffering have a limit. We cannot trample his mercies underfoot forever. Judgment does come, even if we don't like the sound of it. At the end of all of our lives, we stand before a God who is either our Father or our enemy. The choice is ours whether the news is good or bad on that day.

The Good News is that Christ died for you and made it possible for you to have eternal life. The bad news applies if you don't accept the Good News.

| DAY 3 # The Invitation

Jesus told them several other stories to illustrate the Kingdom. He said, "The Kingdom of Heaven can be illustrated by the story of a king who prepared a great wedding feast for his son. Many guests were invited, and when the banquet was ready, he sent his servants to notify everyone that it was time to come. But they all refused! So he sent other servants to tell them, 'The feast has been prepared, and choice meats have been cooked. Everything is ready. Hurry!' But the guests he had invited ignored them and went about their business, one to his farm, another to his store. Others seized his messengers and treated them shamefully, even killing some of them.

"Then the king became furious. He sent out his army to destroy the murderers and burn their city. And he said to his servants, 'The wedding feast is ready, and the guests I invited aren't worthy of the honor. Now go out to the street corners and invite everyone you see.'

"So the servants brought in everyone they could find, good and bad alike, and the banquet hall was filled with guests. But when the king came in to meet the guests, he noticed a man who wasn't wearing the proper clothes for a wedding. 'Friend,' he asked, 'how is it that you are here without wedding clothes?' And the man had no reply. Then the king said to his aides, 'Bind him hand and foot and throw him out into the outer darkness, where there is weeping and gnashing of teeth.' For many are called, but few are chosen."

MATTHEW 22:1-14

If you received an invitation to the inauguration of the President of the United States, politics aside, you probably would consider it an honor and would make every effort to go. Most people would say yes. It is such a privilege to be invited that almost anyone would accept.

Yet how many people hear the call of the gospel and say, "No thanks"? Here it is, as Jesus illustrated in the parable, an invitation from the Creator of the Universe—not just the President of the United States—to attend his Son's wedding banquet. Such an honor! Who would refuse? Sadly, a lot of people in this story do; even more sadly, many people in real life do as well.

The lesson of the parable is clear: when God calls, *answer*. The gracious, longsuffering nature of God is such that he may extend another call, and another, and another . . . but one day time runs out for every person. To state that is not engaging in scare tactics. It is simple, inescapable truth.

Do you sense God speaking to your heart in some way right now? Don't ignore his voice. He may not repeat the message.

When it comes to answering God's invitation, don't put him on call-waiting.

The Right Answer

Then the Pharisees met together to think of a way to trap Jesus into saying something for which they could accuse him. They decided to send some of their disciples, along with the supporters of Herod, to ask him this question: "Teacher, we know how honest you are. You teach about the way of God regardless of the consequences. You are impartial and don't play favorites. Now tell us what you think about this: Is it right to pay taxes to the Roman government or not?"

But Jesus knew their evil motives. "You hypocrites!" he said. "Whom are you trying to fool with your trick questions? Here, show me the Roman coin used for the tax." When they handed him the coin, he asked, "Whose picture and title are stamped on it?"

"Caesar's," they replied.

"Well, then," he said, "give to Caesar what belongs to him. But everything that belongs to God must be given to God." His reply amazed them, and they went away.

MATTHEW 22:15-22

Imagine you're sitting in English class, and the teacher asks the class to write about the main character's motives in the novel you're reading. The teacher gives the class three or four potential motives to write about. As you consider the different options, however, you realize that all appear wrong to you.

In a way the Pharisee's question on taxes, seemingly so straightforward, was meant to trap Jesus into giving a wrong answer. None of the options appeared to be the "right" answer. If Jesus said the people should pay taxes to the hated Romans, he would undoubtedly alienate many of his fellow Jews. If he said no, he would incur the wrath of Rome. Either way, he was set up to lose.

But as before, Jesus refused to allow his adversaries to determine the rules of engagement. In giving his classic reply—"Give to Caesar what belongs to him. But everything that belongs to God must be given to God"—Jesus made a brilliant move. His answer communicated the unmistakable message: *If it bears his image, he has a claim on it.*

What was true of the coin is equally true of humanity: We are made in the image of God (see Genesis 1:26-28). *If it bears his image, he has a claim on it.* All we have and all we are is given to us by the One whose image we bear. That truth should fill us with wonder, awe, and praise for our Creator.

And it should cause us to give back to our Creator what belongs to him—our time, our talents, our love, and our obedience.

Remember whose image you bear, and give God what belongs to him!

DAY 5 trick questions

WEEK THIRTY-NINE

Then some Sadducees stepped forward—a group of Jews who say there is no resurrection after death. They posed this question: "Teacher, Moses gave us a law that if a man dies, leaving a wife but no children, his brother should marry the widow and have a child who will be the brother's heir. Well, there were seven brothers. The oldest married and then died without children. His brother married the widow, but he also died. Still no children. And so it went, one after the other, until each of the seven had married her and died, leaving no children. Finally, the woman died, too. So tell us, whose wife will she be in the resurrection? For all seven were married to her!"

Jesus replied, "Marriage is for people here on earth. But that is not the way it will be in the age to come. For those worthy of being raised from the dead won't be married then. And they will never die again. In these respects they are like angels. They are children of God raised up to new life. But now, as to whether the dead will be raised—even Moses proved this when he wrote about the burning bush. Long after Abraham, Isaac, and Jacob had died, he referred to the Lord as 'the God of Abraham, the God of Isaac, and the God of Jacob.' So he is the God of the living, not the dead. They are all alive to him."

"Well said, Teacher!" remarked some of the teachers of religious law who were standing there. And that ended their questions; no one dared to ask any more. LUKE 20:27-40

If you are faithful in sharing your faith in Christ with others, sooner or later you will encounter someone who is not interested in hearing about it but who *is* interested in trying to trip you up. He or she will pose questions or hypothetical situations designed to demonstrate how implausible your beliefs are. How should you respond?

Jesus' answer to the Sadducees in this passage is quite instructive. The Sadducees weren't really interested in the answer to the dilemma they posed about the woman who married seven brothers in succession. They only wanted to make fun of Jesus' (and others') belief in life after death. Instead of taking the bait, Jesus answered their question in terms they would understand and have to deal with—the clear teaching of Moses that *God is the God of the living,* including Abraham, Isaac, and Jacob, who had been dead hundreds of years at the time Moses wrote those words!

Don't waste time arguing with people who don't want to hear what you have to say. Instead, listen for the question *behind* their questions and lovingly point them to the One who has the answers.

Look for the real issues behind a trick question. Then answer it with Jesus' love and compassion.

What did you learn about Jesus from this week's readings?

What reading this week had the most impact on you? Why?

What do you plan to do about what you have learned this week?

Key Verse:

| DAY 1 ## Laying Down the Law

One of the teachers of religious law was standing there listening to the discussion. He realized that Jesus had answered well, so he asked, "Of all the commandments, which is the most important?"

Jesus replied, "The most important commandment is this: 'Hear, O Israel! The Lord our God is the one and only Lord. And you must love the Lord your God with all your heart, all your soul, all your mind, and all your strength.' The second is equally important: 'Love your neighbor as yourself.' No other commandment is greater than these."

The teacher of religious law replied, "Well said, Teacher. You have spoken the truth by saying that there is only one God and no other. And I know it is important to love him with all my heart and all my understanding and all my strength, and to love my neighbors as myself. This is more important than to offer all of the burnt offerings and sacrifices required in the law."

Realizing this man's understanding, Jesus said to him, "You are not far from the Kingdom of God." And after that, no one dared to ask him any more questions.   MARK 12:28-34

Imagine going to school that has a rule governing every part of your school day. For example, one rule says how many books you can carry between classes, and another one says you can only drink from the water fountain between 10 A.M. and noon. Rules can provide guidance and order, but too many rules can become oppressive.

By the time Jesus came on the scene, the Jewish religious leaders were the arbiters of more than six hundred different laws that governed every aspect of daily life! The religious laws had become an incredible burden for the people to obey, let alone learn. So when this teacher of the law posed his question to Jesus about which commandment was most important, he probably wasn't expecting the answer Jesus gave.

Jesus' answer makes a sharp contrast between God's laws and all the religious regulations. The commandments, Jesus taught, could be summed up in two simple principles: Love God with everything you've got, and love your neighbor. (Check out Deuteronomy 6:5 and Leviticus 19:18.) What could be more basic than that?

When we love God completely and care for others as we do for ourselves, we fulfill the intent and purpose of the Ten Commandments and all the other Old Testament laws. Nothing is cumbersome or burdensome about that.

Let these two principles direct your thoughts, actions, and decisions each day.

DAY 2 In David's Tree

Later, as Jesus was teaching the people in the Temple, he asked, "Why do the teachers of religious law claim that the Messiah will be the son of David? For David himself, speaking under the inspiration of the Holy Spirit, said,
'The LORD said to my Lord, Sit in honor at my right hand until I humble your enemies beneath your feet.'
Since David himself called him Lord, how can he be his son at the same time?" And the crowd listened to him with great interest.   MARK 12:35-37

Researching family trees has become a popular pastime. You probably have relatives who have hit the books to dig up your family history. Maybe they've even put up a website that traces the various branches of your family, going back hundreds of years.

The Jews placed great importance on their family tree, memorizing their lineage back *thousands* of years! They were most interested, however, in the family tree of the promised Messiah, a descendant of King David's royal line, who would come to rule. The Messiah, in the Jews' minds, would be the "son of David." When Jesus pointed out that David actually called the Messiah his *Lord,* he was making the startling statement that he existed before David was born!

Jesus isn't just another link in David's family chain—he's the Son of God. The Jews thought they knew something about the Messiah's background. They were right—Jesus *did* come from a royal line. But they wouldn't listen to what *Jesus* said about himself. He claimed to be king not only of the Jews but also over *all* heaven and earth.

If we try to think of Jesus as just a "good guy" or "teacher" we'll also miss the big picture. Could a truly "good teacher" call himself God if he really wasn't? Jesus made some big statements about his *real* family heritage in the Scriptures. Take a look. Then honestly ask yourself: Who do I believe Jesus is?

Find out what Jesus says about himself in his Word. Then decide to follow him as your Lord.

| DAY 3 showtime

Then Jesus said to the crowds and to his disciples, "The teachers of religious law and the Pharisees are the official interpreters of the Scriptures. So practice and obey whatever they say to you, but don't follow their example. For they don't practice what they teach. They crush you with impossible religious demands and never lift a finger to help ease the burden.

"Everything they do is for show. On their arms they wear extra wide prayer boxes with Scripture verses inside, and they wear extra long tassels on their robes. And how they love to sit at the head table at banquets and in the most prominent seats in the synagogue! They enjoy the attention they get on the streets, and they enjoy being called 'Rabbi.' Don't ever let anyone call you 'Rabbi,' for you have only one teacher, and all of you are on the same level as brothers and sisters. And don't address anyone here on earth as 'Father,' for only God in heaven is your spiritual Father. And don't let anyone call you 'Master,' for there is only one master, the Messiah. The greatest among you must be a servant. But those who exalt themselves will be humbled, and those who humble themselves will be exalted.

MATTHEW 23:1-12

As you and your friend are sitting around talking at the lunch table, a new student walks up and joins you for a few minutes. Everyone is chatty and friendly, but as soon as the new student walks away, watch out! Your friend begins to unload about what a nerd that new kid is, leaving you to wonder what's going on.

We have a tendency to "act" before others. We want to impress them, so we say the right words, smile, and act friendly so others will think well of us. We withhold what we really think about a person and try to put on our best face when we're around others we don't know very well.

In this passage, though, Jesus was addressing a far more serious type of "putting on your best face." Some of the religious leaders at that time were known for their impressive spirituality. They said the right words, they made all the right sacrifices, and they attending all the right temple gatherings. They *looked* holy enough, but they weren't the least bit concerned about *being* holy.

It was, as Jesus said, a show—meant to impress those outside. But it didn't fool Jesus then, and it still doesn't today. Some people say they know a lot about the Bible, but their lives and their actions tell another story.

If we truly are committed to following Jesus, then what we do and say better be for real and not just for show.

Make sure your actions match your beliefs.

WEEK FORTY | DAY 4 **BLinded to the Truth**

"Blind guides! How terrible it will be for you! For you say that it means nothing to swear 'by God's Temple'—you can break that oath. But then you say that it is binding to swear 'by the gold in the Temple.' Blind fools! Which is greater, the gold, or the Temple that makes the gold sacred? And you say that to take an oath 'by the altar' can be broken, but to swear 'by the gifts on the altar' is binding! How blind! For which is greater, the gift on the altar, or the altar that makes the gift sacred? When you swear 'by the altar,' you are swearing by it and by everything on it. And when you swear 'by the Temple,' you are swearing by it and by God, who lives in it. And when you swear 'by heaven,' you are swearing by the throne of God and by God, who sits on the throne.

"How terrible it will be for you teachers of religious law and you Pharisees. Hypocrites! For you are careful to tithe even the tiniest part of your income, but you ignore the important things of the law—justice, mercy, and faith. You should tithe, yes, but you should not leave undone the more important things. Blind guides! You strain your water so you won't accidentally swallow a gnat; then you swallow a camel!

"How terrible it will be for you teachers of religious law and you Pharisees. Hypocrites! You are so careful to clean the outside of the cup and the dish, but inside you are filthy—full of greed and self-indulgence! Blind Pharisees! First wash the inside of the cup, and then the outside will become clean, too."   MATTHEW 23:16-26

The saying "You can't see the forest for the trees" typically refers to someone who is so focused on the details of a particular project or event that he or she is unable to grasp the bigger picture. That person is unable to "see" what is most important.

The religious leaders in this passage were so focused on the minutiae and crossing every religious "T" and dotting every "I" that they entirely missed what was most important to God. Yes, Jesus said, they gave their money as was required, but they overlooked the more important aspects of what God really wanted—to show justice and mercy to others and act in faith. In fact, they were so far off that Jesus called them blind—they were blinded to the God's greater truth.

We act the same way when we refuse to listen to what God is telling us about ourselves. Sometimes that message may come during a sermon at church or in a casual discussion during youth group. We may hear what is being said, but like the Pharisees, ignore it either because we don't see how it applies to us or because we're too focused on the details and the to-do's of our daily routines that we overlook what is more important to God.

When we close ourselves off to God's truth, we become blind ourselves. Without God's Word guiding us, we will wander and stumble like those without sight.

Avoid spiritual blindness by focusing on God's truth.

DAY 5   Hypocrites!
WEEK FORTY

"How terrible it will be for you teachers of religious law and you Pharisees. Hypocrites! You are like whitewashed tombs—beautiful on the outside but filled on the inside with dead people's bones and all sorts of impurity. You try to look like upright people outwardly, but inside your hearts are filled with hypocrisy and lawlessness.

"How terrible it will be for you teachers of religious law and you Pharisees. Hypocrites! For you build tombs for the prophets your ancestors killed and decorate the graves of the godly people your ancestors destroyed. Then you say, 'We never would have joined them in killing the prophets.'

"In saying that, you are accusing yourselves of being the descendants of those who murdered the prophets. Go ahead. Finish what they started. Snakes! Sons of vipers! How will you escape the judgment of hell? I will send you prophets and wise men and teachers of religious law. You will kill some by crucifixion and whip others in your synagogues, chasing them from city to city. As a result, you will become guilty of murdering all the godly people from righteous Abel to Zechariah son of Barachiah, whom you murdered in the Temple between the altar and the sanctuary. I assure you, all the accumulated judgment of the centuries will break upon the heads of this very generation."   MATTHEW 23:27-36

Asked to identify the worst possible criminals in society, where would you look first? Most likely, you would direct someone to the nearest prison that housed convicted murderers, kidnappers, and the like. You probably would not send someone to your church or your youth group or Bible study.

Yet in this passage, Jesus reserved his harshest words and judgment for the religious leaders of his day—the type of people that would most likely be found in the places we hang out every week. Jesus did not mince words when he addressed the Pharisees and religious leaders, repeatedly calling them hypocrites and whitewashed tombs—clean on the outside but dead on the inside.

A hypocrite is someone who fakes who they really are on the *inside*. What's so bad about that? Aren't they only hurting themselves? Not if they are in a position of leadership, as the Pharisees were. By consistently choosing to deceive others about their spirituality, the Pharisees were actively leading others to follow them and leading others away from God.

You probably haven't done anything that would make a policeman, let alone a pastor, bat an eyelid. But who are you *really* on the inside? If all your thoughts could be heard out loud, how would people look at you differently? The Pharisees thought if they *acted* religious, they wouldn't have to worry about important things like holiness, justice, and love. But love and justice are the things that God cares the *most* about. In your inner heart, how much do you care about those things?

Ask God to renew your life from the inside out.

What did you learn about Jesus from this week's readings?

What reading this week had the most impact on you? Why?

What do you plan to do about what you have learned this week?

Key Verse:

WEEKFORTY-ONE

| DAY 1 ## Refusing to be Rescued

"O Jerusalem, Jerusalem, the city that kills the prophets and stones God's messengers! How often I have wanted to gather your children together as a hen protects her chicks beneath her wings, but you wouldn't let me. And now look, your house is left to you, empty and desolate. For I tell you this, you will never see me again until you say, 'Bless the one who comes in the name of the Lord!'"   MATTHEW 23:37-39

Coming right after Jesus had blasted the Pharisees and religious leaders for their blindness and hypocrisy, this short passage offers a startling contrast. We can almost hear the anguish, the pleading in Jesus' voice for his people to come to him for protection and safety before it was too late—and knowing that they would not.

Through these past several passages, we experience a Savior who was both consumed with anger at the religious leaders who were leading the people away from God, and at the same time burned with compassion for his people. We see what broke Jesus' heart and his deep love for both the city and the people.

This passage is a wonderful word picture of how God looks at us and feels about us. Imagine Jesus looking at your school, at your neighborhood, at your community. What would break his heart today? What would anger him? What would make him plead with anguish for us to turn around and come to him for protection?

We worship a God who cares deeply about our hurts and our sinfulness. He is ready and willing to offer us comfort, forgiveness, and help. When you feel hurt and don't know where to turn, remember your Savior, who aches to gather you under his protection as a hen gathers her chicks.

Jesus wants to protect you if you will come to him.

Giving Styles

Jesus went over to the collection box in the Temple and sat and watched as the crowds dropped in their money. Many rich people put in large amounts. Then a poor widow came and dropped in two pennies. He called his disciples to him and said, "I assure you, this poor widow has given more than all the others have given. For they gave a tiny part of their surplus, but she, poor as she is, has given everything she has."   MARK 12:41-44

Walk around a college campus or community and evidence is everywhere of people's generosity—a hospital wing to care for cancer victims, a brand-new library building, a research center, all proudly bearing the name of the donor. What motivated these people to give? Perhaps they had lost a loved one to cancer or wanted to give something back to the community. Maybe they wanted the prestige of having their name on a prominent building.

Whatever the reason, it's true that what motivates giving will differ from person to person. In this short passage, Jesus remarked on two different giving styles, contrasting the rich people who gave large amounts and the poor widow who just dropped in two small coins. The rich gave out of their surplus. It was no big deal for them to give several dozen coins into the temple coffers. The widow, however, Jesus said, gave *everything* she had.

It wasn't the *size* of the gift that mattered to Jesus. It was the heart behind the giving. The poor widow not only gave all she had, but she also gave it willingly to God. It wasn't a chance to show her neighbors how important she was like some of her wealthier counterparts. Her gift was given in love and worship to her heavenly Father.

Giving is an indication of what's important to us. When we give a small portion of what we have, we're no different than the rich people in the passage who gave what was convenient for them. When you give with a thankful attitude and sacrificially, like the widow, your gift, no matter how small or large, will please God.

Give to God with a thankful and generous heart.

| DAY 3 Beware of Fakes

As Jesus was leaving the Temple grounds, his disciples pointed out to him the various Temple buildings. But he told them, "Do you see all these buildings? I assure you, they will be so completely demolished that not one stone will be left on top of another!"

Later, Jesus sat on the slopes of the Mount of Olives. His disciples came to him privately and asked, "When will all this take place? And will there be any sign ahead of time to signal your return and the end of the world?"

Jesus told them, "Don't let anyone mislead you. For many will come in my name, saying, 'I am the Messiah.' They will lead many astray. And wars will break out near and far, but don't panic. Yes, these things must come, but the end won't follow immediately. The nations and kingdoms will proclaim war against each other, and there will be famines and earthquakes in many parts of the world. But all this will be only the beginning of the horrors to come.

"Then you will be arrested, persecuted, and killed. You will be hated all over the world because of your allegiance to me. And many will turn away from me and betray and hate each other. And many false prophets will appear and will lead many people astray. Sin will be rampant everywhere, and the love of many will grow cold. But those who endure to the end will be saved. And the Good News about the Kingdom will be preached throughout the whole world, so that all nations will hear it; and then, finally, the end will come.

"The time will come when you will see what Daniel the prophet spoke about: the sacrilegious object that causes desecration standing in the holy place"—reader, pay attention! "Then those in Judea must flee to the hills. A person outside the house must not go inside to pack. A person in the field must not return even to get a coat. How terrible it will be for pregnant women and for mothers nursing their babies in those days. And pray that your flight will not be in winter or on the Sabbath. For that will be a time of greater horror than anything the world has ever seen or will ever see again. In fact, unless that time of calamity is shortened, the entire human race will be destroyed. But it will be shortened for the sake of God's chosen ones.

"Then if anyone tells you, 'Look, here is the Messiah" or 'There he is,' don't pay any attention. For false messiahs and false prophets will rise up and perform great miraculous signs and wonders so as to deceive, if possible, even God's chosen ones. See, I have warned you." MATTHEW 24:1-25

Every so often there's an account in the newspaper of a person who tries to pass himself or herself off as someone famous. For a time, this phony is able to convince others that he or she is the real deal, using the person's credit cards, assuming the person's identity, until that person is caught and exposed as a fake.

These stories are fascinating, because after reading them we wonder how the person was able to get away with it? How could everyone be so gullible as to believe the impersonator was real and not fake? It's easy to believe we would never be fooled like that.

The truth is, as Jesus pointed out in this passage, this could easily happen to us in terms of spiritual identity. Jesus clearly warned his followers then and now that many will come and claim to be the Messiah returning. Some will claim to have the truth and the ability to give eternal life to those who follow them. And some will go after the fakes, the imposters.

Doubt that's true? Walk into any bookstore today and check out the titles. There are any number of authors and religious experts who claim to have the truth. That's why Jesus gave us this warning—he wanted us to be ready and alert to these fake teachers and false offers of truth.

This passage is a strong reminder that there is only one God, one Son, and only one way to eternal life. As Jesus warned, don't be deceived. Check the claims of others against the truth of God's Word.

Many claim to have truth. Only One does.

| DAY 4 Are you the Messiah?

"So if someone tells you, 'Look, the Messiah is out in the desert,' don't bother to go and look. Or, 'Look, he is hiding here,' don't believe it! For as the lightning lights up the entire sky, so it will be when the Son of Man comes. Just as the gathering of vultures shows there is a carcass nearby, so these signs indicate that the end is near.

"Immediately after those horrible days end, the sun will be darkened, the moon will not give light, the stars will fall from the sky, and the powers of heaven will be shaken.

And then at last, the sign of the coming of the Son of Man will appear in the heavens, and there will be deep mourning among all the nations of the earth. And they will see the Son of Man arrive on the clouds of heaven with power and great glory. And he will send forth his angels with the sound of a mighty trumpet blast, and they will gather together his chosen ones from the farthest ends of the earth and heaven.

"Now learn a lesson from the fig tree. When its buds become tender and its leaves begin to sprout, you know without being told that summer is near. Just so, when you see the events I've described beginning to happen, you can know his return is very near, right at the door. I assure you, this generation will not pass from the scene before all these things take place. Heaven and earth will disappear, but my words will remain forever." MATTHEW 24:26-35

In Are *You My Mother?*, Dr. Seuss wrote about a baby bird who had lost its mother. In an effort to find its mom, the baby bird asks everything from a dog to a bulldozer, "Are *you* my mother?" The tiny bird is confused about the identity of the most important person in its life.

People often are confused about Jesus' identify—whether he is, in fact, God, or just another great moral teacher. But eventually, no one will question his identify. The sky will split open, and everyone will come face to face with the Messiah's glory and power. Just like an earthquake is impossible to ignore, Jesus' return won't be a secret! *Everyone* will see.

Yet, even with the promise of Christ's amazing comeback, attractive promises of freedom *here on earth* still hypnotize some people. Instead of expectantly waiting for Christ, they get antsy and start believing other popular teachings. Their hope and attention are directed away from Jesus. But these "Messiahs" can never save us. Only Christ, whose return *everyone on earth* will know, can give us total freedom.

What "messiahs" tempt you away from Jesus? Make sure you are ready for his return by remaining faithful and trusting only in him.

Live as though Jesus is coming back today. Be ready for his return.

DAY 5 caught by surprise?
WEEK FORTY-ONE

"However, no one knows the day or the hour when these things will happen, not even the angels in heaven or the Son himself. Only the Father knows.

"When the Son of Man returns, it will be like it was in Noah's day. In those days before the Flood, the people were enjoying banquets and parties and weddings right up to the time Noah entered his boat. People didn't realize what was going to happen until the Flood came and swept them all away. That is the way it will be when the Son of Man comes.

"Two men will be working together in the field; one will be taken, the other left. Two women will be grinding flour at the mill; one will be taken, the other left. So be prepared, because you don't know what day your Lord is coming.

"Know this: A homeowner who knew exactly when a burglar was coming would stay alert and not permit the house to be broken into. You also must be ready all the time. For the Son of Man will come when least expected.

"Who is a faithful, sensible servant, to whom the master can give the responsibility of managing his household and feeding his family? If the master returns and finds that the servant has done a good job, there will be a reward. I assure you, the master will put that servant in charge of all he owns. But if the servant is evil and thinks, 'My master won't be back for a while,' and begins oppressing the other servants, partying, and getting drunk—well, the master will return unannounced and unexpected. He will tear the servant apart and banish him with the hypocrites. In that place there will be weeping and gnashing of teeth."

MATTHEW 24:36-51

"Time for a pop quiz!" It's one of the worst phrases to hear from your teacher, especially in the morning. Suddenly, your mind starts racing, *"What was I supposed to have studied? Why did I go out last night? Why aren't pop quizzes outlawed in my state?"* A lot of teachers (to our dismay) enjoy giving pop quizzes. It's all in the surprise—everyone's true knowledge of a subject is revealed immediately.

Jesus' return to earth won't have any warning either. No human knows when Christ will appear. Why all the secrecy? Just like our inability to fake in pop-quizzes, Christ's unexpected coming will reveal his true disciples.

Think of it this way. If we knew the exact time Jesus was coming back, we might wait until the last minute to confess our sins. That wouldn't be real repentance. That little prayer would be as unimportant to us as buying a bus ticket. On the other hand, the prospect of the faithful disappearing in front of the unfaithful should cause us to seriously consider our relationship with Christ. Jesus will come in the blink of an eye. Those who aren't ready will be left behind.

Are you ready for Jesus' return?

Don't let Jesus' return catch you by surprise.

What did you learn about Jesus from this week's readings?

What reading this week had the most impact on you? Why?

What do you plan to do about what you have learned this week?

Key Verse:

| DAY 1 | ## Late for the party |

"The Kingdom of Heaven can be illustrated by the story of ten bridesmaids who took their lamps and went to meet the bridegroom. Five of them were foolish, and five were wise. The five who were foolish took no oil for their lamps, but the other five were wise enough to take along extra oil. When the bridegroom was delayed, they all lay down and slept. At midnight they were roused by the shout, 'Look, the bridegroom is coming! Come out and welcome him!'

"All the bridesmaids got up and prepared their lamps. Then the five foolish ones asked the others, 'Please give us some of your oil because our lamps are going out.' But the others replied, 'We don't have enough for all of us. Go to a shop and buy some for yourselves.'

"But while they were gone to buy oil, the bridegroom came, and those who were ready went in with him to the marriage feast, and the door was locked. Later, when the other five bridesmaids returned, they stood outside, calling, 'Sir, open the door for us!' But he called back, 'I don't know you!'

"So stay awake and be prepared, because you do not know the day or hour of my return."

MATTHEW 25:1-13

"Fashionably late" is an everlasting rule when it comes to parties. Show up too early, and you might look a little too eager or even (gasp) desperate. It's a good idea to be *just* a little late. Be careful though. Sometimes being *too* late for the party means missing out on more than you could imagine.

Jesus set the scene of this story at the reception feast after the wedding. Of course, the bridesmaids wanted to get in on the party (and the food) after the wedding! So they waited around outside for the groom to show up and invite them in. Hours later, when he *finally* arrived, only five of bridesmaids were ready to greet him. The other five had to go on a last-minute shopping run. They missed their chance to join in the party because they weren't ready.

Another party is coming up. Similar to the groom in the story, Jesus *promises* to arrive at an unexpected time. The point is, we need to be ready. When Jesus comes to gather the faithful, we won't have time to get our lives in order. Our relationship with God must begin growing before that time.

If you knew that Jesus was returning tomorrow, what would you change today? Be ready!

| DAY 2 cashing in

"Again, the Kingdom of Heaven can be illustrated by the story of a man going on a trip. He called together his servants and gave them money to invest for him while he was gone. He gave five bags of gold to one, two bags of gold to another, and one bag of gold to the last—dividing it in proportion to their abilities—and then left on his trip. The servant who received the five bags of gold began immediately to invest the money and soon doubled it. The servant with two bags of gold also went right to work and doubled the money. But the servant who received the one bag of gold dug a hole in the ground and hid the master's money for safekeeping.

"After a long time their master returned from his trip and called them to give an account of how they had used his money. The servant to whom he had entrusted the five bags of gold said, 'Sir, you gave me five bags of gold to invest, and I have doubled the amount.' The master was full of praise. 'Well done, my good and faithful servant. You have been faithful in handling this small amount, so now I will give you many more responsibilities. Let's celebrate together!'

"Next came the servant who had received the two bags of gold, with the report, 'Sir, you gave me two bags of gold to invest, and I have doubled the amount.' The master said, 'Well done, my good and faithful servant. You have been faithful in handling this small amount, so now I will give you many more responsibilities. Let's celebrate together!'

"Then the servant with the one bag of gold came and said, 'Sir, I know you are a hard man, harvesting crops you didn't plant and gathering crops you didn't cultivate. I was afraid I would lose your money, so I hid it in the earth and here it is.'

"But the master replied, 'You wicked and lazy servant! You think I'm a hard man, do you, harvesting crops I didn't plant and gathering crops I didn't cultivate? Well, you should at least have put my money into the bank so I could have some interest. Take the money from this servant and give it to the one with the ten bags of gold. To those who use well what they are given, even more will be given, and they will have an abundance. But from those who are unfaithful, even what little they have will be taken away. Now throw this useless servant into outer darkness, where there will be weeping and gnashing of teeth.'"

MATTHEW 25:14-30

What's the first thing you do when a relative sends you a birthday check in the mail? You head to the bank to cash it or put it into savings. If you leave the check tucked away in your room, you won't really benefit from your relative's present (and you risk hurting their feelings). If you don't open or "cash" any gift, then you just waste it.

In this parable, Jesus tells of three servants, each given money to invest for his master. The master *trusted* his servants with this responsibility. Their job was to make a profit for their boss. The exact *amount* of profit really didn't matter; just that his servants made their investments.

God has given every person a set of talents. On top of that, he also gives everyone *opportunities* to invest those talents, to use them to honor him. A responsible person uses his or her talents and abilities to faithfully serve others. When Jesus returns, he will ask everyone to give an account of his or her "profits." Either we will point to specific people we've served and helped, or we'll offer him nothing.

What talents has God given you? How can you use your talents to serve God and help others?

God doesn't focus on how much we **start** with, just how much we produce with what we've been given.

| WEEK FORTY-TWO | DAY 3 | # The Real You

"But when the Son of Man comes in his glory, and all the angels with him, then he will sit upon his glorious throne. All the nations will be gathered in his presence, and he will separate them as a shepherd separates the sheep from the goats. He will place the sheep at his right hand and the goats at his left. Then the King will say to those on the right, 'Come, you who are blessed by my Father, inherit the Kingdom prepared for you from the foundation of the world. For I was hungry, and you fed me. I was thirsty, and you gave me a drink. I was a stranger, and you invited me into your home. I was naked, and you gave me clothing. I was sick, and you cared for me. I was in prison, and you visited me.'

"Then these righteous ones will reply, 'Lord, when did we ever see you hungry and feed you? Or thirsty and give you something to drink? Or a stranger and show you hospitality? Or naked and give you clothing? When did we ever see you sick or in prison, and visit you?' And the King will tell them, 'I assure you, when you did it to one of the least of these my brothers and sisters, you were doing it to me!'

"Then the King will turn to those on the left and say, 'Away with you, you cursed ones, into the eternal fire prepared for the Devil and his demons! For I was hungry, and you didn't feed me. I was thirsty, and you didn't give me anything to drink. I was a stranger, and you didn't invite me into your home. I was naked, and you gave me no clothing. I was sick and in prison, and you didn't visit me.'

"Then they will reply, 'Lord, when did we ever see you hungry or thirsty or a stranger or naked or sick or in prison, and not help you?' And he will answer, 'I assure you, when you refused to help the least of these my brothers and sisters, you were refusing to help me.' And they will go away into eternal punishment, but the righteous will go into eternal life."

MATTHEW 25:31-46

In your circle of friends, there's probably the one person who always is smiling and who always has something positive to say. You enjoy that person because being nice just comes naturally. That person isn't *trying* to be nice; that person is genuine. You get the strong feeling that if you dropped in unexpectedly on this person, he or she still would be smiling and have something nice to say!

The "real you" comes through when no one else is watching. In this passage, two different groups of people are described—those who took the time to help someone else and those who did not. The common link between the two? Both responded in surprise to Jesus' judgment, "Lord, when did we ever see you hungry, or thirsty, or a stranger, or naked?"

Why were they so surprised? Their actions revealed their true character and nature. The one group *always* took the time to help others and therefore served Jesus. Helping others was second nature for them. It was how they always acted all the time. The same was true for those who ignored the needs of others—it was how they acted all the time.

Which group best describes your "natural" response? When no one is looking, do you stop to help the harried mom pick up her groceries, or do you keep walking? Let God give you a heart that sees the needs of others—and the desire to respond to those needs.

Ask Jesus to give you **his** heart to serve others.

| DAY 4 # conspiracy theory

When Jesus had finished saying these things, he said to his disciples, "As you know, the Passover celebration begins in two days, and I, the Son of Man, will be betrayed and crucified."

At that same time the leading priests and other leaders were meeting at the residence of Caiaphas, the high priest, to discuss how to capture Jesus secretly and put him to death. "But not during the Passover," they agreed, "or there will be a riot."   MATTHEW 26:1-5

Most amusement parks feature a racetrack with cars that you can "drive" around. Each car comes equipped with a steering wheel and a gas pedal that you can operate, but in reality, you aren't in control of the car. The cars are guided through the track via electrical cables and a track that keeps them going in the right direction and a safe distance away from the other cars.

There's an illusion of being in control when really the ride operator could shut down the ride with a flick of the switch. In this short passage, the religious leaders thought that they were in control, when in fact God was in control. He could have shut them down with a word.

The religious leaders thought they were being so clever, meeting together to hatch their plot to capture Jesus and kill him. Little did they know that Jesus already knew what they were planning and knew that it was his Father's plan for him. The leaders were not "driving" the plan; they actually were being led to their actions to fulfill God's plan that had been in place since time began.

Sometimes we operate like we can fool God and think that he doesn't know what's going on in our lives. Nothing can be further from the truth. God is constantly at work in our lives, in our circumstances, and in our plans.

We need to trust him and allow him to guide us. He *will* work out all the details of our lives according to his good and eternal plan.

Let God drive your future.

| DAY 5 **dropouts**

The Festival of Unleavened Bread, which begins with the Passover celebration, was drawing near. The leading priests and teachers of religious law were actively plotting Jesus' murder. But they wanted to kill him without starting a riot, a possibility they greatly feared.

Then Satan entered into Judas Iscariot, who was one of the twelve disciples, and he went over to the leading priests and captains of the Temple guard to discuss the best way to betray Jesus to them. They were delighted that he was ready to help them, and they promised him a reward. So he began looking for an opportunity to betray Jesus so they could arrest him quietly when the crowds weren't around.   LUKE 22:1-6

In most groups there comes a time when it's clear who are the faithful members and who are not. Sometimes it's during a difficult period when membership is down, funds are low, and more is required of each member to make the group continue. At those critical junctures, those who have the least commitment to the group simply drop out.

Jesus had invested a great amount of time, teaching, and energy into his twelve chosen disciples. From all appearances, it seemed the disciples were a close-knit group, committed to following him. But at this critical point in Jesus' ministry, it was clear that one of them was never really part of the group.

Judas, once one of Jesus' closest associates, turned from "friend" to Jesus' worst enemy and agreed to betray Jesus into his enemies' hands. Maybe Judas was motivated by money. Maybe he felt disillusioned by Jesus' constant talk of suffering and his death. Maybe he wanted to test Jesus to see if he really was the Messiah. Difficult times were definitely ahead, and Judas chose to drop out.

The amazing part of this sordid story is that Jesus never dropped out of Judas' life. He continued to love him and to reach out to him. Jesus never blasted Judas or even tried to prevent him from carrying out his plot. Had Judas wanted to return to the group, had he asked for Jesus' forgiveness, he most certainly would have received it.

Jesus not only taught love your enemies. He practiced it. He showed us how it was done in the face of the most painful betrayal—by one of his own.

Loving like Jesus did sometimes requires tough love.

What did you learn about Jesus from this week's readings?

What reading this week had the most impact on you? Why?

What do you plan to do about what you have learned this week?

Key Verse:

WEEKFORTY-THREE

DAY 1 | FinaL instructions

Now the Festival of Unleavened Bread arrived, when the Passover lambs were sacrificed. Jesus sent Peter and John ahead and said, "Go and prepare the Passover meal, so we can eat it together."

"Where do you want us to go?" they asked him.

He replied, "As soon as you enter Jerusalem, a man carrying a pitcher of water will meet you. Follow him. At the house he enters, say to the owner, 'The Teacher asks, Where is the guest room where I can eat the Passover meal with my disciples?' He will take you upstairs to a large room that is already set up. That is the place. Go ahead and prepare our supper there." They went off to the city and found everything just as Jesus had said, and they prepared the Passover supper there.   LUKE 22:7-13

Imagine being handed a set of instructions that make no sense to you at all. Basically you have two options: throw away the instructions and try to accomplish the task your own way; or follow the instructions, as strange as they may seem, and trust that the person who wrote them knew what he or she was talking about.

In this passage Peter and John had been given some pretty strange instructions: Look for a man carrying water, follow him, and then ask him about a room for the Passover. Say what, Jesus? A man carrying water? Almost unheard of. That was a woman's job.

They could have opted to nod their heads and then, once they got into Jerusalem, take matters into their own hands. Or they could trust Jesus. Of course, we know that the disciples chose to trust Jesus, and because they did, they were part of an incredible evening that began a series of events that was to change human history forever.

Sometimes it is our obedience in the small matters, in the seemingly insignificant details, that will lead us to incredible opportunities or life-changing events. Does it seem like there is not much going on spiritually in your life right now? Don't overlook the small tasks God has called you to do right now.

Obey God in the small matters so he can use you for more important ones.

| DAY 2 **Dirty work**

Before the Passover celebration, Jesus knew that his hour had come to leave this world and return to his Father. He now showed the disciples the full extent of his love. It was time for supper, and the Devil had already enticed Judas, son of Simon Iscariot, to carry out his plan to betray Jesus. Jesus knew that the Father had given him authority over everything and that he had come from God and would return to God. So he got up from the table, took off his robe, wrapped a towel around his waist, and poured water into a basin. Then he began to wash the disciples' feet and to wipe them with the towel he had around him.

When he came to Simon Peter, Peter said to him, "Lord, why are you going to wash my feet?"

Jesus replied, "You don't understand now why I am doing it; someday you will."

"No," Peter protested, "you will never wash my feet!"

Jesus replied, "But if I don't wash you, you won't belong to me."

Simon Peter exclaimed, "Then wash my hands and head as well, Lord, not just my feet!"

Jesus replied, "A person who has bathed all over does not need to wash, except for the feet, to be entirely clean. And you are clean, but that isn't true of everyone here." For Jesus knew who would betray him. That is what he meant when he said, "Not all of you are clean."

After washing their feet, he put on his robe again and sat down and asked, "Do you understand what I was doing? You call me 'Teacher' and 'Lord,' and you are right, because it is true. And since I, the Lord and Teacher, have washed your feet, you ought to wash each other's feet. I have given you an example to follow. Do as I have done to you. How true it is that a servant is not greater than the master. Nor are messengers more important than the one who sends them. You know these things—now do them! That is the path of blessing"

"I am not saying these things to all of you; I know so well each one of you I chose. The Scriptures declare, 'The one who shares my food has turned against me,' and this will soon come true. I tell you this now, so that when it happens you will believe I am the Messiah. Truly, anyone who welcomes my messenger is welcoming me, and anyone who welcomes me is welcoming the Father who sent me." JOHN 13:1-20

When it comes to chores, what's the one job you hate doing the most? Washing dishes? Mowing the lawn? How about cleaning the bathroom? Every family has jobs to do, and *someone* has to do them. How would you feel getting stuck doing your least favorite chore every day?

Footwashing was one of the most disliked household chores in Jesus' day. In some homes, when guests entered a house, they would remove their sandals and have their feet washed. Naturally, the lowliest servants were handed this duty.

Yet here at the Passover feast, Jesus himself, the King of Heaven, got down on his hands and knees to wash his disciples' feet! Jesus was giving them, and us, a lesson. Those who want to follow Jesus are to humble themselves and *serve* others just as he did. The Christian life involves glorifying God by serving others.

Footwashing in Jesus' time translates into the hundreds of "dirty" tasks we can do today to help our family or neighbors. Sometimes doing the least-wanted job with a good attitude can show people how much God's love changes our hearts.

Pray for the right kind of heart to serve others as Jesus did.

| DAY 3 ## who's number one?

Then at the proper time Jesus and the twelve apostles sat down together at the table. Jesus said, "I have looked forward to this hour with deep longing, anxious to eat this Passover meal with you before my suffering begins. For I tell you now that I won't eat it again until it comes to fulfillment in the Kingdom of God."

Then he took a cup of wine, and when he had given thanks for it, he said, "Take this and share it among yourselves. For I will not drink wine again until the Kingdom of God has come."

Then he took a *loaf* of bread; and when he had thanked God for it, he broke it in pieces and gave it to the disciples, saying, "This is my body, given for you. Do this in remembrance of me." After supper he took another cup of wine and said, "This wine is the token of God's new covenant to save you—an agreement sealed with the blood I will pour out for you.

"But here at this table, sitting among us as a friend, is the man who will betray me. For I, the Son of Man, must die since it is part of God's plan. But how terrible it will be for my betrayer!" Then the disciples began to ask each other which of them would ever do such a thing.

And they began to argue among themselves as to who would be the greatest in the coming Kingdom. Jesus told them, "In this world the kings and great men order their people around, and yet they are called 'friends of the people.' But among you, those who are the greatest should take the lowest rank, and the leader should be like a servant. Normally the master sits at the table and is served by his servants. But not here! For I am your servant. You have remained true to me in my time of trial. And just as my Father has granted me a Kingdom, I now grant you the right to eat and drink at my table in that Kingdom. And you will sit on thrones, judging the twelve tribes of Israel." LUKE 22:14-30

Check it out at any sporting event. Fans on *both* sides of the field chant, "We're number one! We're number one!" Everyone wants to be the best, the greatest, number one. The truth is at the end of the season, whether it's

college football, pro basketball, or whatever the sport, there is only one win-
ner—and a lot of disappointed fans.

Jesus had just demonstrated for his disciples what it meant to be a
servant-leader, yet here were his disciples arguing over who was going
to be the greatest among them in Christ's coming Kingdom. They were
so wrapped up in deciding who was going to be number one that they had
missed out on what Jesus was trying to tell them about his coming death
and resurrection.

It's easy to dismiss the disciples' behavior as being incredibly short-
sighted and self-centered. Yet we often are guilty of acting the same way
when we keep on focus on what's in front of us right now.

What are your concerns today? Do you suppose they will still be concerns
for you 20 years from now, 40 years from now? Don't let the petty demands
of daily life prevent you from missing out on the bigger picture. Jesus *is*
returning. Be ready!

Make Jesus and his concerns No. 1 on your list.

| DAY 4 ## No surprises!

Now Jesus was in great anguish of spirit, and he exclaimed, "The truth is, one of you will betray me!"

The disciples looked at each other, wondering whom he could mean. One of Jesus' disciples, the one Jesus loved, was sitting next to Jesus at the table. Simon Peter motioned to him
to ask who would do this terrible thing. Leaning toward Jesus, he asked, "Lord, who is it?"

Jesus said, "It is the one to whom I give the bread dipped in the sauce." And when he had
dipped it, he gave it to Judas, son of Simon Iscariot. As soon as Judas had eaten the bread,
Satan entered into him. Then Jesus told him, "Hurry. Do it now." None of the others at the
table knew what Jesus meant. Since Judas was their treasurer, some thought Jesus was telling him to go and pay for the food or to give some money to the poor. So Judas left at once,
going out into the night.   JOHN 13:21-30

Pick up the newspaper, and the headline screams about a man who was
convicted of committing a horrendous crime. As you read the story, there's
a quote from a neighbor who said, "He was such a nice guy. He didn't say
very much, but he was always so polite. We couldn't believe he did that."
We often are shocked to discover the truth about others.

The disciples were shocked when Jesus announced during the Passover meal that one of them would betray him. In Matthew's account (Matthew 26:20-30), he describes the disciples as greatly distressed, as they ask, "It's not me, is it?" Perhaps they each knew that they were capable of committing such an act or maybe they realized how much Jesus knew about the insides of their hearts. They were clearly nervous.

Jesus, however, never is shocked by our sin. There is nothing we could do that would surprise him or be unexpected. That might make you a bit nervous, like it did the disciples, until you consider the rest of the story. Even though Jesus knew that Judas was going to betray him, he didn't stop him. And he won't stop us, either. In fact, Jesus will be there waiting for us when we turn to him and ask for forgiveness.

No matter how great a sin you commit, Jesus isn't waiting to scold you and punish you. He is waiting to offer you love, acceptance, and forgiveness.

Jesus isn't shocked by your sin. He's seen it all.

DAY 5 The Truth Hurts

WEEK FORTY-THREE

"Simon, Simon, Satan has asked to have all of you, to sift you like wheat. But I have pleaded in prayer for you, Simon, that your faith should not fail. So when you have repented and turned to me again, strengthen and build up your brothers."

Peter said, "Lord, I am ready to go to prison with you, and even to die with you."

But Jesus said, "Peter, let me tell you something. The rooster will not crow tomorrow morning until you have denied three times that you even know me."

Then Jesus asked them, "When I sent you out to preach the Good News and you did not have money, a traveler's bag, or extra clothing, did you lack anything?"

"No," they replied.

"But now," he said, "take your money and a traveler's bag. And if you don't have a sword, sell your clothes and buy one! For the time has come for this prophecy about me to be fulfilled: 'He was counted among those who were rebels.' Yes, everything written about me by the prophets will come true."

"Lord," they replied, "we have two swords among us."

"That's enough," he said.   LUKE 22:31-38

Ask a friend to critique a term paper or audition piece for orchestra, and what do you really want to hear? At one level, you want honesty, but not if it means being told that the paper is trash or the audition piece is nowhere near what it needs to be. Hearing the truth can sometimes be painful.

It certainly was for Peter. As one of Jesus' more vocal supporters, Peter firmly declared that he was ready to go to prison with Jesus, even die with him if necessary. Imagine how much it must have hurt Peter to hear Jesus tell him the truth: "No, Peter, you won't do that at all. What you are going to do is to deny, not once, but three times, that you even knew me." Ouch.

Are you open to the truth Jesus has to say to you? When you read the Bible, are your heart and mind open to the Holy Spirit's promptings? Pray that he will show you the areas where you need to make changes, no matter how painful they may be.

Remember that Jesus did not leave Peter discouraged and disheartened. He told Peter that he prayed for him and that he would be there when Peter repented and came back to him. Jesus will do the same for you. He will give you the strength you need to accept the truth—and the forgiveness you need when you fail.

Be open to the truth that comes from God's Word.

What did you learn about Jesus from this week's readings?

What reading this week had the most impact on you? Why?

What do you plan to do about what you have learned this week?

Key Verse:

| DAY 1 | **Don't worry?**

"Don't be troubled. You trust God, now trust in me. There are many rooms in my Father's home, and I am going to prepare a place for you. If this were not so, I would tell you plainly. When everything is ready, I will come and get you, so that you will always be with me where I am. And you know where I am going and how to get there."

"No, we don't know, Lord," Thomas said. "We haven't any idea where you are going, so how can we know the way?"

Jesus told him, "I am the way, the truth, and the life. No one can come to the Father except through me. If you had known who I am, then you would have known who my Father is. From now on you know him and have seen him!"

Philip said, "Lord, show us the Father and we will be satisfied."

Jesus replied, "Philip, don't you even yet know who I am, even after all the time I have been with you? Anyone who has seen me has seen the Father! So why are you asking to see him? Don't you believe that I am in the Father and the Father is in me? The words I say are not my own, but my Father who lives in me does his work through me. Just believe that I am in the Father and the Father is in me. Or at least believe because of what you have seen me do.

"The truth is, anyone who believes in me will do the same works I have done, and even greater works, because I am going to be with the Father. You can ask for anything in my name, and I will do it, because the work of the Son brings glory to the Father. Yes, ask anything in my name, and I will do it!" JOHN 14:1-14

Everyone has problems. That's just a fact of life. Whether it's facing rejection at school, losing a spot on the team, finding out your parent has cancer, or being stressed out from too much work at school, our troubles are simply a matter of degree. Some people carry a heavier load than others.

Considering this reality, it's no wonder that people are anxious about their circumstances. It is easy to be overwhelmed by our problems, so it is important to remember Jesus' words to his disciples. He had been telling them for weeks about his pending arrest, his suffering, and his death. It must have finally sunk in with them judging from how Jesus addressed them in this passage.

"Don't be troubled," he began. Easy to say, but hard to put into practice until you understand the rest of Jesus' message. First, he explained, this world is not all there is. There is a heaven, Jesus plainly said, and he is going there to prepare a place for his followers. Not only can we get to heaven, but Jesus will take us there because he *is* the way.

Jesus never sugarcoated life. He never minimized the troubles and trials that his followers would face, then or now. But he also did not leave his followers without hope—the hope that is found in faith through Christ.

Next time you feel crushed under the burden of your problems, remember Jesus' words and his promise: "I will come and get you, so that you will always be with me where I am."

Jesus offers us the way, the truth, and life.

| DAY 2 # together forever
WEEK FORTY-FOUR |

"If you love me, obey my commandments. And I will ask the Father, and he will give you another Counselor, who will never leave you. He is the Holy Spirit, who leads into all truth. The world at large cannot receive him, because it isn't looking for him and doesn't recognize him. But you do, because he lives with you now and later will be in you. No, I will not abandon you as orphans—I will come to you. In just a little while the world will not see me again, but you will. For I will live again, and you will, too. When I am raised to life again, you will know that I am in my Father, and you are in me, and I am in you. Those who obey my commandments are the ones who love me. And because they love me, my Father will love them, and I will love them. And I will reveal myself to each one of them."

Judas (not Judas Iscariot, but the other disciple with that name) said to him, "Lord, why are you going to reveal yourself only to us and not to the world at large?"

Jesus replied, "All those who love me will do what I say. My Father will love them, and we will come to them and live with them. Anyone who doesn't love me will not do what I say. And remember, my words are not my own. This message is from the Father who sent me. I am telling you these things now while I am still with you. But when the Father sends the Counselor as my representative—and by the Counselor I mean the Holy Spirit—he will teach you everything and will remind you of everything I myself have told you.

"I am leaving you with a gift—peace of mind and heart. And the peace I give isn't like the peace the world gives. So don't be troubled or afraid. Remember what I told you: I am going away, but I will come back to you again. If you really love me, you will be very happy for me, because now I can go to the Father, who is greater than I am. I have told you these things before they happen so that you will believe when they do happen.

"I don't have much more time to talk to you, because the prince of this world approaches. He has no power over me, but I will do what the Father requires of me, so that the world will know that I love the Father. Come, let's be going."   JOHN 14:15-31

No one likes to be left alone, but it is particularly tough for young children. If you have ever baby-sat, you probably have witnessed separation anxiety firsthand. The child starts to whimper as the mom puts on her coat and heads for the door. As soon as she utters those words, "I'll be right back; I promise," the child launches into screaming mode. The child doesn't want the mom to leave and doesn't particularly care what the mom promised.

Jesus had been talking openly about his death with the disciples for a long time. He had warned them repeatedly that his time with them was coming to an end. To the disciples, the whole idea pointed to one thought in their minds—abandonment. Why would Jesus leave us? Where will our strength come from now? But Jesus even had a plan for a "replacement" already in place.

The Holy Spirit would take Jesus' place when he returned to the Father. The Holy Spirit doesn't have to stay in a body like Jesus did. He can go *anywhere* and be with *all* believers at the same time! We don't have to understand exactly how this works. What we can hold tight to is the fact that *God is still with us.*

Through faith, you have total access to the Spirit's power, guidance, and presence each day.

Through the Holy Spirit, given by Jesus Christ, God will be with you. That's a promise!

| WEEK FORTY-FOUR | DAY 3 | # The Love connection |

"I am the true vine, and my Father is the gardener. He cuts off every branch that doesn't produce fruit, and he prunes the branches that do bear fruit so they will produce even more. You have already been pruned for greater fruitfulness by the message I have given you. Remain in me, and I will remain in you. For a branch cannot produce fruit if it is severed from the vine, and you cannot be fruitful apart from me.

"Yes, I am the vine; you are the branches. Those who remain in me, and I in them, will produce much fruit. For apart from me you can do nothing. Anyone who parts from me is thrown away like a useless branch and withers. Such branches are gathered into a pile to be burned. But if you stay joined to me and my words remain in you, you may ask any request you like, and it will be granted! My true disciples produce much fruit. This brings great glory to my Father.

"I have loved you even as the Father has loved me. Remain in my love. When you obey me, you remain in my love, just as I obey my Father and remain in his love. I have told you this so that you will be filled with my joy. Yes, your joy will overflow! I command you to love each other in the same way that I love you. And here is how to measure it—the greatest love is shown when people lay down their lives for their friends. You are my friends if you obey me. I no longer call you servants, because a master doesn't confide in his servants. Now you are my friends, since I have told you everything the Father told me. You didn't choose me. I chose you. I appointed you to go and produce fruit that will last, so that the Father will give you whatever you ask for, using my name. I command you to love each other."

JOHN 15:1-17

You try to turn on a lamp and the light doesn't come on. What's the first thing you should do? Check to see if the lamp's plugged in, of course. If the electric connection is broken, the lamp won't work. Without the right connection to the power source, the lamp is useless.

Just like the lamp, we need to be connected to our power source, Jesus. In this passage, Jesus repeatedly reminds his followers that in order for them to be effective and productive for God's kingdom, they need to stay plugged in to him. Without him, their efforts would be futile, useless, without power.

The same is true for us. If we want to love others as Jesus loves, we first must *connect* to Jesus, the *source* of love. With this connection, we tap into the great love Jesus has for us. When we're connected we have the power to love others in a way we couldn't before.

Make sure you are plugged into Jesus' love on a daily basis. Get to know him through the Bible, and then *obey his word*. The next step is to *remain connected* by talking with Jesus through prayer. Let him know what is going on in your life, ask him for his guidance and his power.

Lamps don't work without electricity, and we don't work without staying connected to Jesus.

Keep your connection to Jesus strong.

WEEK FORTY-FOUR | DAY 4 Rough Road Ahead

"When the world hates you, remember it hated me before it hated you. The world would love you if you belonged to it, but you don't. I chose you to come out of the world, and so it hates you. Do you remember what I told you? 'A servant is not greater than the master.' Since they persecuted me, naturally they will persecute you. And if they had listened to me, they would listen to you! The people of the world will hate you because you belong to me, for they don't know God who sent me. They would not be guilty if I had not come and spoken to them. But now they have no excuse for their sin. Anyone who hates me hates my Father, too. If I hadn't done such miraculous signs among them that no one else could do, they would not be counted guilty. But as it is, they saw all that I did and yet hated both of us—me and my Father. This has fulfilled what the Scriptures said: 'They hated me without cause.'

"But I will send you the Counselor— the Spirit of truth. He will come to you from the Father and will tell you all about me. And you must also tell others about me because you have been with me from the beginning.

"I have told you these things so that you won't fall away. For you will be expelled from the synagogues, and the time is coming when those who kill you will think they are doing God a service. This is because they have never known the Father or me. Yes, I'm telling you these things now, so that when they happen, you will remember I warned you. I didn't tell you earlier because I was going to be with you for a while longer."   JOHN 15:18—16:4

Suppose you are taking a trip and need to stop to ask for some directions. The guy at the gas station points out the way, then tells you that one of the roads is filled with potholes. When you get there, the road conditions are not a surprise. You probably take it a bit slowly so as not to damage your car.

Warnings like this prepare us for what's ahead. Since we know what to expect, we're not surprised and we are ready. That's precisely why Jesus gave his disciples this warning. He wasn't trying to discourage them. He wanted them to be fully aware of what to expect—the world *will* hate you, so don't be surprised.

The point is, Jesus wanted his disciples to be ready. He didn't want them to become confused or scared when others opposed them. He wanted them to remember his warning, take heart, and not fall away from their faith.

In many parts of the world today, Christians face persecution and hatred. Even in our country, which enjoys religious freedom, believers are often mocked and ridiculed for their faith.

When you face opposition from friends at school or even at home, remember Jesus' warning and don't be surprised. We don't follow Jesus because it feels good and because it's easy. We follow Jesus because it's true.

Be prepared for rocky roads ahead.

"But now I am going away to the one who sent me, and none of you has asked me where I am going. Instead, you are very sad. But it is actually best for you that I go away, because if I don't, the Counselor won't come. If I do go away, he will come because I will send him to you. And when he comes, he will convince the world of its sin, and of God's righteousness, and of the coming judgment. The world's sin is unbelief in me. Righteousness is available because I go to the Father, and you will see me no more. Judgment will come because the prince of this world has already been judged.

"Oh, there is so much more I want to tell you, but you can't bear it now. When the Spirit of truth comes, he will guide you into all truth. He will not be presenting his own ideas; he will be telling you what he has heard. He will tell you about the future. He will bring me glory by revealing to you whatever he receives from me. All that the Father has is mine; this is what I mean when I say that the Spirit will reveal to you whatever he receives from me."

JOHN 16:5-15

When it comes to the authenticity of Scripture, we know the Old Testament is reliable because Jesus said it was. Throughout his ministry and even after his resurrection, Jesus quoted numerous verses in the Old Testament and pointed to the many prophecies found in the Old Testament that were fulfilled through him.

But what about the New Testament? How do we know that it is reliable? Well, we need to consider the same source—Jesus. In this passage, Jesus was basically giving his disciples a pep talk. He wanted them to know that even though he would soon be going away, the Holy Spirit would come and guide them in "all truth."

That truth, which was revealed to the disciples after Jesus returned to heaven, became the inspiration and the basis for the New Testament. We can be sure of what we read in the New Testament is God's Word because it came from God himself. Read what Jesus promised: "The Spirit will reveal to you whatever he receives from me."

The New Testament Scriptures were reaffirmed by the early church leaders and have been supported through historical research and theological study. But authenticity for the New Testament begins right here with Jesus' promise.

Read the Bible with the confidence that comes from knowing this is the inspired Word of God, from God, and through God.

The Holy Spirit will guide you, too, in all truth as you read God's Word.

What did you learn about Jesus from this week's readings?

What reading this week had the most impact on you? Why?

What do you plan to do about what you have learned this week?

Key Verse:

	DAY 1	## we Are Family
WEEK FORTY-FIVE		

"In just a little while I will be gone, and you won't see me anymore. Then, just a little while after that, you will see me again."

The disciples asked each other, "What does he mean when he says, 'You won't see me, and then you will see me'? And what does he mean when he says, 'I am going to the Father'? And what does he mean by 'a little while'? We don't understand."

Jesus realized they wanted to ask him, so he said, "Are you asking yourselves what I meant? I said in just a little while I will be gone, and you won't see me anymore. Then, just a little while after that, you will see me again. Truly, you will weep and mourn over what is going to happen to me, but the world will rejoice. You will grieve, but your grief will suddenly turn to wonderful joy when you see me again. It will be like a woman experiencing the pains of labor. When her child is born, her anguish gives place to joy because she has brought a new person into the world. You have sorrow now, but I will see you again; then you will rejoice, and no one can rob you of that joy. At that time you won't need to ask me for anything. The truth is, you can go directly to the Father and ask him, and he will grant your request because you use my name. You haven't done this before. Ask, using my name, and you will receive, and you will have abundant joy.

"I have spoken of these matters in parables, but the time will come when this will not be necessary, and I will tell you plainly all about the Father. Then you will ask in my name. I'm not saying I will ask the Father on your behalf, for the Father himself loves you dearly because you love me and believe that I came from God. Yes, I came from the Father into the world, and I will leave the world and return to the Father."

Then his disciples said, "At last you are speaking plainly and not in parables. Now we understand that you know everything and don't need anyone to tell you anything. From this we believe that you came from God."

Jesus asked, "Do you finally believe? But the time is coming—in fact, it is already here—when you will be scattered, each one going his own way, leaving me alone. Yet I am not alone because the Father is with me. I have told you all this so that you may have peace in me. Here on earth you will have many trials and sorrows. But take heart, because I have overcome the world." JOHN 16:16-33

Imagine taking a trip to Washington and deciding that you want to see the president while you are there. Unless you have the proper security clearance, the right credentials, and an appointment, it's going to be a nearly impossible task. No one can just walk in to see the president. With one big exception—the president's family and those closest to him have immediate access to him.

It's the same way with our heavenly Father. Because of Jesus, we are family! We have total and complete access to God. Even the Jews, who were God's chosen people, didn't have direct access to God under the Old Testament system. They had to approach God through an elaborate system of priests and sacrifices.

Jesus was about to introduce a new relationship between God and his people. The disciples could only see the heartache of losing their teacher and friend. They didn't understand that Jesus had to leave them so that they, and all believers, could approach God without a priest, without a sacrifice, without a mediator. Jesus was to become all those—our High Priest, our sacrifice, our mediator—through his death on the cross.

We can approach God directly and personally, not because of our own merit, but because Jesus has made us acceptable to God. Next time you talk to the Father, thank him for the Son.

Remember with God, you're family!

WEEK FORTY-FIVE	DAY 2 **open communication**

When Jesus had finished saying all these things, he looked up to heaven and said, "Father, the time has come. Glorify your Son so he can give glory back to you. For you have given him authority over everyone in all the earth. He gives eternal life to each one you have given him. And this is the way to have eternal life—to know you, the only true God, and Jesus Christ, the one you sent to earth. I brought glory to you here on earth by doing everything you told me to do. And now, Father, bring me into the glory we shared before the world began."

JOHN 17:1-5

Who is your best friend, the one person with whom you share all your secrets, the person who knows what you are going to say before you even say it? Those are the signs of a close, intimate relationship, one that most likely resulted from spending lots of time with that person and keeping the communication lines constantly open.

Jesus had an incredibly close relationship with his Father. While Jesus was on earth he stayed close to his Father in the same way we do—talking to him through prayer. This passage is only the beginning of a long conversation Jesus had with his Father right before the events leading to his crucifixion.

We learn much through this prayer. It is one of the clearest statements in the Gospels of how we can have eternal life—by knowing God the Father through the Son. If eternal life comes through knowing Jesus Christ, the one true God, then prayer is our first avenue to starting that friendship.

Looking at it this way, we can understand why Jesus prayed to the Father. They share the closest relationship possible. While they were apart as Jesus walked the earth, prayer linked them together. The incredible thing is that we've also been given access. And God is waiting to hear from us.

God wants a relationship with you—to know you and be known by you. All it takes is time and open lines of communication between you and God.

Have you talked to God today? He's there.

WEEK FORTY-FIVE | DAY 3 **out of place**

"I have told these men about you. They were in the world, but then you gave them to me. Actually, they were always yours, and you gave them to me; and they have kept your word. Now they know that everything I have is a gift from you, for I have passed on to them the words you gave me; and they accepted them and know that I came from you, and they believe you sent me.

"My prayer is not for the world, but for those you have given me, because they belong to you. And all of them, since they are mine, belong to you; and you have given them back to me, so they are my glory! Now I am departing the world; I am leaving them behind and coming to you. Holy Father, keep them and care for them—all those you have given me—so that they will be united just as we are. During my time here, I have kept them safe. I guarded them so that not one was lost, except the one headed for destruction, as the Scriptures foretold.

"And now I am coming to you. I have told them many things while I was with them so they would be filled with my joy. I have given them your word. And the world hates them because they do not belong to the world, just as I do not. I'm not asking you to take them out of the world, but to keep them safe from the evil one. They are not part of this world any more than I am. Make them pure and holy by teaching them your words of truth. As you sent me into the world, I am sending them into the world. And I give myself entirely to you so they also might be entirely yours." JOHN 17:6-19

If you have ever been to a party where the only person you know is the host, you know what it feels like to be the odd one out. You don't share any common experiences with the other people there. You have nothing to talk about (except maybe the weather). You feel completely out of place, like you don't belong. It's an uncomfortable feeling.

The truth is, as believers, we should feel out of place in this world. Jesus said quite plainly that his followers were not part of this world any more than he was. And because of that—because we have different values, a different allegiance, and different moral standards—the world will hate us. That goes beyond uncomfortable.

Yet Jesus did not ask his Father to take us out of this world. Rather, he asked that God would use us *in* this world. Jesus does not want us to escape from the world or to avoid all non-Christians. He calls his followers to continue his work in spreading the Gospel, telling people about the way to eternal life, and sharing his love and compassion.

Make sure that you are separate *from* the world in your values and beliefs but involved in doing God's work *in* this world.

Don't look for a way out. Look for a way to get involved.

| DAY 4 **Harmony**

"I am praying not only for these disciples but also for all who will ever believe in me because of their testimony. My prayer for all of them is that they will be one, just as you and I are one, Father—that just as you are in me and I am in you, so they will be in us, and the world will believe you sent me.

"I have given them the glory you gave me, so that they may be one, as we are—I in them and you in me, all being perfected into one. Then the world will know that you sent me and will understand that you love them as much as you love me. Father, I want these whom you've given me to be with me, so they can see my glory. You gave me the glory because you loved me even before the world began!

"O righteous Father, the world doesn't know you, but I do; and these disciples know you sent me. And I have revealed you to them and will keep on revealing you. I will do this so that your love for me may be in them and I in them." JOHN 17:20-26

Competition, whether it's in the classroom or on the playing field, is a part of human nature. We want to know who is the smartest, who is the fastest, who is the best. But when it comes to church, competition can be dangerous.

We hear it sometimes in the comments one churchgoer might say about another, "Oh, we have twice as many members as they do," or "We wouldn't go to that church because they don't follow the same order of worship as we do." Even among Christian organizations outside the church, there's competition to get more membership or have the biggest outreach event.

When Jesus prayed for future believers, he didn't ask his Father to give them wealth, health, or even freedom from persecution. Jesus prayed for our *unity*. His great desire was that his followers would be united as he and his Father were.

So what can we do to promote unity among believers? We can pray for other Christians around the world. We can build each other and support our fellow Christians in need with our time and our money. We can avoid gossip and bickering with fellow Christians.

It starts, however, in your neighborhood, at your school, and at your church.

Look for ways to unify rather than divide.

| WEEK FORTY-FIVE | DAY 5 | under pressure |

"Tonight all of you will desert me," Jesus told them. "For the Scriptures say,
'God will strike the Shepherd, and the sheep of the flock will be scattered.''
But after I have been raised from the dead, I will go ahead of you to Galilee and meet you there."
Peter declared, "Even if everyone else deserts you, I never will."
"Peter," Jesus replied, "the truth is, this very night, before the rooster crows, you will deny me three times."
"No!" Peter insisted. "Not even if I have to die with you! I will never deny you!" And all the other disciples vowed the same. MATTHEW 26:31-35

If you are a performer—whether you're a gymnast preparing for the state meet, an instrumentalist practicing for a solo competition, or an actor rehearsing for an audition—you know that the rehearsal or practice is nothing compared to the actual performance. The true test of your ability is how you will perform under pressure. Will you crack or will you succeed?

It was performance time for the disciples—only Jesus knew ahead of time how they would react under intense pressure. And the disciples—particularly Peter—did not like what Jesus had to say about their predicted performance. No way was Peter going to flunk the test when it came to standing up for Jesus. Oh really?

As the saying goes, talk is cheap. We can say we'll never deny Jesus, just like Peter did. We can say that we will never back away from declaring our faith in Christ. We can make all the claims we want about being a Christian, but the only true test of how we will react is when we're challenged.

When not under any pressure, we can declare that we're devoted to Christ. But give us a little opposition, some potential conflict, and we often crumble. Rather than make claims or promises we can't keep, it's better to be honest with Jesus about our real strengths and weaknesses. Besides, he knows already what those are.

Pray to God for more faith. Ask him to give you the strength to "perform under pressure."

If you're cracking under the pressure, ask Jesus to strengthen your faith!

What did you learn about Jesus from this week's readings?

What reading this week had the most impact on you? Why?

What do you plan to do about what you have learned this week?

Key Verse:

WEEK FORTY-SIX

| DAY 1 ## kiLLinq Time

And they came to an olive grove called Gethsemane, and Jesus said, "Sit here while I go and pray." He took Peter, James, and John with him, and he began to be filled with horror and deep distress. He told them, "My soul is crushed with grief to the point of death. Stay here and watch with me."

He went on a little farther and fell face down on the ground. He prayed that, if it were possible, the awful hour awaiting him might pass him by. "Abba, Father," he said, "everything is possible for you. Please take this cup of suffering away from me. Yet I want your will, not mine."

Then he returned and found the disciples asleep. "Simon!" he said to Peter. "Are you asleep? Couldn't you stay awake and watch with me even one hour? Keep alert and pray. Otherwise temptation will overpower you. For though the spirit is willing enough, the body is weak."

Then Jesus left them again and prayed, repeating his pleadings. Again he returned to them and found them sleeping, for they just couldn't keep their eyes open. And they didn't know what to say.

When he returned to them the third time, he said, "Still sleeping? Still resting? Enough! The time has come. I, the Son of Man, am betrayed into the hands of sinners. Up, let's be going. See, my betrayer is here!" MARK 14:32-42

Imagine what it would be like knowing that you were about to be arrested for some trumped-up charge. On top of that you were going to be beaten and tortured. Then you were going to experience a slow and painful death. Wouldn't that be a terrible ordeal to face?

Jesus experienced this painful anticipation in the Garden of Gethsemane. Yet even more than facing arrest, torture, and death on a cross, for Jesus the most painful moment of this experience was being separated from his Father as he became sin for us. Alone and in agony, Jesus cried out, "Is there some other way?"

Some people like to think that it must have been easy for Jesus to die since he's God. After all, Jesus knew the outcome of his death. Still, we will never go through the agony that Jesus felt carrying the sins of the entire world. If we belong to Christ, we will never experience the total separation from God that Jesus did when he took on our sins.

Jesus, in his humanity, struggled with the reality of his separation from his Father. Yet, he willingly submitted to the Father's plan. The only response left for us is gratitude to the One who painfully but willingly took *our* sin and *our* rejection from God.

Jesus is the **only** way to the Father because he took the **only** punishment that completely paid for our sins.

DAY 2 Live Broadcast from the Garden

And even as he said this, Judas, one of the twelve disciples, arrived with a mob that was armed with swords and clubs. They had been sent out by the leading priests and other leaders of the people. Judas had given them a prearranged signal: "You will know which one to arrest when I go over and give him the kiss of greeting." So Judas came straight to Jesus. "Greetings, Teacher!" he exclaimed and gave him the kiss.

Jesus said, "My friend, go ahead and do what you have come for." Then the others grabbed Jesus and arrested him. One of the men with Jesus pulled out a sword and slashed off an ear of the high priest's servant.

"Put away your sword," Jesus told him. "Those who use the sword will be killed by the sword. Don't you realize that I could ask my Father for thousands of angels to protect us, and he would send them instantly? But if I did, how would the Scriptures be fulfilled that describe what must happen now?"

Then Jesus said to the crowd, "Am I some dangerous criminal, that you have come armed with swords and clubs to arrest me? Why didn't you arrest me in the Temple? I was there teaching every day. But this is all happening to fulfill the words of the prophets as recorded in the Scriptures." At that point, all the disciples deserted him and fled.

MATTHEW 26:47-56

For a child who has a splinter in his or her finger that doesn't hurt, trying to convince the child that the best action to take is to dig it out with a sterilized needle is a tough sell. The child's finger doesn't hurt, so why do anything? What the child doesn't understand is that the consequences of leaving the splinter in the finger may be more severe than any momentary discomfort.

The disciples were in a situation where they couldn't see beyond the momentary discomfort. They were under attack, their leader was being arrested, so their first instinct was to get out of there, fighting, if necessary. They saw only defeat and disgrace. They didn't understand, as Jesus pointed out, that these events *had* to unfold if there was going to be complete victory.

This was not easy for Jesus. Just moments before the mob arrived, Jesus prayed in deep agony, fearing the separation from his Father. He could have called on thousands of angels to rescue him, but he had to resist the temptation to avoid the pain and avoid the rejection. Jesus knew, unlike his followers, that unless he went to the cross, our sins could not be forgiven.

Jesus died alone for you, willingly, painfully, obediently. God's kingdom and ultimate plan for the world's salvation advanced not by a show of force, but by a show of faith.

Respond in faith to what Christ has done for you.

| WEEK FORTY-SIX | DAY 3 | split-second response |

But even as he said this, a mob approached, led by Judas, one of his twelve disciples. Judas walked over to Jesus and greeted him with a kiss. But Jesus said, "Judas, how can you betray me, the Son of Man, with a kiss?"

When the other disciples saw what was about to happen, they exclaimed, "Lord, should we fight? We brought the swords!" And one of them slashed at the high priest's servant and cut off his right ear.

But Jesus said, "Don't resist anymore." And he touched the place where the man's ear had been and healed him. Then Jesus spoke to the leading priests and captains of the Temple guard and the other leaders who headed the mob. "Am I some dangerous criminal," he asked, "that you have come armed with swords and clubs to arrest me? Why didn't you arrest me in the Temple? I was there every day. But this is your moment, the time when the power of darkness reigns." LUKE 22:47-53

You probably can't count the number of times either you have said or someone has said to you, "Hey, how ya doing?" or "What's up?" or "What's happening?" You don't really want to take the time to find out what *is* going on in another person's life. You really don't what to know exactly how they are doing. It's just a way of greeting each other that has no real meaning behind the words.

Ironically, Judas used a type of greeting as a signal to betray Jesus—the kiss. In many parts of the world—then and now—a kiss exchanged between men is a common form of greeting that expresses love, respect, and reverence. It would have been a typical greeting between a pupil and his master—the type of exchange expected between Judas and Jesus.

Yet Judas never intended his kiss to show Jesus love, respect, or reverence. His greeting was meaningless because he intended it for another purpose altogether—to betray Jesus.

It's easy to see how Judas' greeting was an empty, hollow gesture because of the result. But what about the practices and gestures in our own lives that have become meaningless? Any time we just go through the motions when we pray or worship or study the Bible, we are, in a sense, betraying Jesus.

Whatever you do, whether it's serving, giving, worshiping, or praying, make sure you're not just doing it for show, but from a heart that is filled with love and thanksgiving.

Guard against insincerity in your relationship with Jesus.

DAY 4 Put to the Test
WEEK FORTY-SIX

So the soldiers, their commanding officer, and the Temple guards arrested Jesus and tied him up. First they took him to Annas, the father-in-law of Caiaphas, the high priest that year. Caiaphas was the one who had told the other Jewish leaders, "Better that one should die for all."

Simon Peter followed along behind, as did another of the disciples. That other disciple was acquainted with the high priest, so he was allowed to enter the courtyard with Jesus. Peter stood outside the gate. Then the other disciple spoke to the woman watching at the gate, and she let Peter in. The woman asked Peter, "Aren't you one of Jesus' disciples?"

"No," he said, "I am not."

The guards and the household servants were standing around a charcoal fire they had made because it was cold. And Peter stood there with them, warming himself.

Inside, the high priest began asking Jesus about his followers and what he had been teaching them. Jesus replied, "What I teach is widely known, because I have preached regularly in the synagogues and the Temple. I have been heard by people everywhere, and I teach nothing in private that I have not said in public. Why are you asking me this question? Ask those who heard me. They know what I said."

One of the Temple guards standing there struck Jesus on the face. "Is that the way to answer the high priest?" he demanded.

Jesus replied, "If I said anything wrong, you must give evidence for it. Should you hit a man for telling the truth?"

Then Annas bound Jesus and sent him to Caiaphas, the high priest.   JOHN 18:12-24

During their junior year, high school students typically take practice tests for college entrance exams. While the practice test gives students a good indicator of how they will perform on the actual exam, it's not the real thing. Only under the pressure of actual testing conditions will students find out well they *really* will perform.

It's like that with spiritual matters as well. Our faith is only as good as it is when tested and under pressure. Take Peter, for example. Surrounded by his peers and his teacher, Peter boldly said that he would never abandon Jesus. But when his faith was put to the real test, Peter failed. Under the pressure of the moment, Peter stumbled.

Like Peter, our faith will be tested many times. And undoubtedly, like Peter, we will falter and fail. But it is only through those times of testing (and yes, failing) that our faith grows and becomes stronger.

You may be asked to pass along some juicy gossip or to help your friend cheat on a test. Or you may be asked about whether you attend church. Right then you have to choose—will you stand for Christ and what is right, or will you deny your faith and do what's wrong?

When these times of testing come, remember Peter and stand strong under the pressure.

Acknowledge Jesus with every opportunity.

DAY 5 only the Religious
WEEK FORTY-SIX

Then the people who had arrested Jesus led him to the home of Caiaphas, the high priest, where the teachers of religious law and other leaders had gathered. Meanwhile, Peter was following far behind and eventually came to the courtyard of the high priest's house. He went in, sat with the guards, and waited to see what was going to happen to Jesus.

Inside, the leading priests and the entire high council were trying to find witnesses who would lie about Jesus, so they could put him to death. But even though they found many who agreed to give false witness, there was no testimony they could use. Finally, two men were found who declared, "This man said, 'I am able to destroy the Temple of God and rebuild it in three days.'"

Then the high priest stood up and said to Jesus, "Well, aren't you going to answer these charges? What do you have to say for yourself?" But Jesus remained silent. Then the high priest said to him, "I demand in the name of the living God that you tell us whether you are the Messiah, the Son of God."

Jesus replied, "Yes, it is as you say. And in the future you will see me, the Son of Man, sitting at God's right hand in the place of power and coming back on the clouds of heaven."

Then the high priest tore his clothing to show his horror, shouting, "Blasphemy! Why do we need other witnesses? You have all heard his blasphemy. What is your verdict?"

"Guilty!" they shouted. "He must die!"

Then they spit in Jesus' face and hit him with their fists. And some slapped him, saying, "Prophesy to us, you Messiah! Who hit you that time?"   MATTHEW 26:57-68

On a scale of one to ten (with ten being the highest), you (or maybe a friend of yours) is off the scale when it comes to being "super-religious." You make sure you attend church every Sunday, prayer meetings before school, Bible study on Wednesday night. You sing the right songs, say the right words, and worship in just the right way. But you are so caught up in "doing religion" that you miss out on what God wants to teach you.

The Pharisees and religious leaders of Jesus' day were guilty of that. They were so busy studying the Scriptures, following the laws, and making sure everyone else did that they missed out on event that the Jewish people have waited hundreds of years for—the coming of the Messiah. They were so involved in "doing religion" that they missed Jesus!

The challenge for us today is not to let anything or anyone keep us from knowing and following Jesus—even Christianity. When your religion becomes more important than relationships, when your study becomes more important than the person you are studying, when rule-keeping becomes more important than faith, it's time to step back and re-evaluate.

Don't let religion keep you from faith in Jesus.

What did you learn about Jesus from this week's readings?

What reading this week had the most impact on you? Why?

What do you plan to do about what you have learned this week?

Key Verse:

WEEKFORTY-SEVEN

| DAY 1 ## you can't tell just one

Meanwhile, Peter was below in the courtyard. One of the servant girls who worked for the high priest noticed Peter warming himself at the fire. She looked at him closely and then said, "You were one of those with Jesus, the Nazarene."

Peter denied it. "I don't know what you're talking about," he said, and he went out into the entryway. Just then, a rooster crowed.

The servant girl saw him standing there and began telling the others, "That man is definitely one of them!" Peter denied it again.

A little later some other bystanders began saying to Peter, "You must be one of them because you are from Galilee."

Peter said, "I swear by God, I don't know this man you're talking about." And immediately the rooster crowed the second time. Suddenly, Jesus' words flashed through Peter's mind: "Before the rooster crows twice, you will deny me three times." And he broke down and cried.   MARK 14:66-72

You see it in every vending machine at school or in the mall. The potato chip brand with the slogan, "You can't eat just one." Have you ever tried to eat just *one?* It's almost impossible! Your hand is back in the bag before your brain even connects. This slogan also fits perfectly for another common action: telling lies. Once you tell one lie, it's difficult not to tell another and another.

Once Peter got rolling he wasn't about to stop. When he started lying about knowing Jesus, he might have thought it was the safest move to make. He just wanted to be close to his master without sticking out too much in the crowd. By the third lie, however, Peter had forgotten why he was even hanging around the courtyard of the Jewish leader's home. Then the rooster crowed . . . Peter was *caught.*

It's called covering our tracks. We lie so that our first lie won't be discovered. Peter told three in a row, and that doesn't compare with some of our track records! It's a painful process to stop and admit we're wrong, but it's even more difficult to unravel the web of lies once we've started spinning. Peter couldn't stop lying until God checked him with a rooster's crow.

What "checks" do you need in your life to stop the cycle of lies? In the end Jesus forgave Peter when he repented. Confess the truth before your lies destroy you. Jesus offers you forgiveness, too.

Lying puts you on the wrong track with others and with God.

DAY 2 ## catch-22

At daybreak all the leaders of the people assembled, including the leading priests and the teachers of religious law. Jesus was led before this high council, and they said, "Tell us if you are the Messiah."

But he replied, "If I tell you, you won't believe me. And if I ask you a question, you won't answer. But the time is soon coming when I, the Son of Man, will be sitting at God's right hand in the place of power."

They all shouted, "Then you claim you are the Son of God?"

And he replied, "You are right in saying that I am."

"What need do we have for other witnesses?" they shouted. "We ourselves heard him say it."   LUKE 22:66-71

The term catch-22 refers to what happens when a person is stuck between two options, neither of which is very attractive. For example, you're listening to CDs in your room when your mom asks, "What are you doing?" No matter how you answer, you know she is going to find something else for you to do. It's a catch-22.

The religious leaders attempted to trap Jesus in a catch-22 of their own making. According to Jewish law Jesus' trial was bogus from the start. For the occasion, the religious leaders had conveniently forgotten all the rules and procedures that governed their judicial process. Then they tried to trap Jesus by asking him if he was the Messiah. However Jesus answered, the Pharisees planned to use that answer against him. Clearly, it was a catch-22.

Jesus didn't fall for their games. Instead, he openly declared one of the most blatant statements of his divinity in the Bible. Surprisingly, we often *miss* it. Jesus simply said, "You are right in saying that I am." In this statement, Jesus proclaimed his divinity by claiming the name God used throughout the Old Testament: "I am."

The Pharisees, on the other hand, immediately caught the connection. But they didn't believe, just as Jesus said they wouldn't. Instead, they accused him of blasphemy.

Jesus' words haven't changed. He still declares, "I am." Some people believe that Jesus never claimed to be God. Others say his claims to deity were made up. But here is the most powerful statement of Jesus' divine nature in the New Testament. "I am."

Don't mistake Jesus' true identity.

| DAY 3

crushed By GuiLt

When Judas, who had betrayed him, realized that Jesus had been condemned to die, he was filled with remorse. So he took the thirty pieces of silver back to the leading priests and other leaders. "I have sinned," he declared, "for I have betrayed an innocent man."

"What do we care?" they retorted. "That's your problem." Then Judas threw the money onto the floor of the Temple and went out and hanged himself. The leading priests picked up the money. "We can't put it in the Temple treasury," they said, "since it's against the law to accept money paid for murder." After some discussion they finally decided to buy the potter's field, and they made it into a cemetery for foreigners. That is why the field is still called the Field of Blood. This fulfilled the prophecy of Jeremiah that says,

"They took the thirty pieces of silver—the price at which he was valued by the people of Israel—and purchased the potter's field, as the Lord directed."   MATTHEW 27:3-10

That feeling has nagged you all day. You know you shouldn't have done it. Whether it's cheating on an exam or blowing up at your friend, bad decisions bring guilt. Why? It takes a lot to silence your conscience. And when you feel guilty you have a choice to make: either repent of the sin that has caused the guilt, or allow the guilt to crush you.

Judas had more reason to feel guilty than any man in history. He had just committed the *ultimate betrayal.* His trusted friend and leader, Jesus, now faced certain death at the hands of his enemies, all because Judas accepted a bribe. Judas' guilt haunted him. Instead of crying out to God in repentance, however, Judas tried to fix the mistake himself. When that didn't work, he fell into depression and sadly decided to end his life.

Judas' betrayal of Jesus had real consequences—it set Jesus' crucifixion in motion. However, Judas didn't think to ask God's forgiveness. This would have cancelled the *eternal* personal consequences of his sin.

When we mess up, we also have to live with the results, and that can be painful. But Jesus' forgiveness lasts way beyond this life. Our hope rests on that truth.

Don't let past mistakes keep you burdened with guilt. Come to God with a repentant heart, and he will forgive you.

Jesus promises to remove your sin from you as far as east is from west.

| DAY 4 # mixing politics with Truth

Jesus' trial before Caiaphas ended in the early hours of the morning. Then he was taken to the headquarters of the Roman governor. His accusers didn't go in themselves because it would defile them, and they wouldn't be allowed to celebrate the Passover feast. So Pilate, the governor, went out to them and asked, "What is your charge against this man?"

"We wouldn't have handed him over to you if he weren't a criminal!" they retorted.

"Then take him away and judge him by your own laws," Pilate told them.

"Only the Romans are permitted to execute someone," the Jewish leaders replied. This fulfilled Jesus' prediction about the way he would die.

Then Pilate went back inside and called for Jesus to be brought to him. "Are you the King of the Jews?" he asked him.

Jesus replied, "Is this your own question, or did others tell you about me?"

"Am I a Jew?" Pilate asked. "Your own people and their leading priests brought you here. Why? What have you done?"

Then Jesus answered, "I am not an earthly king. If I were, my followers would have fought when I was arrested by the Jewish leaders. But my Kingdom is not of this world."

Pilate replied, "You are a king then?"

"You say that I am a king, and you are right," Jesus said. "I was born for that purpose. And I came to bring truth to the world. All who love the truth recognize that what I say is true."

JOHN 18:28-37

When a big election nears, the airwaves are filled with ads supporting one nominee while bashing another. It's difficult to know how much truth is being broadcasted. The facts can get lost when politics mixes with the truth.

As Roman governor, Pilate had a lot of responsibility. Suddenly he was confronted by the Jewish religious leaders, who usually had little to do with Roman politics. In their hatred of Jesus, however, the Pharisees were willing to go through the *secular* government (with its convenient death penalty) to crucify Jesus. When Pilate saw Jesus' innocence, he had to choose between following the truth or making a purely political move.

Pilate believed Jesus was telling the truth, but his idea of truth was twisted. Pilate thought that truth was whatever the *majority* of the people wanted. Thus, without a solid foundation, he let the crowd sway him.

Many people today hold the same ideas as Pilate. They believe truth can be whatever they want it to be. Christians, on the other hand, know that all truth comes from God. God's existence and law do not change just because a person chooses not to believe. Jesus and his Word provide us with the ultimate standard for truth.

Don't let popular thought sway your beliefs or your view of God's truth.

Hold fast to the truth of God's Word and do not waver.

WEEK FORTY-SEVEN | DAY 5 | ## A crowd of influence

Then the entire council took Jesus over to Pilate, the Roman governor. They began at once to state their case: "This man has been leading our people to ruin by telling them not to pay their taxes to the Roman government and by claiming he is the Messiah, a king."

So Pilate asked him, "Are you the King of the Jews?"

Jesus replied, "Yes, it is as you say."

Pilate turned to the leading priests and to the crowd and said, "I find nothing wrong with this man!"

Then they became desperate. "But he is causing riots everywhere he goes, all over Judea, from Galilee to Jerusalem!"

"Oh, is he a Galilean?" Pilate asked. When they answered that he was, Pilate sent him to Herod Antipas, because Galilee was under Herod's jurisdiction, and Herod happened to be in Jerusalem at the time.

Herod was delighted at the opportunity to see Jesus, because he had heard about him and had been hoping for a long time to see him perform a miracle. He asked Jesus question after question, but Jesus refused to answer. Meanwhile, the leading priests and the teachers of religious law stood there shouting their accusations. Now Herod and his soldiers began mocking and ridiculing Jesus. Then they put a royal robe on him and sent him back to Pilate. Herod and Pilate, who had been enemies before, became friends that day.   LUKE 23:1-12

Why are politicians and other elected officials so often exposed for political scandals? There are many reasons, but one major factor that leads to the corruption of many politicians is their willingness to make compromises to stay in power. For some officials, whatever means it takes—legal or not—is worth the price of staying in office.

In this passage is a classic example of two political figures who were so intent on pleasing the other that, in effect, they condemned the only truly innocent man to ever walk this earth to death.

Herod and Pilate both held power positions in the Roman government: Herod, a half-Jew, ruled an area that included Galilee; Pilate was the governor over Samaria and Judea. When the religious leaders brought Jesus to Pilate, he naturally deflected all responsibility back to Herod, for Jesus, a Galilean, fell under his jurisdiction. But soon, Herod sent Jesus back to Pilate. Neither of the rulers knew what to do with Jesus.

Their fear to take a stand against a fierce crowd eventually caused Jesus' death. They stalled and then gave in to save their own skins. Yet both Herod and Pilate originally found Jesus not guilty!

We can act like both these men when we know what is the right action to take but decide not to take it. Peer pressure can be very strong. Instead of being influenced and ruled by it, however, recognize it and accept the fact that certain decisions may result in unpleasant consequences.

Remember Pilate and Herod, and then decide not to follow their footsteps but to be bold in standing up for what you know is right.

Pray for the strength to withstand pressure and stand up for the truth.

What did you learn about Jesus from this week's readings?

What reading this week had the most impact on you? Why?

What do you plan to do about what you have learned this week?

Key Verse:

DAY 1	## Riot!

Now it was the governor's custom to release one prisoner to the crowd each year during the Passover celebration—anyone they wanted. This year there was a notorious criminal in prison, a man named Barabbas. As the crowds gathered before Pilate's house that morning, he asked them, "Which one do you want me to release to you—Barabbas, or Jesus who is called the Messiah?" (He knew very well that the Jewish leaders had arrested Jesus out of envy.)

Just then, as Pilate was sitting on the judgment seat, his wife sent him this message: "Leave that innocent man alone, because I had a terrible nightmare about him last night."

Meanwhile, the leading priests and other leaders persuaded the crowds to ask for Barabbas to be released and for Jesus to be put to death. So when the governor asked again, "Which of these two do you want me to release to you?" the crowd shouted back their reply: "Barabbas!"

"But if I release Barabbas," Pilate asked them, "what should I do with Jesus who is called the Messiah?"

And they all shouted, "Crucify him!"

"Why?" Pilate demanded. "What crime has he committed?"

But the crowd only roared the louder, "Crucify him!"

Pilate saw that he wasn't getting anywhere and that a riot was developing. So he sent for a bowl of water and washed his hands before the crowd, saying, "I am innocent of the blood of this man. The responsibility is yours!"

And all the people yelled back, "We will take responsibility for his death—we and our children!"

So Pilate released Barabbas to them. He ordered Jesus flogged with a lead-tipped whip, then turned him over to the Roman soldiers to crucify him.   MATTHEW 27:15-26

You've probably heard reports of sporting events where a few people have been able to sway the whole crowd. One or two people get out of control, throwing bottles and yelling. Then very quickly, a mob develops. Often innocent people get hurt in the resulting melee.

The Pharisees worked the "crowd dynamics" for their own gain. Using the masses, they saw a way to have the government crucify Jesus. With just a little misinformation passed from person to person, Jesus soon became the most notorious criminal in Jewish history. By the time the governor asked what should be done with Jesus, the crowd enthusiastically screamed, "Crucify him!" Most of the rioters probably didn't know exactly *why* they were shouting. But their actions resulted in the murder of the Son of God.

Crowds act the same way today. Large groups of people will proclaim they're strongly against God. But talk to one of these people alone, and many don't know why they've rejected Jesus. They've just followed the crowd.

Be willing to stand up to the crowd for your beliefs, but also be willing to go one-on-one with those opposing you. You may be surprised at the response once a person is away from the crowd's influence.

Jesus wants us to stand up for what we believe and gently share the truth with others.

DAY 2   the Truth is . . .

"What is truth?" Pilate asked. Then he went out again to the people and told them, "He is not guilty of any crime. But you have a custom of asking me to release someone from prison each year at Passover. So if you want me to, I'll release the King of the Jews."

But they shouted back, "No! Not this man, but Barabbas!" (Barabbas was a criminal.)

Then Pilate had Jesus flogged with a lead-tipped whip. The soldiers made a crown of long, sharp thorns and put it on his head, and they put a royal purple robe on him. "Hail! King of the Jews!" they mocked, and they hit him with their fists.   JOHN 18:38—19:3

We live in a culture where, for many people, truth is relative. What may be true for one person isn't necessarily true for another. Truth is whatever you believe it to be, and it doesn't matter what anyone else might say.

Pilate certainly fell into the "truth is relative" camp. Truth for him was whatever the majority of people agreed with or whatever would best further his own personal power or goals. Ironically, as he asked the question, "What is truth?" he didn't realize that he had come face-to-face with the living Truth.

Only a few chapters earlier, Jesus had made the boldest claim about truth ever spoken: he *was* the truth—the living fulfillment and reality of all God's promises (John 14:6). He spoke the truth; he lived out the truth; he was, and remains, the truth for all ages. Because of this we know that Jesus *is* the only way to God.

In a world where truth is treated as a popularity poll or merely as another option, we can know with confidence the answer to the question, "What is truth?" With so many competing voices today claiming to have the truth, point your friends to Jesus Christ—the source of all truth.

The truth is found in Jesus alone.

DAY 3 control issues

Pilate went outside again and said to the people, "I am going to bring him out to you now, but understand clearly that I find him not guilty." Then Jesus came out wearing the crown of thorns and the purple robe. And Pilate said, "Here is the man!"

When they saw him, the leading priests and Temple guards began shouting, "Crucify! Crucify!"

"You crucify him," Pilate said. "I find him not guilty."

The Jewish leaders replied, "By our laws he ought to die because he called himself the Son of God."

When Pilate heard this, he was more frightened than ever. He took Jesus back into the headquarters again and asked him, "Where are you from?" But Jesus gave no answer. "You won't talk to me?" Pilate demanded. "Don't you realize that I have the power to release you or to crucify you?"

Then Jesus said, "You would have no power over me at all unless it were given to you from above. So the one who brought me to you has the greater sin." JOHN 19:4-11

We all like to believe that we are in control of our situation—whether it's in the classroom, in sports, or even in relationships. We act as if we're calling the shots until something happens that causes us to realize we aren't in control at all.

When it came to his job as governor, Pilate thought he controlled the situation. He held Jesus in custody and he would decide his fate. Isn't *that* power? Then again, the crowd thought *they* had the power to control the situation. They influenced Pilate's every move through the use of fear. If they crowd rioted, Pilate would probably lose his job. And then Pilate heard something surprising: Jesus proclaimed that *he* had the control.

How could Jesus, the "criminal" about to be crucified, have any power over his situation? Well, God *ordained* Pilate's actions because Jesus sacrifice was part of God's plan. There was nothing that occurred that was outside of God's ultimate control and power. In truth, Pilate should have been submitting himself to Jesus' power and control!

No matter whether you feel like you are calling the shots, or if you feel like your life is out of control, God alone holds the power. Our job is to submit to his control and his plan for us.

Remember who is really in control!

| DAY 4 ## Friends in High Places

Then Pilate tried to release him, but the Jewish leaders told him, "If you release this man, you are not a friend of Caesar. Anyone who declares himself a king is a rebel against Caesar."

When they said this, Pilate brought Jesus out to them again. Then Pilate sat down on the judgment seat on the platform that is called the Stone Pavement (in Hebrew, *Gabbatha*). It was now about noon of the day of preparation for the Passover. And Pilate said to the people, "Here is your king!"

"Away with him," they yelled. "Away with him—crucify him!"

"What? Crucify your king?" Pilate asked.

"We have no king but Caesar," the leading priests shouted back.

Then Pilate gave Jesus to them to be crucified.

So they took Jesus and led him away.   JOHN 19:12-16

Pilate made his third mistake in this passage. Already he had refused to recognize the truth, he had mistakenly assumed that he was in control, and here we see him trying to please the wrong person. He wanted to keep in Caesar's good graces, so he took the easy way out.

When Pilate heard the crowd accuse him of not being Caesar's friend if he released Jesus, he had to do some quick calculations. As the Roman governor, Pilate's job was to keep the peace. If reports got back to Caesar that there had been a riot in Jerusalem over this man, Pilate feared it would cost him his job, maybe even his life.

So Pilate chose to please Caesar rather than God. He knew that Jesus was an innocent man, yet he bowed to the pressure of the moment and turned Jesus over to the crowd to be crucified. In Pilate's mind it made more sense politically to sacrifice the life of this seemingly insignificant man than to jeopardize his own power and position.

What sacrifices do we make in our faith? Maybe we are afraid of offending someone by talking about Jesus, so we keep quiet. Maybe we're afraid of losing a job opportunity if we speak up for what is right, so we do nothing.

When you face a difficult decision, remember Pilate. It is more important to please God than to look for the easy way out.

When we know what's right and we don't do it, it's sin.

DAY 5 you wanted what?

The soldiers took him into their headquarters and called out the entire battalion. They dressed him in a purple robe and made a crown of long, sharp thorns and put it on his head. Then they saluted, yelling, "Hail! King of the Jews!" And they beat him on the head with a stick, spit on him, and dropped to their knees in mock worship. When they were finally tired of mocking him, they took off the purple robe and put his own clothes on him again. Then they led him away to be crucified.

A man named Simon, who was from Cyrene, was coming in from the country just then, and they forced him to carry Jesus' cross. (Simon is the father of Alexander and Rufus.) And they brought Jesus to a place called Golgotha (which means Skull Hill). They offered him wine drugged with myrrh, but he refused it. Then they nailed him to the cross. They gambled for his clothes, throwing dice to decide who would get them.

It was nine o'clock in the morning when the crucifixion took place. A signboard was fastened to the cross above Jesus' head, announcing the charge against him. It read: "The King of the Jews." Two criminals were crucified with him, their crosses on either side of his. And the people passing by shouted abuse, shaking their heads in mockery. "Ha! Look at you now!" they yelled at him. "You can destroy the Temple and rebuild it in three days, can you? Well then, save yourself and come down from the cross!"

The leading priests and teachers of religious law also mocked Jesus. "He saved others," they scoffed, "but he can't save himself! Let this Messiah, this king of Israel, come down from the cross so we can see it and believe him!" Even the two criminals who were being crucified with Jesus ridiculed him.   MARK 15:16-32

Just a short time ago, James and John had come with their mother, requesting that Jesus give them special positions in his kingdom. At the time, Jesus told them that they really didn't understand what they were asking (Mark 10:35-39). This passage may have been what Jesus was thinking about when he answered his disciples.

At this point, Jesus was coming into his kingdom. But look at who were on his right and left—the very positions that John and James had requested. Jesus was hung on a cross between two criminals. Not exactly what the two brothers had in mind when they made their request.

The disciples had many misconceptions about Christ's kingdom and what it meant to be a part of it. When James and John made their request, they obviously were thinking about an earthly kingdom and were looking for positions of power and prestige. The reality was that entry into his kingdom was painful and required Jesus to suffer an agonizing death. He died like a criminal without ruling like a king.

We must avoid falling into the trap of thinking that being a Christian will be easy or that it guarantees us a problem-free life. We need to be willing to following Jesus wherever he leads us, no matter what the cost.

Make sure you understand the full cost of following Jesus.

What did you learn about Jesus from this week's readings?

What reading this week had the most impact on you? Why?

What do you plan to do about what you have learned this week?

Key Verse:

DAY 1 Amazing Grace

As they led Jesus away, Simon of Cyrene, who was coming in from the country just then, was forced to follow Jesus and carry his cross. Great crowds trailed along behind, including many grief-stricken women. But Jesus turned and said to them, "Daughters of Jerusalem, don't weep for me, but weep for yourselves and for your children. For the days are coming when they will say, 'Fortunate indeed are the women who are childless, the wombs that have not borne a child and the breasts that have never nursed.' People will beg the mountains to fall on them and the hills to bury them. For if these things are done when the tree is green, what will happen when it is dry?"

Two others, both criminals, were led out to be executed with him. Finally, they came to a place called The Skull. All three were crucified there—Jesus on the center cross, and the two criminals on either side.

Jesus said, "Father, forgive these people, because they don't know what they are doing." And the soldiers gambled for his clothes by throwing dice.

The crowd watched, and the leaders laughed and scoffed. "He saved others," they said, "let him save himself if he is really God's Chosen One, the Messiah." The soldiers mocked him, too, by offering him a drink of sour wine. They called out to him, "If you are the King of the Jews, save yourself!" A signboard was nailed to the cross above him with these words: "This is the King of the Jews."

One of the criminals hanging beside him scoffed, "So you're the Messiah, are you? Prove it by saving yourself—and us, too, while you're at it!"

But the other criminal protested, "Don't you fear God even when you are dying? We deserve to die for our evil deeds, but this man hasn't done anything wrong." Then he said, "Jesus, remember me when you come into your Kingdom."

And Jesus replied, "I assure you, today you will be with me in paradise."   LUKE 23:26-43

Talk to a number of people from different denominations about what it takes to get into heaven, and you will receive a variety of answers. Some may say you have to be baptized first, others may say you need to attend church regularly or live an exemplary life. Here we see that none of those answers are true.

Consider the man on the cross. A convicted criminal, we can assume that he had not lived an exemplary life or even a relatively good life. He probably never stepped inside a synagogue, and he most certainly was not baptized. Clearly, he met none of the above criteria for getting into heaven.

The man was totally powerless. He couldn't move his arms or his legs. His every breath was a struggle. All he could do was confess his guilt and turn to the only One who had the power to save. Clearly, his entrance into heaven was granted because he had put his faith in Jesus.

When we share the gospel with others, people need to know that faith in Jesus is the only requirement for getting into heaven. Like the dying criminal nailed to a cross, we are powerless to do anything on our own but to trust fully in him.

Heaven's entrance exam requires only faith.

| DAY 2   # WWJD?

Carrying the cross by himself, Jesus went to the place called Skull Hill (in Hebrew, *Golgotha*). There they crucified him. There were two others crucified with him, one on either side, with Jesus between them. And Pilate posted a sign over him that read, "Jesus of Nazareth, the King of the Jews." The place where Jesus was crucified was near the city; and the sign was written in Hebrew, Latin, and Greek, so that many people could read it.

Then the leading priests said to Pilate, "Change it from 'The King of the Jews' to 'He said, I am King of the Jews.'"

Pilate replied, "What I have written, I have written. It stays exactly as it is."

When the soldiers had crucified Jesus, they divided his clothes among the four of them. They also took his robe, but it was seamless, woven in one piece from the top. So they said, "Let's not tear it but throw dice to see who gets it." This fulfilled the Scripture that says, "They divided my clothes among themselves and threw dice for my robe." So that is what they did.

Standing near the cross were Jesus' mother, and his mother's sister, Mary (the wife of Clopas), and Mary Magdalene. When Jesus saw his mother standing there beside the disciple he loved, he said to her, "Woman, he is your son." And he said to this disciple, "She is your mother." And from then on this disciple took her into his home.   JOHN 19:17-27

WWJD—What Would Jesus Do—was a popular acrostic that appeared on bracelets, T-shirts, and bumper stickers as a reminder of how Jesus would handle any given situation. Here, in one of the lowest moments of his earthly life, look at what Jesus did.

They had whipped Jesus so that his back was torn into bloody shreds. A crown of long, razor-sharp thorns was pushed into his head so that blood ran down his face. He was beaten with stick, spat upon, and mocked. As he hung naked, gasping for breath, Jesus watched the soldiers at the foot of his cross gamble for his clothes.

Alone, rejected by the world and by his heavenly Father, Jesus suffered the spiritual torture of bearing the sins of the world. And what did Jesus do? In his agony, Jesus spoke words of comfort and care.

He looked down and saw two people he'd be leaving behind: his mother, Mary, and his disciple and friend John. And Jesus cared about what was going to happen to them. Where was Mary, a widow, going to live? Who would take care of her? From the cross, Jesus asked John to take her in.

That's the kind of Savior we have. In the midst of intense pain and suffering, Jesus thought about others with love and compassion. That's our model. That is how we should respond to others as well.

WWJD? Care for the needs of those around you.

| WEEK FORTY-NINE | DAY 3 | ## communication block |

By this time it was noon, and darkness fell across the whole land until three o'clock. The light from the sun was gone. And suddenly, the thick veil hanging in the Temple was torn apart. Then Jesus shouted, "Father, I entrust my spirit into your hands!" And with those words he breathed his last.

When the captain of the Roman soldiers handling the executions saw what had happened, he praised God and said, "Surely this man was innocent." And when the crowd that came to see the crucifixion saw all that had happened, they went home in deep sorrow. But Jesus' friends, including the women who had followed him from Galilee, stood at a distance watching.   LUKE 23:44-49

The Berlin Wall, a symbol of the Cold War, divided communist East Berlin from democracy in West Berlin. With 96 miles of barbed wire and concrete walls guarded by armed soldiers, the Berlin Wall not only acted as a barrier between political ideologies, but also families. When the wall came down in the late eighties, it was a time for joyous reunions and celebration.

There are many types of barriers in our lives, some good and some bad. But all barriers serve to keep people apart.

The very structure of the Jewish temple symbolized a relationship that had a barrier. The temple had three main parts: the outer court where the people worshiped, the Holy Place where the priests worked, and the Most Holy Place where God's presence resided. A huge, heavy curtain separated the Holy Place from the Most Holy Place. Only the high priest was allowed to go beyond the curtain once a year to make sacrifices for the people's sin. It was this curtain that miraculously ripped in two when Jesus died on the cross.

The curtain symbolized a *separation* between God and the nation of Israel. Jesus' death on the cross created a way for all of us to approach God. Now, we can enter directly into God's presence, the Most Holy Place, through Jesus. It's an amazing thing to communicate directly with the living God!

You have total access to God, 24/7/365, because of Jesus' death on the cross and the forgiveness he offers you for your sins.

Don't let any barriers come between you and your holy Father.

Finishing the Job

Jesus knew that everything was now finished, and to fulfill the Scriptures he said, "I am thirsty." A jar of sour wine was sitting there, so they soaked a sponge in it, put it on a hyssop branch, and held it up to his lips. When Jesus had tasted it, he said, "It is finished!" Then he bowed his head and gave up his spirit.

The Jewish leaders didn't want the victims hanging there the next day, which was the Sabbath (and a very special Sabbath at that, because it was the Passover), so they asked Pilate to hasten their deaths by ordering that their legs be broken. Then their bodies could be taken down. So the soldiers came and broke the legs of the two men crucified with Jesus. But when they came to Jesus, they saw that he was dead already, so they didn't break his legs. One of the soldiers, however, pierced his side with a spear, and blood and water flowed out. This report is from an eyewitness giving an accurate account; it is presented so that you also can believe. These things happened in fulfillment of the Scriptures that say, "Not one of his bones will be broken," and "They will look on him whom they pierced."

JOHN 19:28-37

Suppose you have been given a job to do. It's taken you a long time to complete the task, but the day comes when you put the final touches on it and the job's done. That's it. The job is finished. There is nothing more to do.

When Jesus loudly declared, "It is finished!" just before dying, some people might have wondered what he was talking about. Some people might have thought that Jesus was talking about the end of his life. But Jesus knew he would rise again. The "finish" Jesus really referred to was the completion of his work on earth. There was nothing more to do. God's plan of salvation was completed.

With Jesus' death on the cross, final payment had been made for our sins. There is nothing more that we can do. Yet, some people today believe they *have* to do something more. They think they have to live a good life, or attend church regularly, or attend the "right" church. Others believe only by following a long list of man-made rules or saying the right words will their sins be forgiven.

Don't be deceived. Jesus came to finish God's plan of salvation, to pay the full penalty for our sins—once for all (Hebrews 7: 28). Don't follow any human-made rules or rituals to make yourself "right with God." Jesus did it for you with his one time sacrifice for your sins.

The job is finished! Jesus' sacrifice accomplished **perfect** forgiveness for your sins.

DAY 5 stay close

This all happened on Friday, the day of preparation, the day before the Sabbath. As evening approached, an honored member of the high council, Joseph from Arimathea (who was waiting for the Kingdom of God to come), gathered his courage and went to Pilate to ask for Jesus' body. Pilate couldn't believe that Jesus was already dead, so he called for the Roman military officer in charge and asked him. The officer confirmed the fact, and Pilate told Joseph he could have the body. Joseph bought a long sheet of linen cloth, and taking Jesus' body down from the cross, he wrapped it in the cloth and laid it in a tomb that had been carved out of the rock. Then he rolled a stone in front of the entrance. Mary Magdalene and Mary the mother of Joseph saw where Jesus' body was laid.   MARK 15:42-47

You have a problem. All you want to do is call one of your friends for advice. But when you start dialing numbers, all you get is excuses on the other end of the line: "I'm a little busy," or "My other friend's over right now." Often the people who *say* they are our friends leave us right when we need them the most.

Just before Jesus' arrest, his disciples promised *never* to abandon him. They were supposed to be his closest friends! But look at this. Joseph of Arimathea, a man who was not even part of Jesus' inner circle, was one of the *only* people to stand up to honor Jesus' body after his death. As a secret follower of Jesus, Joseph bravely took Jesus' body down from the cross and performed the graveside procedures.

He gives us a good example. If we say we're Jesus' followers, we'll stand up for him when others put our faith down. When the going gets tough, we will be the ones sticking by his side. That's a true friend.

Make sure you are the one to have the courage to stand up and stick with Jesus—no matter what the opposition.

Stick beside Jesus. He will never abandon you.

What did you learn about Jesus from this week's readings?

What reading this week had the most impact on you? Why?

What do you plan to do about what you have learned this week?

Key Verse:

DAY 1 Breaking Down Barriers

The next day—on the first day of the Passover ceremonies—the leading priests and Pharisees went to see Pilate. They told him, 'Sir, we remember what that deceiver once said while he was still alive: 'After three days I will be raised from the dead.' So we request that you seal the tomb until the third day. This will prevent his disciples from coming and stealing his body and then telling everyone he came back to life! If that happens, we'll be worse off than we were at first."

Pilate replied, "Take guards and secure it the best you can." So they sealed the tomb and posted guards to protect it.   MATTHEW 27:62-66

Imagine watching this scene unfold. Jesus had died, his body was in the tomb, but the religious leaders wanted to make sure it stayed there. So they thought if they got a huge stone and rolled it in front of the tomb and posted guards in front of it, no one could get in. More importantly, no one could get out.

From a human standpoint, the tomb was completely sealed. But nothing can stop God's plan, and nothing could have prevented Jesus from leaving the grave. Jesus could have blasted out of the mountain. He could have gone through the stone. The stone was rolled away only so *other* people could see the empty tomb.

There is no stopping God's plan from being fulfilled—not with any physical or human barriers that we might try to erect. Sometimes we get discouraged when we look at the condition of the world we live in. We're tempted to think, "How could God do anything with this world?" and we become discouraged.

We need to remember the empty tomb. God alone has the power to overcome any obstacle, to transform hard hearts into soft ones, and ultimately, to accomplish his plans for this world. There *is* no stopping God.

Trust in the One who has the power to break through the grave.

DAY 2 stranger than Fiction

But very early on Sunday morning the women came to the tomb, taking the spices they had prepared. They found that the stone covering the entrance had been rolled aside. So they went in, but they couldn't find the body of the Lord Jesus. They were puzzled, trying to think what could have happened to it. Suddenly, two men appeared to them, clothed in dazzling robes. The women were terrified and bowed low before them. Then the men asked, "Why are you looking in a tomb for someone who is alive? He isn't here! He has risen from the dead! Don't you remember what he told you back in Galilee, that the Son of Man must be betrayed into the hands of sinful men and be crucified, and that he would rise again the third day?"

Then they remembered that he had said this. So they rushed back to tell his eleven disciples—and everyone else—what had happened. The women who went to the tomb were Mary Magdalene, Joanna, Mary the mother of James, and several others. They told the apostles what had happened, but the story sounded like nonsense, so they didn't believe it. However, Peter ran to the tomb to look. Stooping, he peered in and saw the empty linen wrappings; then he went home again, wondering what had happened.   LUKE 24:1-12

Life is often stranger than fiction. A lot of times, the story line of a movie is easier to believe than some of the events in your own life, especially if you've had that one amazing, *true* story that no one believed! It can be so frustrating!

These women faced the same dilemma. How could they explain that Jesus' *sealed* tomb wasn't sealed anymore? That there had been an earthquake and angels, not to mention the disappearance of Jesus' body? Who would accept a story like that?

The women immediately went to the people most likely to believe their story—the eleven remaining disciples. Jesus had shared with them the details and the ultimate outcome of his arrest, his suffering, his death, *and* his resurrection. Certainly these men would accept their story! But they didn't. To the disciples, their story "sounded like nonsense."

It must have been discouraging. These women had the greatest, most incredible news to share, and no one would believe them. The same is true for us when we try to share our faith and are met with disbelief. Despite our enthusiasm and our excitement, no one is buying our story.

Don't be discouraged. Whether anyone believes or not, the story remains true. Persist in your faith and in sharing with others the greatest news you have ever received.

Continue to show others the "proof" of the Resurrection in your life.

DAY 3 DO YOU understand NOW?

Early Sunday morning, while it was still dark, Mary Magdalene came to the tomb and found that the stone had been rolled away from the entrance. She ran and found Simon Peter and the other disciple, the one whom Jesus loved. She said, "They have taken the Lord's body out of the tomb, and I don't know where they have put him!"

Peter and the other disciple ran to the tomb to see. The other disciple outran Peter and got there first. He stooped and looked in and saw the linen cloth lying there, but he didn't go in. Then Simon Peter arrived and went inside. He also noticed the linen wrappings lying there, while the cloth that had covered Jesus' head was folded up and lying to the side. Then the other disciple also went in, and he saw and believed—for until then they hadn't realized that the Scriptures said he would rise from the dead. Then they went home.   JOHN 20:1-10

How do you react when you hear some unbelievable news? Maybe you try to confirm the news through another source. Maybe you try to check out the facts yourself. Or maybe you simply discount the story. In this passage, we see Peter and John checking out the facts of the women's unbelievable story and arriving at life-changing belief.

At first, Peter and John just saw the evidence—the stone rolled away and the empty tomb. But it was still confusing. There could be any number of explanations: the Roman soldiers had moved the body during the night; someone might have stolen the body; they went to the wrong tomb. Then they investigated further, going inside the tomb. Peter noticed the linen cloth lying to the side—certainly no one stealing or removing a body would leave the grave clothes behind.

At last, John entered the tomb, looked at the evidence, and "believed." Understanding flooded him—Jesus rose from the dead just as he had predicted. The two disciples put together all the evidence and finally *understood* the significance of what had happened.

Where are you in this story? Do you know the facts about Christianity but remain unsure what it all means? Are you still checking out the facts, or are you at the place where you have put it all together?

Consider *all* the evidence. What more do you need?

Let the reality of the Resurrection change your life.

powerful witness

Mary was standing outside the tomb crying, and as she wept, she stooped and looked in. She saw two white-robed angels sitting at the head and foot of the place where the body of Jesus had been lying. "Why are you crying?" the angels asked her.

"Because they have taken away my Lord," she replied, "and I don't know where they have put him."

She glanced over her shoulder and saw someone standing behind her. It was Jesus, but she didn't recognize him. "Why are you crying?" Jesus asked her. "Who are you looking for?"

She thought he was the gardener. "Sir," she said, "if you have taken him away, tell me where you have put him, and I will go and get him."

"Mary!" Jesus said.

She turned toward him and exclaimed, "Teacher!"

"Don't cling to me," Jesus said, "for I haven't yet ascended to the Father. But go find my brothers and tell them that I am ascending to my Father and your Father, my God and your God."

Mary Magdalene found the disciples and told them, "I have seen the Lord!" Then she gave them his message. JOHN 20:10-18

Many churches teach new Christians to share their faith first by describing their life before they met Christ, second, explaining how they met Jesus, and finally, describing how their lives have changed because of trusting in him. Mary Magdalene, the central figure in this passage, had an incredible testimony to share.

Before Mary met Jesus, she had been possessed by seven demons (Luke 8:2) and her life had been total misery. Although we don't know all the specifics, Jesus encountered Mary and freed her from the demons. She was forever changed and became a devoted follower of her Lord.

So it is only natural to find her outside Jesus' tomb weeping, overcome with grief at losing her friend, teacher, and Savior. Mary was so distraught that at first, she didn't even recognize Jesus when he appeared to her. She never expected to see his face again this side of heaven. It was only after Jesus called her name that Mary realized who was standing before her.

Earlier Mary had been one of the first to report to the disciples that the tomb was empty. Now after meeting the risen Lord, she ran back to the disciples with greater news, "I have seen the Lord. He is alive!"

Mary was able to witness to the disciples with power because she had seen the risen Jesus. When we understand the significance of Jesus' death and resurrection in our own lives, we too can witness with power.

Have you encountered the risen, living Lord?

| DAY 5 # The Proper Response

The women ran quickly from the tomb. They were very frightened but also filled with great joy, and they rushed to find the disciples to give them the angel's message. And as they went, Jesus met them. "Greetings!" he said. And they ran to him, held his feet, and worshiped him. Then Jesus said to them, "Don't be afraid! Go tell my brothers to leave for Galilee, and they will see me there." MATTHEW 28:8-10

Who is the most famous person you have ever met? Some people have been fortunate enough to meet the President; others maybe have encountered a sports hero or a famous rock singer. Even if the person is only the local mayor, coming into the presence of someone who is well-known and has a position of power requires a response of respect and esteem.

Several women who came to Jesus' tomb on the third day were in for their very own encounter with a person whose position of power and authority demanded an appropriate response. Even though the women had seen Jesus' empty tomb *and* an angel, they never expected to see their Savior standing in front of them. As soon as they saw Jesus and recognized him, the women *raced* to him and held on for dear life! They had the right response!

Our encounter with Jesus, the living God, should produce the same reaction: awe, worship, and humility. Often, we initially respond to God in this way. And other people can see it. Yet sometimes we treat our relationship with Jesus as an afterthought. Our response to him lacks that esteem, respect, and worship that he so richly deserves.

How would you describe your response to Jesus lately? If you need to refresh and renew your relationship with him, don't worry. Just as Jesus openly embraced the worship and adoration of those women, he will accept your response.

Approach Jesus with the worship and respect he so richly deserves.

What did you learn about Jesus from this week's readings?

What reading this week had the most impact on you? Why?

What do you plan to do about what you have learned this week?

Key Verse:

DAY 1 the cover-up

As the women were on their way into the city, some of the men who had been guarding the tomb went to the leading priests and told them what had happened. A meeting of all the religious leaders was called, and they decided to bribe the soldiers. They told the soldiers, "You must say, 'Jesus' disciples came during the night while we were sleeping, and they stole his body.' If the governor hears about it, we'll stand up for you and everything will be all right." So the guards accepted the bribe and said what they were told to say. Their story spread widely among the Jews, and they still tell it today.   MATTHEW 28:11-15

Politicians today often want to put their own "spin" on a story that is either unflattering or controversial for them. In fact, the procedure is so common that the men and women hired to do this are known as "spin doctors." Their primary function is to put bad news in the best possible light.

In this passage, the religious leaders decided to "spin" the news that Jesus' body was missing from the tomb. They knew that Jesus had predicted that he would rise again after three days, and they thought they had prevented that from happening by sealing the tomb with a huge stone.

So what did they do? They resorted to bribery and concocted a story that Jesus' disciples had come and stolen his body. But there still were problems with the story. First, no self-respecting Roman soldier would be caught sleeping on the job—at least not one who wanted to keep his life. Second, if the disciples were able to roll away the stone and get Jesus' body out, how could they have overcome the armed guards?

The problem is that many people still buy that story today. Jesus' resurrection still causes a stir among people. People will deny it, ignore it, or try to explain it away.

There is another option, however. You can accept the eyewitness accounts of the women and the disciples who were at the cross, who went to the tomb, and who *saw* the risen Christ.

Believe! Jesus has risen and is alive!

the wrong Direction

That same day two of Jesus' followers were walking to the village of Emmaus, seven miles out of Jerusalem. As they walked along they were talking about everything that had happened. Suddenly, Jesus himself came along and joined them and began walking beside them. But they didn't know who he was, because God kept them from recognizing him.

"You seem to be in a deep discussion about something," he said. "What are you so concerned about?"

They stopped short, sadness written across their faces. Then one of them, Cleopas, replied, "You must be the only person in Jerusalem who hasn't heard about all the things that have happened there the last few days."

"What things?" Jesus asked.

"The things that happened to Jesus, the man from Nazareth," they said. "He was a prophet who did wonderful miracles. He was a mighty teacher, highly regarded by both God and all the people. But our leading priests and other religious leaders arrested him and handed him over to be condemned to death, and they crucified him. We had thought he was the Messiah who had come to rescue Israel. That all happened three days ago. Then some women from our group of his followers were at his tomb early this morning, and they came back with an amazing report. They said his body was missing, and they had seen angels who told them Jesus is alive! Some of our men ran out to see, and sure enough, Jesus' body was gone, just as the women had said."   LUKE 24:13-24

Disappointment—whether it's because you didn't win the class election or you because you didn't get selected for the varsity squad—often can cause us to focus on our dashed plans and withdraw from others. When we do that we disconnect from the very people who can help support us during those times.

The two disciples in this passage had watched their teacher and leader be arrested, beaten, crucified, and buried—all in the span of three days. They knew about the empty tomb, but they didn't understand what it meant. All their hopes for rescue Israel from the tyranny of Rome had died at the cross with Jesus.

They were so engrossed in their own despair and disappointment that they didn't recognize Jesus as he walked alongside them. To make the situation worse, they were heading in the wrong direction, away from Jerusalem and the comfort and support of the other believers there.

We are likely to miss out on Jesus and the support of others when we become so preoccupied with our own broken dreams and frustrated plans. Only when we focus on Jesus can we experience the power and help he can bring through the Spirit and fellowship with others.

Look for Jesus in the midst of your disappointment.

| DAY 3 | # The Perfect Ending

Then Jesus said to them, "You are such foolish people! You find it so hard to believe all that the prophets wrote in the Scriptures. Wasn't it clearly predicted by the prophets that the Messiah would have to suffer all these things before entering his time of glory?" Then Jesus quoted passages from the writings of Moses and all the prophets, explaining what all the Scriptures said about himself.

By this time they were nearing Emmaus and the end of their journey. Jesus would have gone on, but they begged him to stay the night with them, since it was getting late. So he went home with them. As they sat down to eat, he took a small loaf of bread, asked God's blessing on it, broke it, then gave it to them. Suddenly, their eyes were opened, and they recognized him. And at that moment he disappeared!

They said to each other, "Didn't our hearts feel strangely warm as he talked with us on the road and explained the Scriptures to us?" And within the hour they were on their way back to Jerusalem, where the eleven disciples and the other followers of Jesus were gathered. When they arrived, they were greeted with the report, "The Lord has really risen! He appeared to Peter!"

Then the two from Emmaus told their story of how Jesus had appeared to them as they were walking along the road and how they had recognized him as he was breaking the bread.   LUKE 24:25-35

Sometimes when you read a novel and get to the end, you're disappointed with how the story turned out. You were hoping for a different ending than the one written by the author. The two disciples in this passage also had hoped for a different ending to the events they had just witnessed in Jerusalem.

If they had written the script, they would have had God come down and rescue Jesus from the cross. They would have had the armies of heaven descend upon Jerusalem to drive out the hated Romans. Victory would have been theirs as Jesus took his rightful place on the throne in Jerusalem.

Fools, Jesus called them, because they didn't understand that real victory was achieved in his suffering, his death, and ultimately, in his resurrection—just as the Old Testament prophets had predicted. Jesus' suffering *was* his path to glory.

The message of the suffering servant is no more popular and accepted today than it was then. People still would rather follow the power brokers of this world than a Savior whose values call for humility, servanthood, and submission.

Yet we have all of the Old Testament prophecies in addition to the witness of the New Testament apostles and the history of the Christian church to testify to Jesus' victory over death—a victory that leads to eternal life in God's heavenly kingdom.

Which ending would you prefer?

Don't be foolish and ignore the victory found in the Suffering Servant.

| DAY 4 seeing isn't always believing

And just as they were telling about it, Jesus himself was suddenly standing there among them. He said, "Peace be with you." But the whole group was terribly frightened, thinking they were seeing a ghost! "Why are you frightened?" he asked. "Why do you doubt who I am? Look at my hands. Look at my feet. You can see that it's really me. Touch me and make sure that I am not a ghost, because ghosts don't have bodies, as you see that I do!" As he spoke, he held out his hands for them to see, and he showed them his feet.

Still they stood there doubting, filled with joy and wonder. Then he asked them, "Do you have anything here to eat?" They gave him a piece of broiled fish, and he ate it as they watched.   LUKE 24:36-43

The saying goes "Seeing is believing," but sometimes that's not exactly the case. Sometimes something so spectacular, so amazing, so incredibly unbelievable happens that you will say, "I can't believe what I just saw. That didn't really happen, did it?"

The disciples found themselves in one of those situations when Jesus suddenly appeared among them. You can almost hear them saying, "I can't believe what I'm seeing." Although they didn't vocalize it, Jesus knew what they were thinking because he said, "Why do you doubt who I am?" In other words, why don't you believe what you are seeing?

We tend to be like the disciples when we discount answers to prayers, or when we are skeptical about the incredible testimony of a hardened sinner whose life has turned around because he or she finally "saw" Jesus. "Why do you doubt who I am?"

We may not be able to see Jesus with our human eyes, but we have the advantage of God's Word written down for us. We have the advantage of thousands of testimonies of believers that have been passed down. We have all of church history to "see" Jesus at work in human events.

"Why do you doubt who I am?" Jesus asks.

See Jesus at work and believe!

| DAY 5 Believing isn't always seeing

One of the disciples, Thomas (nicknamed the Twin), was not with the others when Jesus came. They told him, "We have seen the Lord!" But he replied, "I won't believe it unless I see the nail wounds in his hands, put my fingers into them, and place my hand into the wound in his side."

Eight days later the disciples were together again, and this time Thomas was with them. The doors were locked; but suddenly, as before, Jesus was standing among them. He said, "Peace be with you." Then he said to Thomas, "Put your finger here and see my hands. Put your hand into the wound in my side. Don't be faithless any longer. Believe!"

"My Lord and my God!" Thomas exclaimed.

Then Jesus told him, "You believe because you have seen me. Blessed are those who haven't seen me and believe anyway."

Jesus' disciples saw him do many other miraculous signs besides the ones recorded in this book. But these are written so that you may believe that Jesus is the Messiah, the Son of God, and that by believing in him you will have life. JOHN 20:24-31

Some people won't believe anything without seeing it for themselves. They doubt practically everything. We often call this type of person a "Doubting Thomas." This nickname, in fact, is based on one disciple's response to news of Jesus' resurrection.

Thomas must have thought that the rest of the disciples were trying to play a trick on him. But Thomas actually *did* miss Jesus' appearance to the disciples after his resurrection. Now the group's exciting news made Thomas response doubtfully, "I'd have to see it to believe it."

When Thomas finally encountered the risen Christ, Jesus did not put him down, but rather affirmed Thomas' faith in him by telling him to touch his wounds and believe. Jesus isn't surprised or afraid of our doubts. When doubts lead to questions, and questions lead to answers, and when the answers are accepted, doubts can help lead to Jesus.

Only when doubts about spiritual issues become stubbornness and that becomes a habitual response to anything spiritual, can doubts become an obstacle to having a relationship with Christ.

It's okay to have doubts. Jesus knows and accepts that. Use your doubts to ask questions and allow your faith to grow stronger.

Don't let your doubts stop you from seeing Jesus.

What did you learn about Jesus from this week's readings?

What reading this week had the most impact on you? Why?

What do you plan to do about what you have learned this week?

Key Verse:

DAY 1 | jesus on the job

Later Jesus appeared again to the disciples beside the Sea of Galilee. This is how it happened. Several of the disciples were there—Simon Peter, Thomas (nicknamed the Twin), Nathanael from Cana in Galilee, the sons of Zebedee, and two other disciples.

Simon Peter said, "I'm going fishing."

"We'll come, too," they all said. So they went out in the boat, but they caught nothing all night.

At dawn the disciples saw Jesus standing on the beach, but they couldn't see who he was. He called out, "Friends, have you caught any fish?"

"No," they replied.

Then he said, "Throw out your net on the right-hand side of the boat, and you'll get plenty of fish!" So they did, and they couldn't draw in the net because there were so many fish in it.

Then the disciple whom Jesus loved said to Peter, "It is the Lord!" When Simon Peter heard that it was the Lord, he put on his tunic (for he had stripped for work), jumped into the water, and swam ashore. The others stayed with the boat and pulled the loaded net to the shore, for they were only out about three hundred feet. When they got there, they saw that a charcoal fire was burning and fish were frying over it, and there was bread.

"Bring some of the fish you've just caught," Jesus said. So Simon Peter went aboard and dragged the net to the shore. There were 153 large fish, and yet the net hadn't torn.

"Now come and have some breakfast!" Jesus said. And no one dared ask him if he really was the Lord because they were sure of it. Then Jesus served them the bread and the fish. This was the third time Jesus had appeared to his disciples since he had been raised from the dead.   JOHN 21:1-14

Listen to any news report and stories about politics, war, or natural disasters dominate the headlines. Rarely do you see a news flash about someone flunking a test, or going for a job interview, or breaking up with a boyfriend (or girlfriend). Yet that's where we live day in and day out. Sometimes it's hard to think that God would bother with the everyday details of your life when there are so many serious issues.

Yet as the disciples discovered, that is exactly where Jesus revealed himself to them next—during their daily routine. Several had gone to the Sea of Galilee to fish. We don't know exactly why they went. Maybe they were hungry. Maybe they had to make some money. But it was while they were occupied that Jesus came to see them.

Jesus meets us right where we are as well, in the classroom, with our friends, in the dorm. It's in those seemingly mundane times that Jesus teaches us. Peter is a perfect example. Even though he was an experienced fisher, Peter didn't catch one fish all night. Yet when he followed Jesus' advice, he came back with a loaded net. Jesus provided what was important for his disciples, and wants to provide for us as well.

Jesus wants to participate in every aspect of your life. There is not one area or detail that is too insignificant for his attention.

Expect Jesus to meet you right where you are.

DAY 2 second chances

After breakfast Jesus said to Simon Peter, "Simon son of John, do you love me more than these?"

"Yes, Lord," Peter replied, "you know I love you."

"Then feed my lambs," Jesus told him.

Jesus repeated the question: "Simon son of John, do you love me?"

"Yes, Lord," Peter said, "you know I love you."

"Then take care of my sheep," Jesus said.

Once more he asked him, "Simon son of John, do you love me?"

Peter was grieved that Jesus asked the question a third time. He said, "Lord, you know everything. You know I love you."

Jesus said, "Then feed my sheep. The truth is, when you were young, you were able to do as you liked and go wherever you wanted to. But when you are old, you will stretch out your hands, and others will direct you and take you where you don't want to go." Jesus said this to let him know what kind of death he would die to glorify God. Then Jesus told him, "Follow me." JOHN 21:15-19

Maybe you've messed up at school, forgetting to turn in an assignment or flunking a test. Or maybe you've let your friend down by forgetting an important meeting you had with them. Whatever the reason, when we have blown it, the best words we can hear are "I'm giving you another chance."

Peter knew he had let Jesus down terribly. At a time when Jesus most needed the support of his friends, Peter three times had denied even know-ing Jesus. It probably was the lowest moment of his life. Yet here was

Jesus, giving him a second chance to prove himself as a true disciples and follower.

Jesus asked Peter three times if he loved him—a fact that was not lost on Peter. Jesus' questions completely removed the cloud of Peter's denials and he was forgiven. In asking Peter three times if he loved him, Jesus also was looking for more than a superficial response. It's one thing to say you love Jesus, but the real test is your willingness to serve him. Peter passed both tests and became one of the early church's most committed servants.

The good news is that Jesus offers us second chances when we mess up. If we turn to him and confess, he will forgive us and restore us. Then, like Peter, we can become committed and wholehearted disciples.

When you mess up, let Jesus restore you.

DAY 3 your own story

Peter turned around and saw the disciple Jesus loved following them—the one who had leaned over to Jesus during supper and asked, "Lord, who among us will betray you?" Peter asked Jesus, "What about him, Lord?"

Jesus replied, "If I want him to remain alive until I return, what is that to you? You follow me." So the rumor spread among the community of believers that that disciple wouldn't die. But that isn't what Jesus said at all. He only said, "If I want him to remain alive until I return, what is that to you?"

This is that disciple who saw these events and recorded them here. And we all know that his account of these things is accurate.

And I suppose that if all the other things Jesus did were written down, the whole world could not contain the books.   JOHN 21:20-25

It's human nature to compare ourselves with others. Sometimes we do it to feel better about ourselves: "I'm not as bad off as that person" or "At least I have my own car." Sometimes we compare ourselves with others because we want to know why: "Why was that person selected for the team and I wasn't?" or "Why don't we live in a bigger house?"

Peter had just been informed how he would die as Jesus' follower. So he looked at John, and wanted to know about him. Was the same death predicted for John—and why not? Peter wanted to compare his ending with John's ending.

Jesus, however, wasn't about to engage in the comparison game. It wasn't

Peter's business to know about what was going to happen to John. All Peter needed to do was follow the path that Jesus had set out for him.

God has a story for each one of us, and no two stories will be the same. He may call one person to serve him by leading a huge ministry and another to serve him by teaching Sunday school. Whatever story God has planned for you, resist the temptation to test your devotion to God or to question God's justice by comparing yourself with others.

Follow God's path for you and don't compare!

| | DAY 4 | your assignment is . . .
WEEK FIFTY-TWO |

Then the eleven disciples left for Galilee, going to the mountain where Jesus had told them to go. When they saw him, they worshiped him—but some of them still doubted!
Jesus came and told his disciples, "I have been given complete authority in heaven and on earth. Therefore, go and make disciples of all the nations, baptizing them in the name of the Father and the Son and the Holy Spirit. Teach these new disciples to obey all the commands I have given you. And be sure of this: I am with you always, even to the end of the age."
MATTHEW 28:16-20

This passage has become known as Jesus' Great Commission—his final instructions to his followers. After the events of the Jesus' death and resurrection, the disciples probably wished that they had listened more closely and carefully to what Jesus had to say. Undoubtedly, they were listening carefully by this time—and so should we.

Jesus challenged his disciples with a *commission,* kind of like a job assignment. The disciples were to spread Jesus' message to the entire earth, making *new* disciples. Baptism would unite believers in symbolizing spiritual death and resurrection with Jesus. And the best part was, the disciples didn't have to go alone. The Holy Spirit would be with them all the way.

Jesus' Great Commission is our calling too. The message of God's love and forgiveness is for people of all nations. But we don't have to travel far—our job starts right at our front door with our friends and neighbors. The job requirements? Someone who's willing to speak up about God's incredible love.

You have the message. Think of how it's changed your life. Jesus has also promised to stick by your side through everything. So what are you waiting for?

To whom can you talk to about Jesus today?

Jesus in Genesis!

Then he said, "When I was with you before, I told you that everything written about me by Moses and the prophets and in the Psalms must all come true." Then he opened their minds to understand these many Scriptures. And he said, "Yes, it was written long ago that the Messiah must suffer and die and rise again from the dead on the third day. With my authority, take this message of repentance to all the nations, beginning in Jerusalem: 'There is forgiveness of sins for all who turn to me.' You are witnesses of all these things.

"And now I will send the Holy Spirit, just as my Father promised. But stay here in the city until the Holy Spirit comes and fills you with power from heaven."

Then Jesus led them to Bethany, and lifting his hands to heaven, he blessed them. While he was blessing them, he left them and was taken up to heaven. They worshiped him and then returned to Jerusalem filled with great joy. And they spent all of their time in the Temple, praising God. LUKE 24:44-53

Walk into a classroom and hand the teacher an unsigned note saying school has been dismissed for the afternoon, and the teacher will question the authority behind that note. But if the principal of the school were to bring in the same note, the teacher wouldn't have any problem accepting its authenticity.

The disciples had been given a "note" to take to the world—that there is forgiveness of sins for all who turn to Jesus. That's not all that he gave them before returning to heaven—Jesus also gave them the authority needed to back up that message through the Scriptures.

Jesus showed the disciples the countless prophecies found throughout Scripture that he had fulfilled through his death and resurrection. All of Scripture pointed to him, and it was the authoritative proof that God's plan for salvation had been accomplished through his Son, Jesus Christ.

We also need to take Jesus' message to the world, and when we do, we have the same proof available to us. When people question the validity of Christianity, open their minds to understand the Scriptures. Point to the prophecies, such as Jesus' suffering in Psalm 22 and Isaiah 53, or his resurrection in Psalm 16:9-11, that were fulfilled in Christ.

Jesus has left you with a message that has authority and power. He has given you all you need to point people to him.

Tell the story of salvation with authority.

What did you learn about Jesus from this week's readings?

What reading this week had the most impact on you? Why?

What do you plan to do about what you have learned this week?

Key Verse:

topical index

Use this index, arranged by topics, as a quick and easy reference guide for Gospel passages and devotionals relating to a specific subject.

FORGIVENESS

FUTURE

GIFTS/TALENTS

GIVING

GOD THE FATHER

GOD'S WORD